CW00801562

PORTABLE

CIXOUS

European Perspectives

EUROPEAN PERSPECTIVES

A Series in Social Thought and Cultural Criticism

Lawrence D. Kritzman, Editor

European Perspectives presents outstanding books by leading European thinkers. With both classic and contemporary works, the series aims to shape the major intellectual controversies of our day and to facilitate the tasks of historical understanding.

For a complete list of books in the series, see pages 000–00.

····· THE ·····

PORTABLE

Cixous

EDITED BY

MARTA
SEGARRA

COLUMBIA UNIVERSITY PRESS   NEW YORK

Columbia University Press

Publishers Since 1893

New York   Chichester, West Sussex

Copyright © 2010 Columbia University Press

All rights reserved

Library of Congress Cataloging-in-Publication Data

Cixous, Hélène, 1937–

[Selections. English. 2010]

The portable Cixous / edited by Marta Segarra.

p. cm. — (European perspectives)

Includes bibliographical references.

ISBN 978-0-231-14530-5 (cloth: alk. paper) —

ISBN 978-0-231-14531-2 (pbk.: alk. paper) —

ISBN 978-0-231-51782-9 (e-book)

1. Segarra, Marta. II. Title. III. Series.

PQ2663. I9A6   2010

848'.91409—dc22   2009013341

Casebound editions of Columbia University Press books are printed on permanent
and durable acid-free paper.

Printed in the United States of America

c 10 9 8 7 6 5 4 3 2 1

p 10 9 8 7 6 5 4 3 2 1

References to Internet Web sites (URLs) were accurate at the time of writing. Neither
the author nor Columbia University Press is responsible for Web sites that may have
expired or changed since the book was prepared.

CONTENTS

ACKNOWLEDGMENTS

For granting me access to some of the texts gathered here, for allowing me absolute freedom in my choices among and comments upon them, and for her generosity in offering the previously unpublished texts included in the reader, I would like to express my gratitude to Hélène Cixous, without whom this book could not have been completed. Special thanks to Judith G. Miller, who accepted the task of editing—and did so brilliantly—part 6 on theater. More special thanks are extended to those who translated the texts that have not yet been published in English: Beverley Bie Brahic, Peggy Kamuf, Laurent Milesi, and Eric Prenowitz (who also offered me information and advice on English texts by Cixous). I also thank the translators and publishers of the already published texts, especially Antoinette Fouque and Joanna Delorme for their generosity. I am, as well, indebted to Lawrence D. Kritzman and Verena A. Conley for their advice on the first steps of the project, to Jennifer Crewe and Afua Adusei and to Susan Pensak at CUP, to Susan Sellers, and to Anna Casas and Víctor Escudero who helped in the correction of scanned texts. And, finally, I warmly thank Marianne Choquet for reading, and sometimes rewriting, my texts.

A section of the bibliography is based on that of Cixous's works by Eric Prenowitz and Marguerite Sandré, which only runs until 2005. I thank them for permitting me to use their work.

The editor and publisher would like to thank the following for permission to include the material collected here: every effort has been made to trace the copyright holders, but if any have been inadvertently overlooked, the publisher will be pleased to make the necessary arrangements at the first opportunity.

"The Laugh of the Medusa," first published in French as "Le rire de la Méduse" in *L'Arc* no. 61 (1975). English version published in *Signs* 1, no. 4 (Summer 1976): 875–93. Copyright © 1976 University of Chicago Press.

"Coming to Writing," first published in French as "La venue à l'écriture," in *La Venue à l'écriture*, by Hélène Cixous, Madeleine Gagnon, and Annie Leclerc (Union Générale d'Éditeurs, 1977). English version reprinted by permission of the publisher from Hélène Cixous, *Coming to Writing and Other Essays*, pp. 7–16, ed. Deborah Jenson (Cambridge: Harvard University Press). Copyright © 1991 the president and fellows of Harvard College.

"Tales of Sexual Difference," first published in French as "Contes de la différence sexuelle," in Mara Negrón, ed., *Lectures de la différence sexuelle*, pp. 31–68. Copyright © 1994 Des Femmes–Antoinette Fouque. The editor thanks Antoinette Fouque and Éditions des Femmes for their gracious permission to translate this text and all those listed here whose rights they hold.

A Real Garden, first published in French as *Un vrai jardin* (L'Herne, 1971). Copyright © 1999 Des Femmes–Antoinette Fouque.

Osnabrück, first published in French as *Osnabrück*, pp. 219–30. Copyright © 1999 Des Femmes–Antoinette Fouque.

"Letter-Beings and Time," previously unpublished in English or in the original French (entitled "Les Lettres et le Temps"). The French version was presented by Cixous as a lecture at the Museu d'Art Contemporani de Barcelona (MACBA), under the title "Si près d'Alger," in February 2007. The English version was presented as a lecture for a conference held at the State University of New York–Albany, organized by David Wills in April 2007. Copyright © Hélène Cixous.

"Lemonade Everything Was So Infinite," first published in French as *Limonade tout était si infini*, pp. 233–50. Copyright © 1982 Des Femmes–Antoinette Fouque.

"Love of the Wolf," first published in French in *La Métaphore*, no. 2 (Spring), La Différence (1994): 13–37. The English version appeared in Hélène Cixous, *Stigmata: Escaping Texts* (Routledge, 1998). Copyright © Hélène Cixous. English version copyright © Laurent Lourson. The editor thanks Hélène Cixous and Laurent Lourson for permission to reproduce this text.

"On February 12, I committed an Error," from *Love Itself in the Letter Box* (Polity, 2008), pp. 133–42. First published in French as *L'Amour même dans la boîte aux lettres*, pp. 181–92. Copyright © 2005 Éditions Galilée.

"Dedication to the Ostrich," from *Manna for the Mandelstams for the Mandelas*, pp. 1–22, translated by Catherine A. MacGillivray. First published in French as *Manne aux Mandelstams aux Mandelas* (Des Femmes–Antoinette Fouque, 1988). Copyright © 1994 the Regents of the University of Minnesota.

Messiah first appeared as *Messie*, pp. 103–116. Copyright © 1988 Des Femmes–Antoinette Fouque.

"My Three-Legged Dog," from *The Day I Wasn't There*, pp. 9–16. English translation copyright © 2006 Northwestern University Press. Originally published in French in 2000 under the title *Le Jour où je n'étais pas là*. Copyright © 2000 by Éditions Galilée. All rights reserved. Used with permission.

"Second Skin," from *Portrait of Jacques Derrida as a Young Jewish Saint*, pp. 111–23. First published in French as *Portrait de Jacques Derrida en jeune saint juif* (Éditions Galilée, 2001). Copyright © 2004 Columbia University Press.

"About *Style* (A Question to H. Cixous and J. Derrida)," from *Lengua por venir/Langue à venir: Seminario de Barcelona*, by Hélène Cixous and Jacques Derrida, edited by Marta Segarra, pp. 77–84. Copyright © 2004 Icaria Editorial. The editor thanks Hélène Cixous and Marguerite Derrida for their permission to translate and publish this excerpt.

"Today," from *Insister of Jacques Derrida*, pp. 41–52. First published in French as *Insister: À Jacques Derrida* (Éditions Galilée, 2006). Copyright © 2007 Edinburgh University Press.

"The Name of Oedipus: Song of the Forbidden Body," from *Plays by French and Francophone Women: A Critical Anthology*, pp. 305–12, by Christiane P. Makward and Judith G. Miller. First published in French as *Le Nom d'Œdipe: Chant du corps interdit* (Des Femmes–Antoinette Fouque, 1978). Copyright © 1994 the University of Michigan Press.

The Indiad or India of Their Dreams, translated by Donald Watson, included in Susan Sellers, ed., *The Hélène Cixous Reader* (Routledge, 1994). First appeared in French as *L'Indiade, ou l'Inde de leurs rêves, et quelques écrits sur le théâtre*, Théâtre du Soleil, 1987. Copyright © Hélène Cixous.

Rouen, the Thirtieth Night of May '31, published as *Rouen, la Trentième Nuit de Mai 31*, pp. 57–67. Copyright © 1991 Éditions Galilée.

The Blindfolded Fiancée or Amelait. Original title in French, unpublished: "La Fiancée aux yeux bandés." Copyright © 2004 Hélène Cixous.

····· T H E ·····

P O R T A B L E

CIXOUS

HÉLÈNE CIXOUS: BLOOD AND LANGUAGE

Hélène Cixous is undoubtedly one of the most influential theorists and innovative writers in contemporary literature. The enormous number of references to her work in academic courses and journals and the critical studies and symposia devoted to her texts only make this distinction more evident. Translations into a wide range of languages—including English, Spanish, German, Italian, Swedish, and Japanese—also attest to the international recognition of her oeuvre. As a writer who consistently breaks down the boundaries of genre, Hélène Cixous poses many intellectual challenges with her texts, which, though rooted in the practices of fiction and criticism, also depart from them. In spite of her celebrity, Jacques Derrida (who published two books and several shorter essays on Cixous's work) pointed out that there was, in general, a "profound misunderstanding" of it,[1] especially in the United States: many readers limited their knowledge of Cixous's writing to the theoretical texts she wrote in the seventies, which had a great impact on feminist theory and gender studies. Although this situation should have changed by now, as most of Cixous's recent fiction has been translated into English, it seems that she is still considered mainly a theorist or even a "philosopher"—a appellation she does not acknowledge—and is thus criticized for being abstruse and not giving concrete directions that could be taken as a "method." The writer herself considers her texts— apart from her plays—above all poetic, but, in fact, as the present collection clearly shows, they defy any attempt at classification by genre. For editorial reasons, Cixous's first books bore subtitles: "novel" (replaced since 1975 by "fiction"), "essay" or "theater," and in bibliographies her work is often assigned to one of these categories. As one may see reading the texts selected here, theory cannot be separated from fiction in her writing as it combines autobiographical and fictional narrative with philosophical and poetic reflection. It can even be said that Hélène Cixous's peculiar "genius"—to use a word that Derrida suggested in this context—lies in her ability to interweave fiction, theory, and living, as Verena A. Conley asserted.[2]

This volume, The Portable Cixous, is a selection of short texts and excerpts of Hélène Cixous's work, from the beginning of her career (A Real Garden was published in 1971, and Cixous's first book appeared in 1967) until the present (including an unpublished text written in 2007), with a special emphasis on the last decade. The aim of this chronological bias is to make this collection a new and useful contribution—The Hélène Cixous Reader by Susan Sellers (1994) includes only earlier texts—while allowing the reader to have a comprehensive view of Cixous's amazingly broad oeuvre (more than seventy books and hundreds of articles published since 1964). Moreover, most of Cixous's contributions to readers or collections (on women's studies, for instance) come from her work published in the seventies, such as her famous "The Laugh of the Medusa,"[3] which has been said to be the most widely quoted feminist text. Cixous's writing and thought has evolved since then, and The Portable Cixous explores these new developments in her oeuvre, while not forgetting her classic older texts. Since 1997, more or less (when OR: Les lettres de mon père appeared), critics have signaled a turn in Cixous's work, the recurrence of certain images and themes—in the musical sense—that, being already present in her world, stand out with more intensity in recent texts (her childhood in Algeria, a reflection on Jewishness, the impact of dreams in her writing . . .). Her oeuvre, increasingly subtle, welcomes fruitful exchanges between literature, philosophy, psychoanalysis, and the arts. The main purpose of this book is not to offer access to Cixous's still untranslated texts (although nearly half the selected excerpts have not been previously published in English and have been translated by some of the best in the field: Beverley Bie Brahic, Peggy Kamuf, Laurent Milesi, Judith G. Miller, and Eric Prenowitz); the collection aims rather to make an original and significant contribution both by making available in one place a number of Cixous's more recent texts and, especially, by organizing them in a way that enables an English-speaking reader to better appreciate the depth and breadth of this innovative writing and its relation to the areas of gender, fiction, theater, theory, Jewish studies, and postcolonial studies. Moreover, the critical introductions that open each section intend to provide readers with a new lens through which to approach an extremely compelling oeuvre, sometimes considered difficult.

For these reasons, the texts are not grouped here according to genre; in order to facilitate a better understanding of Cixous's importance and originality as a writer and thinker, they are distributed in six relevant "areas" or "fields"—in the geographic sense—of the author's territory. One may wonder why precisely six, and not five or seven. Without resorting to numerology, many reasons to choose the number six may be found: following the geographic image, there are said to be six continents—but some maintain that there are five, or seven; six, being a "unitary perfect number" in mathematics, is also a symbol of imperfection—which may be considered one of the aporias that are characteristic of deconstruction; according to Genesis, on the sixth day mankind was created, and, more ironically, since Cixous has explained her feeling of nonbelonging to the country that is hers, six could refer to *L'Hexagone* (the hexagon), which is a French nickname for France, alluding to its form on the map. However, the crux of the numeric argument is that Cixous's writing is singular and plural at the same time; her work speaks a specific language—Frédéric-Yves Jeannet has called it "the Cixaldien"[4]—that stands out as one of the most peculiar and original in contemporary literature, yet through its richness and intentional ambiguity its meanings multiply until infinity.

Part 1, "Writing and Dreaming the Feminine," addresses the point of sexual difference, central in Hélène Cixous's texts, especially in those written during the seventies, when she committed herself to the feminist movement—although she always refused to acknowledge the feminist label, explaining that, at least in France, it had a restricted and biased meaning with which she did not identify. She uses the term *sexual difference(s),* preferably in the plural, to elude firm categories like dividing human beings into two opposed groups: "men" and "women." Cixous defends the concept (particularly in the third text of this section, "Tales of Sexual Difference," written in 1990) that sexual difference(s) is/are always in motion, in women as much as men—a statement that contradicts the accusation of essentialism sometimes inflicted on her thinking. In Cixous's deservedly celebrated essay, "The Laugh of the Medusa" (1975),[5] she strongly reacts against the deep-rooted prejudices that prevented women from fulfilling themselves and that linked femininity with death. The author encourages woman to "write her self," through a "feminine practice of writing," also called *écriture féminine*. This concept has been—and still is—extremely fruitful, although it has often been misunderstood as referring exclusively to women's writing. Cixous makes it clear that *écriture féminine* can be produced by men or women writers, as masculinity and femininity exist in every human being. She never defined this practice— that would be contrary to its purpose and also to her adherence to so-called deconstruction—but its meaning may be grasped reading both her fiction, where she performs it, and also her essays on other writers such as Clarice Lispector. Hélène Cixous explained in *Rencontre terrestre* that, after her encounter with Antoinette Fouque—the founder of the publishing house Éditions des femmes and a renowned activist for women's rights in France—she realized that she had to engage herself in the women's liberation movement, and she did so by publishing only in this house for twenty-five years and, of course, by writing "proclaiming texts" such as "The Laugh of the Medusa" or *Writing the Orange* (1979). In these works she speaks in the name of women to women, despite her resistance to fixed identities such as this one and in the mood of a magical "wishful thinking"—these are her words—that may make changes happen. In the mid-seventies Cixous also began to write on other women writers, in search not of a genealogy, as Virginia Woolf put it, but of female writing "companions," such as the Brazilian novelist Clarice Lispector (1920–1977)—to whom she devoted a book, *L'Heure de Clarice Lispector* (1989), among other essays—the Russian poets Anna Akhmatova (1889–1966) and Marina Tsvetaeva (1892–1941)—"Love of the Wolf," a text included in part 3, refers to one of Tsvetaeva's short stories—and the Austrian writer Ingeborg Bachmann (1926–1973). However, Cixous's literary "friends" are not only women; also included, among others, are Shakespeare, Heinrich von Kleist, Montaigne, and Stendhal.

Most of these writers belong to literature in English, German, and French, Hélène Cixous's three main languages, favored by her mixed origins: she was born in a Francophone environment, but her mother spoke German; then she, herself, chose English as her second/third language and became a specialist in English literature. Part 2 of the reader, "The Origins: Algeria and Germany," focuses on the fundamental theme of belonging in Cixous's writing, not because she essentializes her origins, but, on the contrary, because she problematizes the notion of belonging itself. With it, other concepts are also deconstructed, such as homeland, mother language, nationality, "cultural heritage," the "proper name," and even "identity," as Jacques Derrida pointed out in *Geneses, Genealogies, Genres, and Genius*. Hélène Cixous was born to Jewish parents in Algeria in 1937, when the country was still a French colony. Her father was native Algerian—that is to say, officially "French"—and her German-speaking mother came from a European region that was successively German then French, following the historic circumstances of the twentieth century. The whole family suffered not only legal and social antisemitism during the Second World War—to the point of being deprived of their French nationality—but also the contempt and hostility of the Arab Algerians who fought for independence since the end of that war and deemed Algerian Jews, in general, strangers and traitors. Hélène Cixous was, since her early childhood, acutely aware of these hostilities and contradictions, which can be applied to all forms of colonialism, and her work has therefore also been read from a postcolonial point of view. Moreover, many of her mother's relatives who lived in Europe were deported and died in concentration camps. This awareness of injustice, along with the knowledge that it usually leads to tragedy, made her a "rebel" and, as she was too young to actually react against it, it pushed her to seek refuge in reading. She has written in *Rencontre terrestre* that, at the time, she chose an "imaginary nationality," that is to say, a "literary nationality." Literature soon became her world, one that she has never left. This does not mean that hers is a world apart from "reality"; on the contrary, for Cixous, living, writing, and reading are inextricably interwoven. This is one reason her writing defies any classification and combines theory, fiction, and autobiography. Cixous's first works—such as *A Real Garden*, published in 1971 and included in this section—alluded more obscurely than recent texts to these biographical facts. *OR: Les lettres de mon père* (1997) was the first book that explicitly narrated some of the most lasting—and painful—memories of her life. This fiction was devoted to her father, who died when she was a child, and it was shortly followed by a narrative on her mother's origins: *Osnabrück*, published in 1999 (an excerpt of which is also included here). However, these books were preceded by *Rootprints* (1994), which can be considered an essay, while containing pictures of her ancestors and relatives. *The Reveries of the Wild Woman* and *The Day*

I Wasn't There (a chapter excerpt of which is included in part 4), both published in 2000, emphasize this autobiographical inspiration, while focusing on two different moments of Cixous's life: her early childhood and her father's death in the first, and the birth and death of her second child, who suffered from Down syndrome, in the second. One of her most recent books, *Si près* (2007), relates her return to Algeria after a thirty-year absence and a moving visit to her father's grave. *Ciguë: Vieilles femmes en fleurs* (2008) expresses her dread at her aging mother's death as a means of exorcising it.

All the tragic events suffered by the author are considered—in a typically Cixousian reversal—as "extraordinary luck" or "chance" because they allowed her to "share the experience of humanity, crime, fiction, and punishment." Cixous once told Frédéric-Yves Jeannet that, in order to write, "inaugurally, one needs the wound." And, if one hears the echo of Dostoevsky in the quote prior to this last one, it is because, in addition to having suffered an initial wound, there is also the need for "the letters of the wound": "blood and language." This enables us to understand how young Hélène Cixous's love of reading was not just a means to escape an ugly everyday life, nor necessarily a first step of entry to literature as a writer, but rather a lifelong passion and eventually a way for her to conceive her own writing. She practices what she has called "readwriting," a constant hospitality to texts from other poets, writers, and thinkers, such as Freud's (especially in her play *Portrait of Dora* [1976], inspired by Freud's famous patient), but also many others: Dante's *Divine Comedy*, the Bible, the Egyptian and Tibetan Books of the Dead (in *La*, 1976), Balzac's short stories, Proust's *Remembrance of Things Past* . . . Cixous frequently pays homage to literature and its saving power (for instance, in *Love Itself in the Letter Box* (2005), a chapter of which is included in part 3); this homage is one sense of the key word *letter(s)* in Cixous's world, referring to *belles lettres* or literature. However, this receptivity to others' texts—which can be called intertextuality—consists not only of a tribute to her passion for literature but also of a subtle dialogue, sometimes an ironic (mis)appropriation or, on other occasions, a passionate "digestion" on her most cherished works. Finally, Cixous's linguistic environment has also had an influence on her writing itself: though she has declared never having doubted the choice of French as her literary language—she has often expressed her love for the French idiom—she has also acknowledged her feeling of having broken into it and of her nonbelonging to French culture because of her "other" origins. As Jacques Derrida stated, Cixous's writing could only take place inside the French language, and it is "untranslatable"—yet the philosopher also said that the only possible translation is the one that translates the untranslatable. Cixous used a beautiful image in *Rencontre terrestre* to describe the place of different languages in her writing: she rows a French boat, but with German and English oars. These languages (and others, such as Latin, too) intertwine through her own, "deterritorial-izing" it.

This linguistic plurality in the interior of one language, as well as the hospitality to other texts in other languages in "readwriting," is characteristic of Hélène Cixous's conception of alterity. Part 3, entitled "Love (and) the Other," deals with this relation to the other, which constitutes one of the main concerns of her thought. Cixous's living experiences, as we have already seen, made her very sensitive to everything related to personal as well as collective identities. Both are always defined in relation to an "other," meaning any or all those who are not *me* or who do not belong to *my* community—or race, class, nation, etc. This profound section on *me* and *the other* defines the traditional Western conception of the subject, also called the Platonic or the Cartesian subject, named after the two philosophers who formalized it. The Enlightenment established that rationalist conception of a unified and impervious subject, but since the nineteenth century—and especially over the twentieth—philosophy, literature, and psychoanalysis have more and more depicted a split and fractured subject, traversed by alterity: one whose limits, instead of being solid barriers, are prone to being pierced and fading. Cixous has inscribed herself in that tendency, emphasized in postmodern literature and art and also in poststructuralist thinking. However, her originality lies, first, in her poetic way of reflecting on the subject and, second, in her insistence on stressing that otherness is always already *inside* the subject and not exterior to it. Cixous deconstructs therefore the opposition between interior/exterior, singular/plural, and the subject/the other. Moreover, she does not make a theoretical demonstration, but *performs* it through her writing, which has thus been called a *poethics*,[6] melding poetics and ethics together. As we have already perceived, in Cixous's oeuvre and thought everything is related to writing and language. This does not make her an elitist, idealist, or apolitical writer—as she has sometimes been caricatured; on the contrary, she is an innovative thinker and writer who explores new paths related to fundamental questions for all human beings. For instance, in the first text of part 3 (an excerpt of the book *Limonade tout était si infini*, 1982), through an anecdote narrated by Franz Kafka, Cixous reflects on how to respect differences while not putting "an other" before "the others."

In earlier texts such as "Sorties" (in *The Newly Born Woman*, 1975) Cixous related the capacity to welcome alterity to "femininity" and the so-called *écriture féminine*; it is in this sense that we can interpret her polemic and famous sentence: "Today, writing is women's." Writing nourishes itself with alterity, with the others that are within *me*, maybe unknowingly: "our women, our monsters, our jackals, our arabs," in Cixous's words. However, even her first texts—which are much more "experimental" than the essays of the seventies and her fiction of the last decade—deal with this "bunch of great human themes" evoked in universal literature, as she states in *Rencontre terrestre*. Her first published book—a collection of short stories (or, more accurately, of "fragments") outrageously entitled *Le Prénom de Dieu* (God's first name, 1967)—already contains the seeds of all the motifs and images found in her subsequent work. There is a substantial difference, though, between these "demonic" texts (such as *Les Commencements*, 1970; *Angst*, 1977; or *Ananké*, 1979)—which Cixous herself did not recognize after having written them and had thus the uncanny feeling of not being their author—and the seemingly more controlled ones of later times. Cixous considers these first works close to "bleeding" or "sobbing." They sprang, as a "burst," or came, as a "tempest," displaying "visions" or "hallucinations" that made her fear madness. These texts did not come from the author's will and reason but from her unconscious feelings, thoughts, and dreams. They allowed her to feel the experience of the split subject, but also to realize the richness of the language stemming from the inner self—the space of alterity, too, and thus the most subjective and the most universal. Moreover, this writing that recognizes the unconscious's place—not pretending to master language but letting it flow freely—stresses the role of the signifier, no longer linking to a reduced set of signifieds. In an interview Cixous explained that we no longer listen to "everyday language" because "we have always heard it" and that, therefore, poetic language should "give birth to the innumerable languages of which it is pregnant."[7] Such a conception of writing is not far from the Russian formalists' theories on poetic language—which had great influence in French postmodern poetics. However, even Cixous's more playful and apparently formalistic texts—such as *Partie* (1979), where the author acknowledges the influences of Lewis Carroll and Joyce's *Finnegans Wake*—are linked to alterity. In *Coming to Writing* it is stated that "there is a language . . . in all tongues. A language at once unique and universal that resounds in each national tongue when a poet speaks it." It is a poetic language, she offers, formed by "the milk of love" and "the honey of my unconscious." One may recognize in this description the conjunction of singularity and universality so characteristic of Cixous's writing.

The relation between the subject and the other is also associated with another eternal theme in art and literature: love. We can hate or fear the other, and thus try to keep him or her away, or we can feel attracted to and even want to possess the other. That feeling, which may be more commonly known as desire, Hélène Cixous prefers to call love. The last two texts of part 3 contain this signifier, love, in their title: "Love of the Wolf" (1994) and *Love Itself* (2005). The latter is an excerpt from one of the author's more recent books and is the story of a passion (as was *Souffles,* 1975, defined by the writer as a "book of desire") between the female narrator and a man, but it is also the story of her passion for literature. "Love of the Wolf" can be classified as an essay—if this distinction has any meaning in Cixous's work—that elaborates on a text by Marina Tsvetaeva and might be said to develop a theory of love (if that were not contrary to Cixous's practices). She deconstructs the traditional image of the relationship between wolf and lamb—itself an ancient story (present in Aeschylus, Plato, and La Fontaine) of the power relation implicit in love. She does so in order to illustrate a "love-other" that, though it does not evade the yearning for appropriation—or, more accurately, for devouring the other—does manage not to yield to this craving. For the writer, as she herself has declared, love is always equivalent to "passion, absoluteness, condition of living and staying alive." She confesses that love is one of the three "legs" of her existence—the other two being "writing" and "living" itself (*Rencontre terrestre*).

The fact that Cixous uses animals to illustrate her arguments is not accidental. As many critics have pointed out, animals play a leading role in her world. Part 4, "The Animal," is devoted to this topic: while animality has always been conceived in opposition to humanity—and, in this sense, animals represent the radically different other (to man)—in Cixous's universe they also embody alterity, but they are not separated from human beings. Animals—particularly certain dogs and cats—represent the loved and loving other embedded in the self. They also often personify the innocence, unselfishness, and sacrifice that are related to true love. For instance, the first excerpt of this section, "Dedication to the Ostrich" (from the book *Manna for the Mandelstams for the Mandelas*, 1988), identifies these two historic freedom fighters (the Russian Osip Mandelstam and the South African Nelson Mandela) with the image of the ostrich, as it takes on a mythical and even sacred meaning. There are many other different animals in Cixous's menagerie, and some of them evoke literary or legendary beasts: the lamb and the wolf (also a reference to "Little Red Riding Hood," fairy tales being another frequent intertext in Cixous's writing), the donkey (alluding to Abraham), and the mole (echoing Shakespeare). Nevertheless, the cat occupies the leading role: *Messie* (1996), a fragment of which has been reproduced in this section, is the major "character" in the book titled by her name. In the typical Cixousian manner of mixing fact and fiction, her cats are both dear companions in *real* life as well as exemplary figures of the intimate and respectful loving relation to the other in her work. Cats are domestic animals who share a human's everyday life, but, as felines, they keep a distance and a mystery that may remind one of the irreducibility of difference and alterity (they can thus be considered *uncanny* in the Freudian sense of being familiar and unfamiliar at the same time).

Dogs also make an appearence in Cixous: the author stated in *Stigmata* (1999) that the dog was her "former and first animal," referring to a precise dog named Fips, a puppy that her father brought home as a present for the children. But her father died shortly after, and the rest of the family could not properly take care of the dog, who was doomed to spend the rest of his life stuck in the garden and tormented by their Arab neighbors. Fips is therefore a symbol of the violence and injustice that surrounded Cixous during her childhood, and in several texts he becomes a sort of martyr, representative of all the innocents who were sacrificed without knowing why they were being tortured. This is also the case of the "three-legged dog" who appears in the third text of this section, in the excerpt from *The Day I Wasn't There* (2000). The title of this book refers to the day the narrator's son died while she was absent. This "inexact" child, born with a flaw (which is also a blessing, as he is the most innocent of creatures), melds with the abandoned three-legged dog she encounters but cannot adopt. Compassion, love, guilt, and admiration complexly intertwine in this narrator who is acutely sensitive to all the injustices and abandonments—in the sense of forsaking and being forsaken—that are constitutive of life. Fips gets thus muddled with the narrator's father, her son, and herself.

In addition to those already mentioned, there are other animals in Cixous's world, some of which can be regarded as "primal." In *Ciguë* (2008), the writer speaks of the "Primal Squirrel," evoked for the first time in *Tombe* (1973, reedited in 2008), and refers to a plausibly real experience she had in New York years earlier: she saw a squirrel whose head was buried in the ground—while the other visible half of the body was very still—and thought it strangely dead until the animal suddenly jumped and *resurrected*. For the author, this uncanny scene signaled her entrance into literature: "because of a Squirrel in Washington Square my life changed to literature." This scene demonstrates the "extensive use" of metaphor (*Rootprints*) that is particular to Hélène Cixous: although this squirrel symbolizes the capacity of literature to bring the dead back—to obliterate the effect of death—it is also a *real* animal in an amazing situation. In her world, animals are real and metaphorical at the same time. As Derrida noted in *Geneses, Genealogies, Genres, and Genius,* it is on this "undecidability" among factual, fictional, invented, dreamed, or else fantasized events that rests the "secret" of literature: its magic and its unlimited power.

Part 5, "Derrida," concerns the special relationship between Jacques Derrida's thought—one of the most radically innovative and influential in the twentieth century—and Hélène Cixous's writing. Derrida is widely known as the "father" of deconstruction, which is not a philosophical method or theory, but rather a new way of reading texts and, therefore, a new way of looking at the world. His origins are similar to Cixous's: he, too, was born in Algeria to Jewish parents, albeit seven years before her and in another town. They did not meet until the early sixties, when they began an intense friendship, both personal and intellectual, which lasted until his death in 2004 and endures beyond it. Hélène Cixous said in *Rootprints* that they came "from the same garden," and that he was her privileged "other." She has extensively written on Jacques Derrida, and two of the three texts of this fifth section are excerpted from her book-length essays on the philosopher's work (*Portrait of Jacques Derrida as a Young Jewish Saint*, 2001; *Insister of Jacques Derrida*, 2006). Some critics rush to the conclusion that Cixous, as a writer, is "influenced" by Derrida's philosophy, but their relationship was much more of an exchange consisting of a mutual identification in many fields (as we can see in the third text, extracted from a seminar Cixous and Derrida gave together at the University of Barcelona). One may consider that Cixous's writing carries out—without being preceded by any theoretical frame—what Derrida defined as *dissemination,* showing that language does not function by binary oppositions but that every signifier is related to many others, even some that are apparently contradictory. As she already wrote in *Neutre* (1972), writing becomes therefore a "celebration of the signifier," of its unlimited and mysterious richness. This is why Cixous's verbal creativity cannot be regarded as a solely playful, witty, or formalistic invention, or a purely intellectual game, because its aim is to disclose the immense possibilities of the signifier. According to Derrida—whose argument concurs with what the author herself has explained about her writing methods—one of Cixous's greatest features is her capacity to let the unconscious flow freely through her writing. This is based on "the most powerfully calculated . . . watchful and deliberate strategy," at the same time allowing space for "the most spontaneous living breath of the word" (*H.C. for Life, That Is to Say* . . . —Derrida's other book on Cixous). The allusion to breathing is significant, because (especially feminist) critics have often described Cixous's manner—in relation to *écriture féminine*—as "writing the body," meaning that she does not rely mainly on rationality but incorporates the body's rhythms, humors, and moods. However, as Derrida specifies, she does not practice a totally *automatic* writing, but stays watchful in "an impeccable vigil." "Vigil" is opposed to sleep, and thus to dream, but dreaming occupies a central place in Cixous's approach to writing. In a beautiful image, the philosopher says that "she writes by dream, . . . as one would say to navigate by sail or wind." The author recognizes the important role of dreams in her writing, and she has even published a *book of dreams* entitled *Dream I Tell You* (2003), which gathers several short accounts of actual dreams, obviously sifted through the act of writing them down in a communicative form. Derrida returned, in *Geneses, Genealogies, Genres, and Genius* to this essential place of dreams in Cixous's work, and in so doing he stressed the originality of her "translation" of nocturnal dreams into daytime writing. The genesis of Cixous's writing—an original and revealing process—has become increasingly interesting to critics as her manuscripts have become progressively available to scholars (since her donation of most of them to the Bibliothèque nationale de France in Paris). A useful collection of Cixous's writing notebooks is also in print, edited and translated into English by Susan Sellers.

This "breathing" of Cixous's writing is also enhanced by her particular use of punctuation, which is often against or on the fringes of French linguistic rules. She comments on it in *Rencontre terrestre*, pointing out that this special punctuation stands for the "respiration" and "cardiac contractions" of the text, while also improving its ambiguity. Amphibology—typical of dreams and of all the unconscious's productions—is perhaps the most powerful and characteristic rhetoric device in Cixous's texts. The subsequent difficulty for the reader to identify *the one* meaning of some sentences and words feeds the richness of her textual universe, yet is also responsible, sometimes, for its lack of transparency—a quality, however, that is not to be considered literary. We are back to deconstruction's conception of language as more complex than a system of binary oppositions. Jacques Derrida, who also exercised the chances of ambiguity in his own writing, linked this characteristically Cixousian trait to dream as well and commented on the concept of *rêvexistence* ("dreamexistence"), a word she coined; this signifier is full of meaning, as it evokes Eve (her mother's name, along with all the biblical echoes it carries) and also, the English words *eve, even,* and, above all, *event*—a relevant concept both in Derrida's and Cixous's thought. Cixous pays much attention to letters—this statement can be interpreted in every sense of the word—however, here we are referring to the alphabet. In her world there are key words and also key letters, such as *G/J* (often pronounced in the same way in French): this letter appears twice in her father's name (Georges), in Derrida's (Jacques), in her personal address (*je* meaning "me" in French), in her homeland (Algeria), and in other significant words in her world such as *orange*. This recurrence can be visual, but more often the writer resorts to orality, that is to say, to the voice. Though her texts are very *written*, they also talk and sing—which is a sign of their poetic nature. Responding to a statement of Frédéric-Yves Jeannet, who appreciates—as many other critics—a certain evolution in Cixous's writing since the end of the nineties (in the sense of giving an increasing place to narrative and "anecdote"), the author suggests that there are, rather, two "regimes" in her work: one of "blows" ("crushes, drama, crises, amputations") and one of "time." They are not successive in her career but simultaneous, and we can find both in the same book—often including passages where lines are poetically disposed.

This is also a matter of reading: the majority of Cixous's texts allow a "poetic" or "fragmented"—these are her words—reading or a narrative, linear one.

The "time" regime in Hélène Cixous's oeuvre may respond not only to a narrative mood that prevails in some texts or passages but also to her acute sensitivity toward present time and its political circumstances. Besides her involvement in women's writing and the women's movement, Cixous has engaged and still engages herself actively in various political causes, not only related to women but also to prisoners, political refugees, and immigrants. At the beginning of her career, this political activity was seemingly detached from her literary work, and she soon felt the necessity to link them. Cixous describes in *Rencontre terrestre* how, in the mid seventies, she felt her writing to be too "lyrical" and "intimate," and she wondered "how to give voice to the massacred." She then published *Révolutions pour plus d'un Faust* (1975), before finding that theater could be a more suitable genre for this political vein. Part 6, "The Theater of Hélène Cixous: Re-memberings, Re-fashionings, and Revenants," edited with an introduction by Judith G. Miller, focuses on this significant field of Cixous's work, of which the non-French readership is generally unaware—among English-speaking readers, at least until Eric Prenowitz collected four of them into *Selected Plays by Hélène Cixous* (2004), which also contains two essays by Cixous on theater. The fact that this last part of our reader is based on a genre criterion is not contradicted by the statement that Cixous's writing withstands any categorization by traditional genres such as novel, essay, or poetry. The author herself has always maintained that she considers her plays apart from her fiction and that they should be critically addressed separately from the rest of her work. She has even suggested that she arrived at theater by chance, because she met some people who convinced her that it would be interesting and even politically useful to write for the stage. Besides, theater is not only based on writing, and Cixous stresses that her plays are the fruit of special encounters and of collective work, especially those staged by Ariane Mnouchkine's Théâtre du Soleil. However, this does not mean that her dramatic work is completely different from the rest, as sometimes suggested. The vivid dialogues and some of the scenes in her fiction are truly theatrical; on the other hand, we cannot consider her fiction to be a purely literary game (as if this expression had any meaning): it also addresses political questions, as already discussed.

A major originality of Cixous's theater is that it includes contemporary characters and real historical events. For instance, one of her best-known plays, *The Terrible But Unfinished Story of Norodom Sihanouk, King of Cambodia* (1985), staged the genocide of the Cambodian people by the Khmer Rouge party, which had taken place a few years before the production. *The Indiad or India of Their Dreams* (1987)—for which Cixous spent several months in India—gives voice to Gandhi; and *The Perjured City* (1994) speaks, in an allusive way, to a contemporary political scandal related to the death of some people infected with HIV+ blood through transfusions made in French hospitals—when those responsible were aware of the danger. These and other plays are attuned to present time, and Hélène Cixous acknowledges that she is "sensitive to present" in the way that present also contains past and future. As Derrida states, she also breaks the boundaries between "historic memory and political urgency" (*Geneses, Genealogies, Genres, and Genius*). The main character in *Rouen, the Thirtieth Night of May '31* (2001) is thus a historic figure, Joan of Arc, and *The Blindfolded Fiancée or Amelait* (2004, unpublished)—excerpts from both are included here—refers to Hamlet (or "Amelait," which is pronounced alike in French). Hélène Cixous is influenced by Shakespeare, but also by ancient Greek theater.

Nevertheless, Cixous's plays are not to be separated from the rest of her oeuvre because they belong to a different genre, have a different style, are not completely in the hands of the author, or are focused on political events instead of personal circumstances, as her fiction is. Political events are also "personal metaphors," says the author. In fact, one of her writing's most powerful traits is that it erases the border between what is personal and what is collective, between the singular and the plural, the subjective and the universal. If one thinks, like Derrida, that literature is characterized by its irreducible singularity and, at the same time, by the fact that it is a universalizing experience, we—woman or man and even maybe also cat—are able to recognize ourselves in Cixous's texts.

Finally, Hélène Cixous is also a renowned professor and scholar who lectures around the world—she is Doctor Honoris Causa in several universities in Europe and America—but has taught mostly in France and the United States. She began her academic career in 1959 as an English professor, then shifted to comparative literature and women's studies. She was responsible for founding a new university in Paris inspired by the principles of May 68—the Université Paris 8–Vincennes. There she gathered some of the most outstanding thinkers of the twentieth century, such as Michel Foucault and Gilles Deleuze, and she founded the first women's studies center in Europe (Centre d'Études Féminines, now Centre de Recherche en Études Féminines et en Études de Genre). It has been thirty years since she began giving a seminar—in recent years at the Collège international de Philosophie—attended by scholars from different parts of the world. Verena A. Conley—who is also the author of the first book written in English on Cixous—edited and translated a selection of this seminar, unpublished in French.

In conclusion, the most striking feature of Hélène Cixous's work is its capacity to cross, with the elegant pace—as well as the jumps—of a cat, the boundaries between genres, disciplines, genders, fact and fiction, conscious and unconscious, vigil and dream . . . thus questioning and holing into these barriers, making them permeable. On the other hand, Hélène Cixous's oeuvre is, fortunately, still open to the future, as she continues publishing articles and books prolifically. The directions it will take in the future cannot be foreseen—for example, Cixous has always had a great interest in music and painting, and her writing on visual arts has increased lately. No collection of her texts could therefore be considered up-to-date, and any attempt to capture her oeuvre's movements is doomed to failure. Nonetheless, this volume means to be a comprehensive collection of her texts, including a variety of intersecting subjects and perspectives, that will hopefully broaden an appreciation of Hélène Cixous's work, opening debates and inspiring new research.

1

WRITING AND DREAMING THE FEMININE

Hélène Cixous is celebrated worldwide as a feminist theorist, mostly because of the power of some widely disseminated texts she published in the seventies. "The Laugh of the Medusa," which appeared as an article in 1975, is one of the most reproduced and quoted essays in feminist and gender studies. However, its popularity has created a misunderstanding: Cixous's writing is often assimilated only to feminist theory, and especially to what is called French feminism in the States, whereas, as we have seen in the introduction, her work largely exceeds this field. The author—as she explains in *Rootprints*—believes that her fiction more faithfully characterizes her writing than these well-known essays. She also reminds us that they were written in a precise historical moment, at a time that she considered it necessary to take a firm position for "women" as a group socially and symbolically oppressed by patriarchy. Nevertheless, Cixous has never given up reflecting on sexual difference—or, more to the point, sexual difference*s*, in the plural that she likes to specify. In her subsequent work Cixous slightly modified not her thought but her way of expressing it. We can appreciate this evolution in the excerpts reproduced in this section. "The Laugh of the Medusa" constitutes a feminist manifesto, a cogent call to all women regardless of culture or situation, to realize their strength and capacity to change the world. Written in a forceful style, the author, in first person, addresses the reader ("woman") in second and in the imperative mood. The originality of the text lies in the combination of this mood with very poetic language. It is this combination that makes "The Laugh of the Medusa" so beautiful and effective. In "Coming to

Writing," Cixous links women's ability to transform the world more precisely to an access to speech and writing, still maintaining her elated tone. Finally, in the third and final excerpt, from "Tales of Sexual Difference," a change can be observed. Without losing force, this essay (composed in 1990, fifteen years later than the first two) is written in another, more ponderous and philosophical manner.

"The Laugh of the Medusa," one of the earliest Cixous essays devoted to sexual difference, attacks two myths that define femininity in a negative way. The first qualifies women as "the dark continent" (an expression used by Napoleon), meaning that men not only have to penetrate it in order to gain knowledge, but they also must "pacify" it, that is colonize it, as Europe did with Africa. Freud appropriated this point and went further with it, stating that woman, and especially woman's sexuality, was an "enigma." This conception is linked to the fact that the female sex is traditionally considered unrepresentable, associated with death. Cixous, however, declares that "*the Dark continent is neither dark nor unexplorable,*" but also adds that "we are dark and we are beautiful." The second myth is that of the femme fatale, here symbolized by the mythological figure of the Medusa who turns men into stone when they dare to look her in the eye. To this Cixous replies: "You only have to look at the Medusa straight on to see her. And she's not deadly. She's beautiful and she's laughing."

"The Laugh of the Medusa" is a feminist text in the sense that it seeks to empower women while denouncing their ageless oppression under patriarchal social structures. A major part of the text's originality consists in how it tightly links the repression of women's bodies to the repression of their writing. It calls on women to break the symbolic and effective silence to which they have been reduced. Cixous mentions the poor number of women writers in the history of literature, but she believes, as well, that women should write differently: "Writing has been run by a libidinal and cultural—hence political, typically masculine—economy," which has "perpetuated" the repression of women. It is true that "some poets"—such as Heinrich von Kleist (1777–1811), author of *Penthesilea,* a play about this Amazon queen— have imagined women who do not fit into the traditional image of femininity. However, in narrative fiction the majority of writers, men and women, have been guided by the empire of reason—*phallocentrism*— which is masculine and hence can be called *phallogocentrism* (from *phallus, logos*—meaning "word" and "reason"—and "center").

Cixous encourages women to "write [their] self." She speaks to and about "woman" in the singular, specifying that "there is . . . no general woman, no one typical woman" and refusing "to confuse the biological and the cultural." Therefore, she can assert that some writing "inscribes femininity," whether authored by a woman (she mentions the French writers Colette and Marguerite Duras) or by a man (e.g., Jean Genet). Masculinity and femininity are present inside both men and women, an idea rendered by the concept of *bisexuality*. This word, however, is often misunderstood, assimilated to the "neuter" or to the fantasy of a "total being." The author refers to this concept as the "presence of both sexes" in everyone. A "feminine practice of writing"—which one cannot systematize without reducing and thus betraying its complexity—might be characterized by "writing with the body." This bodily involvement in writing entails letting the unconscious flow like oil springing forth from a pit. Women, in general, are more prone than men to let the unconscious free, because, since women have been led astray of the *logos*, they put up less barriers against their own drives. The author suggests that woman's speech is closer to the "voice," being more "impassioned" and personal: "she draws her story into history"—which is exactly what she Cixous is doing with her work. Women are also more willing than men to recognize the presence of the other in themselves, and the writer uses the metaphor of maternity to symbolize women's greater tolerance for alterity (because, as she says later in the text, "the child is the other, but the other without violence"). Therefore, it can be metaphorically said that woman "writes in white ink" (in an allusion to breast-feeding).

All these very poetic images are combined with a highly committed and even prophetic tone in the text. The voice who speaks in the first person proclaims that a new age for women is to come when the "New Woman" will replace the "old" one, and that writing constitutes precisely "*the very possibility of change.*"[1] Moreover, women's liberation will imply a fundamental modification of all other power relations. In this sense, "The Laugh of the Medusa" inscribes itself both in the path of feminism and in the women's liberation movement of the seventies. With feminism, it shares its two main aims: "to destroy" (the ancient oppression) and "to project" (a better present and future). It is also interesting to note that this essay was originally published in a special issue of a journal devoted to Simone de Beauvoir,[2] whose positions are quite distant from Cixous's. Sentences such as "Text: my body" or

"Let the priests tremble, we're going to show them our sexts,"[3] are at a great remove from Beauvoir's thought and style and much closer to postmodern feminist positions.

"Coming to writing" (1977) describes, as its title suggests, how the author became a writer, but the chosen excerpt focuses especially on the obstacles she encountered along her way. "How would I have written," asks the narrator, being "no one": "Everything in me joined forces to forbid me to write: History, my story, my origin, my sex." In the same line of thought as "The Laugh of the Medusa," Hélène Cixous claims here that women have been pushed aside from writing, as they have from many other social and political activities. The voice who speaks compares herself to a "mouse," a small and despised animal, while writers seem like "eagles" and "prophets" to her. However, her sex is not the only "bad reason" to prevent her from writing: she is also marked by her Jewishness in the time of concentration camps and by her being born in the French colony of Algeria. These are *real* facts, considering Hélène Cixous's biography, but they are also symbolic of the exclusions one can suffer. The author coins the neologism "Jewoman" (*Juifemme*) to express the banishment of those who are not considered part of the community from the "world." (More than two decades later, Judith Butler would write about those who are so excluded that even their death cannot be mourned.)[4]

Nevertheless, the first and main obstacle a woman encounters when she wants to write comes from herself, from her belief that she has no right to do it—because, from the time they are girls, women are prevented from "flying" and from "thieving"—Cixous uses the French verb *voler*, which will become one of her favorite words, meaning both to fly and to steal. Following her predilection for fairy tales, she alludes to "Little Red Riding Hood" to exemplify how girls were traditionally doomed to a "destiny of restriction and oblivion" due to having been misled to limit their activities mainly to the care of their appearance (they were "mummified . . . into prettiness") excluding anything that had to do with imagination (to fly) or brave opposition (to steal). That is why girls, like Little Red Riding Hood, got lost in the forest and never came to a destination, such as writing. Having assumed this fate, most women did not feel permitted to act otherwise, and that is how and why they became their first and own censors. The narrator thus describes her "shame" in front of her desire: her "passion" to write. Her shame is not only due to the fact that she is a woman but also that, coming from "Africa," she feels excluded from Western tradition. She discovers "culture" at the age of eighteen, marveling at its richness but feeling excluded from it, in the same way that she is expelled from a cathedral because of her bare arms. Nevertheless, she "takes" this culture by passionately reading its works. The image that Cixous uses to express this intense feeling of appropriation is a physical one: the narrator "ate, sucked, suckled, kissed" these texts, like a fervid lover. She is hence capable of stealing this culture, which is not hers, and of flying free from it. Writing begins by reading, in response to the expression of love she finds in books, and, for her, writing will always be linked to love, even assimilated to "saying its names, giving thanks for its caresses." More precisely, reading cannot be understood simply as a first step that leads to writing, yet they are inseparable; Cixous later invented the verb *lirécrire* ("readwrite") to show that, for her, both activities make one single gesture. Obviously, she is referring to her devotion to the many authors who have inspired her (such as Montaigne, Kleist, Balzac, or Proust), but the concept of readwrite goes further. Cixous alludes likewise to the fact that there is a continuity between literary texts, which can be called intertextuality, not only in the sense of authors quoting each other, but almost as if all their books were parts of a single text.

Yet writing was not a choice for the narrator: it imposed itself as an order, in the same way that a prophet speaks urged by God. However, in this case, the order was neither given by a god nor an external structure: it came from "deep down inside," from her inner self, like lava emerging from an erupting volcano. As we saw in "The Laugh of the Medusa," such writing comes from the body and originates in the unconscious, like a dream. Dreams, being productions of the unconscious, are very present in Cixous's texts, and this one is no exception. At its beginning, the narrator explains a dream she had, related to her incapacity to write: in it a sick woman loses a hand ("the hand that writes"), but, instead of giving up, she is told: "Learn to write with the other hand." This is a powerful metaphor for saying that she must write in a different way than the dominant one of the past. Her lack of "grounds from which to write" (she has "no legitimate place, no land, no fatherland, no history of [her] own"), even though it makes her coming to writing much more difficult, is in fact a blessing because it enables her to create with less hindrance. For instance, her first "lack" is language; her mixed origins and the historical features of the time she was born (in a colonized Algeria adhering to Nazi anti-Jewish laws) left her without a "legitimate tongue": "In German I sing; in English I disguise my self; in French I fly, I thieve." French is thus a choice for her, as she has no "right" to write in it—Jacques Derrida, who shared similar origins with Cixous, brilliantly developed the same idea in *Monolingualism of the Other*.[5] More exactly, she does not write *in* French (because she is not allowed to pass this "door," to enter this forbidden "garden") but *writes French*, an expression that suggests a more intimate and loving relationship with language, like the one Hélène Cixous has with words. Having "no roots" becomes an asset instead of a handicap, in a sense close to the concept of *deterritorialization* conceived by Gilles Deleuze and Félix Guattari.[6]

The third excerpt of this section, "Tales of Sexual Difference" (published in 1994) was conceived as a dialogue with Jacques Derrida—who wrote the text "Ants" in response—for a conference on "Readings of Sexual Difference," held in Paris in 1990. In it Hélène Cixous returns to the ideas displayed in her earlier texts, but here puts the emphasis on the difficulty of defining what "sexual difference" is. She calls it D.S. (from its initials in French), pronounced in French the same as *déesse*, which means "goddess." Cixous also identifies sexual difference with a "fairy tale." These allusions to the supernatural indicate that S.D.—as we might call it in English—is, at the same time, elusive and extremely pervasive because of its "magical" power. Its most characteristic feature is, however, that it cannot be stopped: S.D. is in perpetual motion, always "passing": "She-who-passes is her name." (It is worth noting that D.S. is also the name of a "mythical" French car—Roland Barthes included it in his *Mythologies*[7]—launched in 1955, that reigned until the seventies as a most admired model. This allusion adds a humorous note, typical of Cixous's style.) Although S.D. cannot be captured (or taken in a picture, as the author says), that does not mean it does not exist. Men and women are generally different because they are driven by culture to different destinies. Resorting to a well-known fairy tale, Cixous affirms that only a girl can notice the emperor's nudity,[8] since most boys are already engaged in a "phallocratic destiny." That is to say, men—save the "poets"—are trapped in an imposed image of masculinity that is based on rivalry for power.

As for women, they carry difference "as a burden," they embody it, while men are often assimilated to the nonmarked or the neuter. (In this sense, circumcision, a topic on which Derrida has written extensively,[9] is evoked here as the inscription of difference on the masculine body and, thus, as a feminization of it.) Sexual difference is "hidden" in woman's body, states Cixous, alluding to the traditional belief that the female body lacks the penis and is therefore both physically and symbolically castrated, i.e., set aside from power. Contrary to tradition yet again, the author praises the woman's body for being turned to the "interior," understood here not as the viscera but as the "interior earth" everybody comes from. Maternity—as in "The Laugh of the Medusa"—is therefore a feminine feature that touches not only women who have had children but also every woman and even some men. Every woman has the child "written in [her] flesh," because of a "transmitted, inherited" memory, which goes from grandmother to mother to daughter and to granddaughter. However, if one thinks that Cixous is being "essentialist" here—attributing special properties to women and men because of their biological differences—this impression is denied by her next statement: "very often a 'woman' is not a woman nor a 'man' a man." This puzzling sentence can be interpreted as a distinction between the usual epithets *man* and *woman*, which separate human beings in two different—and opposite—categories, and the actual persons, who are always composite.

Here Hélène Cixous is arguing for a postmodern conception of the subject as one who is no longer conceived of as solely an individual (from Latin *individuus*, "indivisible") with definite limits that separate her from the other. As we shall see in part 3 ("Love (and) the Other"), the subject is multiple because he is traversed by alterity and, in so being, is the very place of difference(s). Hélène Cixous places herself in line with postmodern thinkers such as Gilles Deleuze and, above all, Jacques Derrida, who overcame the Cartesian subject and suggested a new way of conceiving it. In the text we are introducing, it is said that everyone, man or woman, is "an ensemble of x elements." The traditional question "Who am I?" can therefore be replaced by a new one, "Who are I?" ("Qui sont-je?"), which uses the plural to indicate the inherent multiplicity of the subject. But in the original French there is a play with the signifier—typical of Cixous's writing: *sont-je* is homophonous with *songe*, "dream." This is equivalent to admitting that self-knowledge is impossible, that "Who am/are I?" is an unanswerable question. Cixous's poetic turn of phrase: "we are blind people who paint our own portraits" is a quotation of a contemporary text by Derrida.[10] The mention of the dream is also, as already seen, an allusion to the unconscious nature of the inner self as well as to the impossibility of the subject's knowing himself. This impossibility is not only obedient to the subject's multiplicity but also to the fact that these identities are extremely heterogeneous, in perpetual motion: "Our interior identifications are innumerable: grandfather, granddaughter, brother (without counting the vegetable, animal, chemical, phonic, astral elements . . .)." Here the writer is talking specifically of women, because she considers women to be more prone to various identifications than men, who are, in general, "occupied by predominantly masculine elements." On the contrary, women are "ensembles that are occupied, populated, naturalized, grafted by a certain number of shares of otherness." Again, this is not a question of nature but of culture: Cixous specifies that it occurs "in the social-political scene today," which means that the situation may change.

Moreover, this distinction between men and women is a frail one, because sexual difference can also be assimilated to "the networks of identifications always trembling and always exchanged between men and women." Finally, S.D. is more a question of "resemblance" than of "difference"; it occurs in "exchange," and it is always moving "from the one to the other." It is in this sense that we can understand Cixous's polemical statement that writing is always feminine, because the text is a privileged place where sexual difference is at stake, where it can leave "traces that last long enough." Writing enables us to modify the traditional identifications that conform masculinity and femininity. Among its gifts, we can find the power "to invent" ourselves.

THE LAUGH OF THE MEDUSA
(1975)

I shall speak about women's writing: about *what it will do*. Woman must write her self: must write about women and bring women to writing, from which they have been driven away as violently as from their bodies—for the same reasons, by the same law, with the same fatal goal. Woman must put herself into the text—as into the world and into history—by her own movement.

The future must no longer be determined by the past. I do not deny that the effects of the past are still with us. But I refuse to strengthen them by repeating them, to confer upon them an irremovability the equivalent of destiny, to confuse the biological and the cultural. Anticipation is imperative.

Since these reflections are taking shape in an area just on the point of being discovered, they necessarily bear the mark of our time—a time during which the new breaks away from the old, and, more precisely, the (feminine) new from the old (*la nouvelle de l'ancien*). Thus, as there are no grounds for establishing a discourse, but rather an arid millennial ground to break, what I say has at least two sides and two aims: to break up, to destroy; and to foresee the unforeseeable, to project.

I write this as a woman, toward women. When I say "woman," I'm speaking of woman in her inevitable struggle against conventional man; and of a universal woman subject who must bring women to their senses and to their meaning in history. But first it must be said that in spite of the enormity of the repression that has kept them in the "dark"—that dark which people have been trying to make them accept as their attribute—there is, at this time, no general woman, no one typical woman. What they have *in common* I will say. But what strikes me is the infinite richness of their individual constitutions: you can't talk about *a* female sexuality, uniform, homogeneous, classifiable into codes—any more than you can talk about one unconscious resembling another. Women's imaginary is inexhaustible, like music, painting, writing: their stream of phantasms is incredible.

I have been amazed more than once by a description a woman gave me of a world all her own which she had been secretly haunting since early childhood. A world of searching, the elaboration of a knowledge, on the basis of a systematic experimentation with the bodily functions, a passionate and precise interrogation of her erotogeneity. This practice, extraordinarily rich and inventive, in particular as concerns masturbation, is prolonged or accompanied by a production of forms, a veritable aesthetic activity, each stage of rapture inscribing a resonant vision, a composition, something beautiful. Beauty will no longer be forbidden.

I wished that that woman would write and proclaim this unique empire so that other women, other unacknowledged sovereigns, might exclaim: I, too, overflow; my desires have invented new desires, my body knows unheard-of songs. Time and again I, too, have felt so full of luminous torrents that I could burst—burst with forms much more beautiful than those which are put up in frames and sold for a stinking fortune. And I, too, said nothing, showed nothing; I didn't open my mouth, I didn't repaint my half of the world. I was ashamed. I was afraid, and I swallowed my shame and my fear. I said to myself: You are mad! What's the meaning of these waves, these floods, these outbursts? Where is the ebullient, infinite woman who, immersed as she was in her naïveté, kept in the dark about herself, led into self-disdain by the great arm of parental-conjugal phallocentrism, hasn't been ashamed of her strength? Who, surprised and horrified by the fantastic tumult of her drives (for she was made to believe that a well-adjusted normal woman has a . . . divine composure), hasn't accused herself of being a monster? Who, feeling a funny desire stirring inside her (to sing, to write, to dare to speak, in short, to bring out something new), hasn't thought she was sick? Well, her shameful sickness is that she resists death, that she makes trouble.

And why don't you write? Write! Writing is for you, you are for you; your body is yours, take it. I know why you haven't written. (And why I didn't write before the age of twenty-seven.) Because writing is at once too high, too great for you, it's reserved for the great—that is, for "great men;" and it's "silly." Besides, you've written a little, but in secret. And it wasn't good, because it was in secret, and because you punished yourself for writing, because you didn't go all the way; or because you wrote, irresistibly, as when we would masturbate in secret, not to go further, but to attenuate the tension a bit, just enough to take the edge off. And then as soon as we come, we go and make ourselves feel guilty—so as to be forgiven; or to forget, to bury it until the next time.

Write, let no one hold you back, let nothing stop you: not man; not the imbecilic capitalist machinery, in which publishing houses are the crafty, obsequious relayers of imperatives handed down by an economy that works against us and off our backs; and not *yourself*. Smug-faced readers, managing editors, and big bosses don't like the true texts of women—female-sexed texts. That kind scares them.

I write woman: woman must write woman. And man, man. So only an oblique consideration will be found here of man; it's up to him to say where his masculinity and femininity are at: this will concern us once men have opened their eyes and seen themselves clearly.[1]

Now women return from afar, from always: from "without," from the heath where witches are kept alive; from below, from beyond "culture;" from their childhood which men have been trying desperately to make them forget, condemning it to "eternal rest." The little girls and their "ill-mannered" bodies immured, well-preserved, intact unto themselves, in the mirror. Frigidified. But are they ever seething underneath! What an effort it takes—there's no end to it—for the sex cops to bar their threatening return. Such a display of forces on both sides that the struggle has for centuries been immobilized in the trembling equilibrium of a deadlock.

Here they are, returning, arriving over and again, because the unconscious is impregnable. They have wandered around in circles, confined to the narrow room in which they've been given a deadly brainwashing. You can incarcerate them, slow them down, get away with the old Apartheid routine, but for a time only. As soon as they begin to speak, at the same time as they're taught their name, they can be taught that their territory is black: because you are Africa, you are black. Your continent is dark. Dark is dangerous. You can't see anything in the dark, you're afraid. Don't move, you might fall. Most of all, don't go into the forest. And so we have internalized this horror of the dark.

Men have committed the greatest crime against women. Insidiously,
violently, they have led them to hate women, to be their own enemies,
to mobilize their immense strength against themselves, to be the exe-
cutants of their virile needs. They have made for women an antinarcis-
sism! A narcissism which loves itself only to be loved for what women
haven't got! They have constructed the infamous logic of antilove.

We the precocious, we the repressed of culture, our lovely mouths
gagged with pollen, our wind knocked out of us, we the labyrinths,
the ladders, the trampled spaces, the bevies—we are black and we are
beautiful.

We're stormy, and that which is ours breaks loose from us without
our fearing any debilitation. Our glances, our smiles, are spent; laughs
exude from all our mouths; our blood flows and we extend ourselves
without ever reaching an end; we never hold back our thoughts, our
signs, our writing; and we're not afraid of lacking.

What happiness for us who are omitted, brushed aside at the scene
of inheritances; we inspire ourselves and we expire without running
out of breath, we are everywhere!

From now on, who, if we say so, can say no to us? We've come back
from always.

It is time to liberate the New Woman from the Old by coming to
know her—by loving her for getting by, for getting beyond the Old
without delay, by going out ahead of what the New Woman will be,
as an arrow quits the bow with a movement that gathers and separates
the vibrations musically, in order to be more than her self.

I say that we must, for, with a few rare exceptions, there has not yet
been any writing that inscribes femininity; exceptions so rare, in fact,
that, after plowing through literature across languages, cultures, and
ages,[2] one can only be startled at this vain scouting mission. It is well
known that the number of women writers (while having increased
very slightly from the nineteenth century on) has always been ridicu-
lously small. This is a useless and deceptive fact unless from their species of female writers we do not first deduct the immense majority
whose workmanship is in no way different from male writing, and
which either obscures women or reproduces the classic representations
of women (as sensitive—intuitive—dreamy, etc.).[3]

Let me insert here a parenthetical remark. I mean it when I speak
of male writing. I maintain unequivocally that there is such a thing as
marked writing; that, until now, far more extensively and repressively

than is ever suspected or admitted, writing has been run by a libidinal and cultural—hence political, typically masculine—economy; that this is a locus where the repression of women has been perpetuated, over and over, more or less consciously, and in a manner that's frightening since it's often hidden or adorned with the mystifying charms of fiction; that this locus has grossly exaggerated all the signs of sexual opposition (and not sexual difference), where woman has never *her* turn to speak—this being all the more serious and unpardonable in that writing is precisely *the very possibility of change*, the space that can serve as a springboard for subversive thought, the precursory movement of a transformation of social and cultural structures.

Nearly the entire history of writing is confounded with the history of reason, of which it is at once the effect, the support, and one of the privileged alibis. It has been one with the phallocentric tradition. It is indeed that same self-admiring, self-stimulating, self-congratulatory phallocentrism.

With some exceptions, for there have been failures—and if it weren't for them, I wouldn't be writing (I-woman, escapee)—in that enormous machine that has been operating and turning out its "truth" for centuries. There have been poets who would go to any lengths to slip something by at odds with tradition—men capable of loving love and hence capable of loving others and of wanting them, of imagining the woman who would hold out against oppression and constitute herself as a superb, equal, hence "impossible" subject, untenable in a real social framework. Such a woman the poet could desire only by breaking the codes that negate her. Her appearance would necessarily bring on, if not revolution—for the bastion was supposed to be immutable—at least harrowing explosions. At times it is in the fissure caused by an earthquake, through that radical mutation of things brought on by a material upheaval when every structure is for a moment thrown off balance and an ephemeral wildness sweeps order away, that the poet slips something by, for a brief span, of woman. Thus did Kleist expend himself in his yearning for the existence of sister-lovers, maternal daughters, mother-sisters, who never hung their heads in shame. Once the palace of magistrates is restored, it's time to pay: immediate bloody death to the uncontrollable elements.

But only the poets—not the novelists, allies of representationalism. Because poetry involves gaining strength through the unconscious and because the unconscious, that other limitless country, is the place where the repressed manage to survive: women, or as Hoffmann would say, fairies.

She must write her self, because this is the invention of a *new insurgent* writing which, when the moment of her liberation has come, will allow her to carry out the indispensable ruptures and transformations in her history, first at two levels that cannot be separated.

a) Individually. By writing her self, woman will return to the body which has been more than confiscated from her, which has been turned into the uncanny stranger on display—the ailing or dead figure, which so often turns out to be the nasty companion, the cause and location of inhibitions. Censor the body and you censor breath and speech at the same time.

Write your self. Your body must be heard. Only then will the immense resources of the unconscious spring forth. Our naphtha will spread, throughout the world, without dollars—black or gold—nonassessed values that will change the rules of the old game.

To write. An act which will not only "realize" the decensored relation of woman to her sexuality, to her womanly being, giving her access to her native strength; it will give her back her goods, her pleasures, her organs, her immense bodily territories which have been kept under seal; it will tear her away from the superegoized structure in which she has always occupied the place reserved for the guilty (guilty of everything, guilty at every turn: for having desires, for not having any; for being frigid, for being "too hot;" for not being both at once; for being too motherly and not enough; for having children and for not having any; for nursing and for not nursing . . .)—tear her away by means of this research, this job of analysis and illumination, this emancipation of the marvelous text of her self that she must urgently learn to speak. A woman without a body, dumb, blind, can't possibly be a good fighter. She is reduced to being the servant of the militant male, his shadow. We must kill the false woman who is preventing the live one from breathing. Inscribe the breath of the whole woman.

b) An act that will also be marked by woman's *seizing* the occasion to *speak*, hence her shattering entry into history, which has always been based *on her suppression*. To write and thus to forge for herself the antilogos weapon. To become *at will* the taker and initiator, for her own right, in every symbolic system, in every political process.

It is time for women to start scoring their feats in written and oral language.

Every woman has known the torment of getting up to speak. Her heart racing, at times entirely lost for words, ground and language slipping away—that's how daring a feat, how great a transgression it is for a woman to speak—even just open her mouth—in public. A double distress, for even if she transgresses, her words fall almost always upon the deaf male ear, which hears in language only that which speaks in the masculine.

It is by writing, from and toward women, and by taking up the challenge of speech which has been governed by the phallus, that women will confirm women in a place other than that which is reserved in and by the symbolic, that is, in a place other than silence. Women should break out of the snare of silence. They shouldn't be conned into accepting a domain which is the margin or the harem.

Listen to a woman speak at a public gathering (if she hasn't painfully lost her wind). She doesn't "speak," she throws her trembling body forward; she lets go of herself, she flies; all of her passes into her voice, and it's with her body that she vitally supports the "logic" of her speech. Her flesh speaks true. She lays herself bare. In fact, she physically materializes what she's thinking; she signifies it with her body. In a certain way she *inscribes* what she's saying, because she doesn't deny her drives, the intractable and impassioned part they have in speaking. Her speech, even when "theoretical" or political, is never simple or linear or "objectified," generalized: she draws her story into history.

There is not that scission, that division made by the common man between the logic of oral speech and the logic of the text, bound as he is by his antiquated relation—servile, calculating—to mastery. From which proceeds the niggardly lip service which engages only the tiniest part of the body, plus the mask.

In women's speech, as in their writing, that element which never stops resonating, which, once we've been permeated by it, profoundly and imperceptibly touched by it, retains the power of moving us—that element is the song: first music from the first voice of love which is alive in every woman. Why this privileged relationship with the voice? Because no woman stockpiles as many defenses for countering the drives as does a man. You don't build walls around yourself, you don't forego pleasure as "wisely" as he. Even if phallic mystification has generally contaminated good relationships, a woman is never far from "mother" (I mean outside her role functions: the "mother" as non-name and as source of goods). There is always within her at least a little of that good mother's milk. She writes in white ink.

Woman for women.—There always remains in woman that force which produces/is produced by the other—in particular, the other woman. *In* her, matrix, cradler; herself giver as her mother and child; she is her own sister-daughter. You might object, "What about she who is the hysterical offspring of a bad mother?" Everything will be changed once woman gives woman to the other woman. There is hidden and always ready in woman the source; the locus for the other. The mother, too, is a metaphor. It is necessary and sufficient that the best of herself be given to woman by another woman for her to be able to love herself and return in love the body that was "born" to her. Touch me, caress me, you the living no-name, give me my self as myself. The relation to the "mother," in terms of intense pleasure and violence, is curtailed no more than the relation to childhood (the child that she was, that she is, that she makes, remakes, undoes, there at the point where, the same, she others herself). Text: my body—shot through with streams of song; I don't mean the overbearing, clutchy "mother" but, rather, what touches you, the equivoice that affects you, fills your breast with an urge to come to language and launches your force; the rhythm that laughs you; the intimate recipient who makes all metaphors possible and desirable; body (body? bodies?), no more describable than god, the soul, or the Other; that part of you that leaves a space between yourself and urges you to inscribe in language your woman's style. In women there is always more or less of the mother who makes everything all right, who nourishes, and who stands up against separation; a force that will not be cut off but will knock the wind out of the codes. We will rethink womankind beginning with every form and every period of her body. The Americans remind us, "We are all Lesbians;" that is, don't denigrate woman, don't make of her what men have made of you.

Because the "economy" of her drives is prodigious, she cannot fail, in seizing the occasion to speak, to transform directly and indirectly *all* systems of exchange based on masculine thrift. Her libido will produce far more radical effects of political and social change than some might like to think.

Because she arrives, vibrant, over and again, we are at the beginning of a new history, or rather of a process of becoming in which several histories intersect with one another. As subject for history, woman always occurs simultaneously in several places. Woman un-thinks[4] the unifying, regulating history that homogenizes and channels forces, herding contradictions into a single battlefield. In woman, personal history blends together with the history of all women, as well as national and world history. As a militant, she is an integral part of all liberations. She must be farsighted, not limited to a blow-by-blow interaction. She foresees that her liberation will do more than modify power relations or toss the ball over to the other camp; she will bring about a mutation in human relations, in thought, in all praxis: hers is not simply a class struggle, which she carries forward into a much vaster movement. Not that in order to be a woman-in-struggle(s) you have to leave the class struggle or repudiate it; but you have to split it open, spread it out, push it forward, fill it with the fundamental struggle so as to prevent the class struggle, or any other struggle for the liberation of a class or people, from operating as a form of repression, pretext for postponing the inevitable, the staggering alteration in power relations and in the production of individualities. This alteration is already upon us—in the United States, for example, where millions of night crawlers are in the process of undermining the family and disintegrating the whole of American sociality.

The new history is coming; it's not a dream, though it does extend beyond men's imagination, and for good reason. It's going to deprive them of their conceptual orthopedics, beginning with the destruction of their enticement machine.

It is impossible to *define* a feminine practice of writing, and this is an impossibility that will remain, for this practice can never be theorized, enclosed, coded—which doesn't mean that it doesn't exist. But it will always surpass the discourse that regulates the phallocentric system; it does and will take place in areas other than those subordinated to philosophico-theoretical domination. It will be conceived of only by subjects who are breakers of automatisms, by peripheral figures that no authority can ever subjugate.

Hence the necessity to affirm the flourishes of this writing, to give form to its movement, its near and distant byways. Bear in mind to begin with (1) that sexual opposition, which has always worked for man's profit to the point of reducing writing, too, to his laws, is only a historico-cultural limit. There is, there will be more and more rapidly pervasive now, a fiction that produces irreducible effects of femininity. (2) That it is through ignorance that most readers, critics, and writers of both sexes hesitate to admit or deny outright the possibility or the pertinence of a distinction between feminine and masculine writing. It will usually be said, thus disposing of sexual difference: either that all writing, to the extent that it materializes, is feminine; or, inversely— but it comes to the same thing—that the act of writing is equivalent to masculine masturbation (and so the woman who writes cuts herself out a paper penis); or that writing is bisexual, hence neuter, which again does away with differentiation. To admit that writing is precisely working (in) the in-between, inspecting the process of the same and of the other without which nothing can live, undoing the work of death—to admit this is first to want the two, as well as both, the ensemble of the one and the other, not fixed in sequences of struggle and expulsion or some other form of death but infinitely dynamized by an incessant process of exchange from one subject to another. A process of different subjects knowing one another and beginning one another anew only from the living boundaries of the other: a multiple and inexhaustible course with millions of encounters and transformations of the same into the other and into the in-between, from which woman takes her forms (and man, in his turn; but that's his other history).

In saying "bisexual, hence neuter," I am referring to the classic conception of bisexuality, which, squashed under the emblem of castration fear and along with the fantasy of a "total" being (though composed of two halves), would do away with the difference experienced as an operation incurring loss, as the mark of dreaded sectility.

To this self-effacing, merger-type bisexuality, which would conjure away castration (the writer who puts up his sign: "bisexual written here, come and see," when the odds are good that it's neither one nor the other), I oppose the *other bisexuality* on which every subject not enclosed in the false theater of phallocentric representationalism has founded his/her erotic universe. Bisexuality: that is, each one's location in self (*repérage en soi*) of the presence—variously manifest and insistent according to each person, male or female—of both sexes, nonexclusion either of the difference or of one sex, and, from this "self-permission," multiplication of the effects of the inscription of desire, over all parts of my body and the other body.

Now it happens that at present, for historico-cultural reasons, it is women who are opening up to and benefiting from this vatic bisexuality which doesn't annul differences but stirs them up, pursues them, increases their number. In a certain way, "woman is bisexual;" man—it's a secret to no one—being poised to keep glorious phallic monosexuality in view. By virtue of affirming the primacy of the phallus and of bringing it into play, phallocratic ideology has claimed more than one victim. As a woman, I've been clouded over by the great shadow of the scepter and been told: idolize it, that which you cannot brandish. But at the same time, man has been handed that grotesque and scarcely enviable destiny (just imagine) of being reduced to a single idol with clay balls. And consumed, as Freud and his followers note, by a fear of being a woman! For, if psychoanalysis was constituted from woman, to repress femininity (and not so successful a repression at that—men have made it clear), its account of masculine sexuality is now hardly refutable; as with all the "human" sciences, it reproduces the masculine view, of which it is one of the effects.

Here we encounter the inevitable man-with-rock, standing erect in his old Freudian realm, in the way that, to take the figure back to the point where linguistics is conceptualizing it "anew," Lacan preserves it in the sanctuary of the phallos (Ø) "sheltered" from *castration's lack*! Their "symbolic" exists, it holds power—we, the sowers of disorder, know it only too well. But we are in no way obliged to deposit our lives in their banks of lack, to consider the constitution of the subject in terms of a drama manglingly restaged, to reinstate again and again the religion of the father. Because we don't want that. We don't fawn around the supreme hole. We have no womanly reason to pledge allegiance to the negative. The feminine (as the poets suspected) affirms: " . . . And yes," says Molly, carrying *Ulysses* off beyond any book and toward the new writing; "I said yes, I will Yes."

The Dark Continent is neither dark nor unexplorable.—It is still unexplored only because we've been made to believe that it was too dark to be explorable. And because they want to make us believe that what interests us is the white continent, with its monuments to Lack. And we believed. They riveted us between two horrifying myths: between the Medusa and the abyss. That would be enough to set half the world laughing, except that it's still going on. For the phallologocentric sublation[5] is with us, and it's militant, regenerating the old patterns, anchored in the dogma of castration. They haven't changed a thing: they've theorized their desire for reality! Let the priests tremble, we're going to show them our sexts!

Too bad for them if they fall apart upon discovering that women aren't men, or that the mother doesn't have one. But isn't this fear convenient for them? Wouldn't the worst be, isn't the worst, in truth, that women aren't castrated, that they have only to stop listening to the Sirens (for the Sirens were men) for history to change its meaning? You only have to look at the Medusa straight on to see her. And she's not deadly. She's beautiful and she's laughing.

Men say that there are two unrepresentable things: death and the feminine sex. That's because they need femininity to be associated with death; it's the jitters that gives them a hard-on! for themselves! They need to be afraid of us. Look at the trembling Perseuses moving backward toward us, clad in apotropes. What lovely backs! Not another minute to lose. Let's get out of here.

Let's hurry: the continent is not impenetrably dark. I've been there often. I was overjoyed one day to run into Jean Genet. It was in *Pompes funèbres*.[6] He had come there led by his Jean. There are some men (all too few) who aren't afraid of femininity.

Almost everything is yet to be written by women about femininity: about their sexuality, that is, its infinite and mobile complexity, about their eroticization, sudden turn-ons of a certain minuscule-immense area of their bodies; not about destiny, but about the adventure of such and such a drive, about trips, crossings, trudges, abrupt and gradual awakenings, discoveries of a zone at one time timorous and soon to be forthright. A woman's body, with its thousand and one thresholds of ardor—once, by smashing yokes and censors, she lets it articulate the profusion of meanings that run through it in every direction—will make the old single-grooved mother tongue reverberate with more than one language.

We've been turned away from our bodies, shamefully taught to ignore them, to strike them with that stupid sexual modesty; we've been made victims of the old fool's game: each one will love the other sex. I'll give you your body and you'll give me mine. But who are the men who give women the body that women blindly yield to them? Why so few texts? Because so few women have as yet won back their body. Women must write through their bodies, they must invent the impregnable language that will wreck partitions, classes, and rhetorics, regulations and codes, they must submerge, cut through, get beyond the ultimate reserve-discourse, including the one that laughs at the very idea of pronouncing the word "silence," the one that, aiming for the impossible, stops short before the word "impossible" and writes it as "the end."

Such is the strength of women that, sweeping away syntax, breaking that famous thread (just a tiny little thread, they say) which acts
for men as a surrogate umbilical cord, assuring them—otherwise they
couldn't come—that the old lady is always right behind them, watching them make phallus, women will go right up to the impossible.
. . .

Translated by Keith Cohen and Paula Cohen

2

COMING TO WRITING
(1976)

. . .

I'm afraid: that life will become foreign. That it will no longer be this nothing that makes immediate sense in my body, but instead, outside me, will surround me and beset me with Its question; that it will become the enigma, the irrational, the roll of the die; the final blow.

Terror: life arrest, death sentence:[1] every child's Terror. Perhaps being adult means no longer asking yourself where you come from, where you're going, who to be. Discarding the past, warding off the future? Putting history in place of yourself? Perhaps. But who is the woman spared by questioning? Don't you, you too, ask yourself: who am I, who will I have been, why-me, why-not-me? Don't you tremble with uncertainty? Aren't you, like me, constantly struggling not to fall into the trap? Which means you're in the trap already, because the fear of doubting is already the doubt that you fear. And why can't the question of why-am-I just leave me in peace? Why does it throw me off balance? What does it have to do with my woman-being? It's the social scene, I think, that constrains you to it; history that condemns you to it. If you want to grow, progress, stretch your soul, take infinite pleasure in your bodies, your goods, how will you position yourself to do so? You are, you too, a Jewoman, trifling, diminutive, mouse among the mouse people, assigned to the fear of the big bad cat. To the diaspora of your desires; to the intimate deserts. And if you grow, your desert likewise grows. If you come out of the hole, the world lets you know that there is no place for your kind in its nations.

"Why did you put me in the world if only for me to be lost in it?"

Determining whom to put this question to is beyond you.

Sometimes I think I began writing in order to make room for the wandering question that haunts my soul and hacks and saws at my body; to give it a place and time; to turn its sharp edge away from my flesh; to give, seek, touch, call, bring into the world a new being who won't restrain me, who won't drive me away, won't perish from very narrowness.

Because of the following dream:

My rejection of sickness as a weapon. There is a self that horrifies me. Isn't she dead yet? Done for. I fear her death. There, on that great bed. Sad, horribly so. Her sickness: cancer. A diseased hand. She herself is the sickness.[2] Will you save her by cutting off the hand? Overcome the atrocious, anguishing disgust, not at death but at the condemnation, the work of sickness. My whole being is convulsed. Tell her what must be said: "You have two hands. If one hand can't live, cut it off. You have twomorrow.[3] When one hand doesn't work, replace it with the other hand. Act. Respond. You've lost the hand that writes? Learn to write with the other hand." And with it-her-self-me-her-hand, I begin to trace on the paper. And now at once there unfurls a perfect calligraphy, as if she had always had this writing in that other hand. If you die, live.

With one hand, suffering, living, putting your finger on pain, loss. But there is the other hand: the one that writes.

A GIRL IS BEING KILLED[4]

In the beginning, I desired.

"What is it she wants?"

"To live. Just to live. And to hear myself say the name."

"Horrors! Cut out her tongue!"

"What's wrong with her?"

"She can't keep herself from flying!"[5]

"In that case, we have special cages."

Who is the Superuncle who hasn't prevented a girl from flying, the flight of the thief, who has not bound her, not bandaged the feet of his little darling, so that they might be exquisitely petite, who hasn't mummified her into prettiness?

Wouldn't you first have needed the "right reasons" to write? The reasons, mysterious to me, that give you the "right" to write? But I didn't know them. I had only the "wrong" reason; it wasn't a reason, it was a passion, something shameful—and disturbing; one of those violent characteristics with which I was afflicted. I didn't "want" to write. How could I have "wanted" to? I hadn't strayed to the point of losing all measure of things. A mouse is not a prophet. I wouldn't have had the cheek to go claim my book from God on Mount Sinai, even if, as a mouse, I had found the energy to scamper up the mountain. No reasons at all. But there was madness. Writing was in the air around me. Always close, intoxicating, invisible, inaccessible. I undergo writing! It came to me abruptly. One day I was tracked down, besieged, taken. It captured me. I was seized. From where? I knew nothing about it. I've never known anything about it. From some bodily region. I don't know where. "Writing" seized me, gripped me, around the diaphragm, between the stomach and the chest, a blast dilated my lungs and I stopped breathing.

Suddenly I was filled with a turbulence that knocked the wind out of me and inspired me to wild acts. "Write." When I say "writing" seized me, it wasn't a sentence that had managed to seduce me, there was absolutely nothing written, not a letter, not a line. But in the depths of the flesh, the attack. Pushed. Not penetrated. Invested. Set in motion. The attack was imperious: "Write!" Even though I was only a meager anonymous mouse, I knew vividly the awful jolt that galvanizes the prophet, wakened in mid-life by an order from above. It's a force to make you cross oceans. Me, write? But I wasn't a prophet. An urge shook my body, changed my rhythms, tossed madly in my chest, made time unlivable for me. I was stormy. "Burst!" "You may speak!" And besides, whose voice is that? The Urge had the violence of a thunderclap. Who's striking me? Who's attacking me from behind? And in my body the breath of a giant, but no sentences at all. Who's pushing me? Who's invading? Who's changing me into a monster? Into a mouse wanting to swell to the size of a prophet?

A joyful force. Not a god; it doesn't come from above. But from an inconceivable region, deep down inside me but unknown, as if there might exist somewhere in my body (which, from the outside, and from the point of view of a naturalist, is highly elastic, nervous, lively, thin, not without charm, firm muscles, pointed nose always quivering and damp, vibrating paws) another space, limitless; and there, in those zones which inhabit me and which I don't know how to live in, I feel them, I don't live them, they live me, gushing from the wellsprings of my souls, I don't see them but I feel them, it's incomprehensible but that's how it is. There are sources. That's the enigma. One morning, it all explodes. My body experiences, deep down inside, one of its panicky cosmic adventures. I have volcanoes on my lands. But no lava: what wants to flow is breath. And not just any old way. The breath "wants" a form.[6] "Write me!" One day it begs me, another day it threatens. "Are you going to write me or not?" It could have said: "Paint me." I tried. But the nature of its fury demanded the form that stops the least, that encloses the least, the body without a frame, without skin, without walls, the flesh that doesn't dry, doesn't stiffen, doesn't clot the wild blood that wants to stream through it—forever. "Let me through, or everything goes!"

What blackmail could have made me give in to this breath? Write? Me? Because it was so strong and furious, I loved and feared this breath. To be lifted up one morning, snatched off the ground, swung in the air. To be taken by surprise. To find in myself the possibility of the unexpected. To fall asleep a mouse and wake up an eagle! What delight! What terror. And I had nothing to do with it, I couldn't help it. And worse, each time the breathing seized me, the same misery was repeated: what began, in spite of myself, in exultation, proceeded, because of myself, in combat, and ended in downfall and desolation. Barely off the ground: "Hey! What are you doing up there? Is that any place for a mouse? For shame!" Shame overcame me. There is no lack on earth, so there was no lack in my personal spaces, of guardians of the law, their pockets filled with the "first stone" to hurl at flying mice. As for my internal guardian—whom I didn't call superego at the time—he was more rapid and accurate than all the others: he threw the stone at me before all the other-relatives, masters, prudent contemporaries, compliant and orderly peers—all the noncrazy and antimouse forces—had the chance to let fire. I was the "fastest gun." Fortunately! My shame settled the score without scandal. I was "saved."

Write? I didn't think of it. I dreamed of it constantly, but with the chagrin and the humility, the resignation and the innocence, of the poor. Writing is God. But it is not your God. Like the Revelation of a cathedral: I was born in a country where culture had returned to nature—had become flesh once again. Ruins that are not ruins, but hymns of luminous memory, Africa sung by the sea night and day. The past wasn't past. Just curled up like the prophet in the bosom of time. At the age of eighteen, I discovered "culture." The monument, its splendor, its menace, its *discourse*. "Admire me. I am the spirit of Christianity. Down on your knees, offspring of the bad race. Transient. I was erected for my followers. Out, little Jewess. Quick, before I baptize you." "Glory": what a word! A name for armies or cathedrals or lofty victories; it wasn't a word for Jewoman. Glory, stained-glass windows, flags, domes, constructions, masterpieces—how to avoid recognizing your beauty, keep it from reminding me of my foreignness?

One summer I get thrown out of the cathedral of Cologne. It's true that I had bare arms; or was it a bare head? A priest kicks me out. Naked. I felt naked for being Jewish, Jewish for being naked, naked for being a woman, Jewish for being flesh and joyful!,—So I'll take all your books. But the cathedrals I'll leave behind. Their stone is sad and male.

The texts I ate, sucked, suckled, kissed. I am the innumerable child of their masses.

But write? With what right? After all, I read them without any right, without permission, without their knowledge.

The way I might have prayed in a cathedral, sending their God an impostor-message.

Write? I was dying of desire for it, of love, dying to give writing what it had given to me. What ambition! What impossible happiness. To nourish my own mother. Give her, in turn, my milk? Wild imprudence.

No need for a severe superego to prevent me from writing: nothing in me made such an act plausible or conceivable. How many workers' children dream of becoming Mozart or Shakespeare?

Everything in me joined forces to forbid me to write: History, my story, my origin, my sex. Everything that constituted my social and cultural self. To begin with the necessary, which I lacked, the material that writing is formed of and extracted from: language. You want—to Write? In what language? Property, rights, had always policed me: I learned to speak French in a garden from which I was on the verge of expulsion for being a Jew. I was of the race of Paradise-losers. Write French? With what right? Show us your credentials! What's the password? Cross yourself! Put out your hands, let's see those paws! What kind of nose is that?

I said "write French." One writes *in*. Penetration. Door. Knock before entering. Strictly forbidden.

"You are not from here. You are not at home here. Usurper!"

"It's true. No right. Only love."

Write? Taking pleasure as the gods who created the books take pleasure and give pleasure, *endlessly*; their bodies of paper and blood; their letters of flesh and tears; they put an end to the end. The human gods, who don't know what they've done; what their visions, their words, do to us. How could I have not wanted to write? When books took me, transported me, pierced me to the entrails, allowed me to feel their disinterested power; when I felt loved by a text that didn't address itself to me, or to you, but to the other; when I felt pierced through by life itself, which doesn't judge, or choose, which touches without designating; when I was agitated, torn out of myself, by love? When my being was populated, my body traversed and fertilized, how could I have closed myself up in silence? Come to me, I will come to you. When love makes love to you, how can you keep from murmuring, saying its names, giving thanks for its caresses?

You can desire. You can read, adore, be invaded. But writing is not granted to you. Writing is reserved for the chosen. It surely took place in a realm inaccessible to the small, to the humble, to women. In the intimacy of the sacred. Writing spoke to its prophets from a burning bush. But it must have been decided that bushes wouldn't dialogue with women.

Didn't experience prove it? I thought it addressed itself not to ordinary men, however, but only to the righteous, to beings fashioned out of separation, for solitude. It asked everything of them, took everything from them, it was merciless and tender, it dispossessed them entirely of all riches, all bonds, it lightened them, stripped them bare; then it granted them passage: toward the most distant, the nameless, the endless. It gave them leave—this was a right and a necessity. They would never arrive. They would never be found by the limit. It would be with them, in the future, like no one.

Thus, for this elite, the gorgeous journey without horizon, beyond everything, the appalling but intoxicating excursion toward the never-yet-said.

But for you, the tales announce a destiny of restriction and oblivion; the brevity, the lightness of a life that steps out of mother's house only to make three little detours that lead you back dazed to the house of your grandmother, for whom you'll amount to no more than a mouthful. For you, little girl, little jug of milk, little pot of honey, little basket, experience reveals it, history promises you this minute alimentary journey that brings you back quickly indeed to the bed of the jealous Wolf, your ever-insatiable grandmother, as if the law ordained that the mother should be constrained to sacrifice her daughter, to expiate the audacity of having relished the good things in life in the form of her pretty red offspring. Vocation of the swallowed up, voyage of the scybalum.

So for the Sons of the Book: research, the desert, inexhaustible space, encouraging, discouraging, the march straight ahead. For the daughters of the housewife: the straying into the forest. Deceived, disappointed, but brimming with curiosity. Instead of the great enigmatic duel with the Sphinx, the dangerous questioning addressed to the body of the Wolf: What is the body for? Myths end up having our hides. Logos opens its great maw, and swallows us whole.

Speaking (crying out, yelling, tearing the air, rage drove me to this endlessly) doesn't leave traces: you can speak—it evaporates, ears are made for not hearing, voices get lost. But writing! Establishing a contract with time. Noting! Making yourself noticed!!!

"Now *that* is forbidden."

All the reasons I had for believing I didn't have the right to write, the good, the less good, and the really wrong reasons: I had no grounds from which to write. No legitimate place, no land, no fatherland, no history of my own.

Nothing falls to me by right—or rather everything does, and no more so to me than to any other.

"I have no roots: from what sources could I take in enough to nourish a text? Diaspora effect.

"I have no legitimate tongue. In German I sing; in English I disguise myself; in French I fly, I thieve. On what would I base a text?

"I am already so much the inscription of a divergence that a further divergence is impossible. They teach me the following lesson: you, outsider, fit in. Take the nationality of the country that tolerates you. Be good, return to the ranks, to the ordinary, the imperceptible, the domestic."

Here are your laws: you will not kill, you will be killed, you will not steal, you will not be a bad recruit, you will not be sick or crazy (this would be a lack of consideration for your hosts), you will not zigzag.

You will not write. You will learn to calculate. You will not touch. In whose name would I write?

You, write? But who do you think you are? Could I say: "It's not me, it's the breath!"? "No one." And this was true: I didn't think I was anyone.

This was in fact what most obscurely worried me and pained me: being no one. Everyone was someone, I felt, except me. I was no one. "Being" was reserved for those full, well-defined, scornful people who occupied the world with their assurance, took their places without hesitation, were at home everywhere where I "was"-n't except as an infraction, intruder, little scrap from elsewhere, always on the alert. The untroubled ones. "To be?" What selfconfidence! I thought to myself: "I could have not been." And: "I will be." But to say "I am"? I who? Everything that designated me publicly, that I made use of—you don't turn down an oar when you're drifting—was misleading and false. I didn't deceive myself, but, objectively, I deceived the world. My true identification papers were false. I wasn't even a little girl, I was a fearful and wild animal, and I was ferocious (although they may have suspected this). Nationality? "French." Not my fault! *They* put me in the position of imposture. Even now, I sometimes feel pushed to explain myself, to excuse myself, to rectify, like an old reflex. For at least I believed, if not in the truth of being, in a rigor, a purity of language. If a given word turned to the practice of lying, it was because it was being mistreated. Twisted, abused, used idiotically.

"I am": who would dare to speak like God? Not I . . . *What* I was, if that could be described, was a whirlwind of tensions, a series of fires, ten thousand scenes of violence (history had nourished me on this: I had the "luck" to take my first steps in the blazing hotbed between two holocausts, in the midst, in the very bosom of racism, to be three years old in 1940, to be Jewish, one part of me in the concentration camps, one part of me in the "colonies").

So all my lives are divided between two principal lives, my life up above and my life down below. Down below I claw, I am lacerated, I sob. Up above I pleasure. Down below, carnage, limbs, quarterings, tortured bodies, noises, engines, harrow. Up above, face, mouth, aura; torrent of the silence of the heart.

Translated by Deborah Jenson, with Ann Liddle and Susan Sellers

3

TALES OF SEXUAL DIFFERENCE
(1990)

. . .

I am afraid. I hope this fear will let go of me. A long time ago, thinking about today, I wrote: "I see only obstacles; I am afraid." That has not changed. Here we are him you, she me and him, in the same place, no, I mean in the same room, no, I meant at the same hour. The time is the same. And at the same time and facing us, no, rather around us or rather in me—I'm having a hard time saying "us" at the moment—and in him, that is, in you, the question, that is, the fear, this "story" of "sexual difference." Or perhaps it is a tale? Or else it's a joke, it might be a game, and if it is a fairy tale, then it is the fairy that makes the difference, the *difference fairy*.[1] Yes, I realize that in talking of a fairy I am a bit less afraid. I sense that with the help of a fairy I can say and do whatever comes, and above all whatever I believe and thus think, without worrying that what "I think," as soon as it is said, will instantly be annihilated by a great blow of reason, of my reason, not necessarily his reason, or denial. I am afraid. But why?

Because what is happening now is a scene that happens in dreams. An exam scene: I must prove I and you, she and he, sheshe and hehe, not without shehe and heshe, etc. Must I prove the most improbable thing in the world: the truth, the obvious fact?

I am going to have to photograph *the difference that passes by*. "D.S.," as I call it, when I write it silently.[2] The goddess (who) passes. She-who-passes is her name.

Clarice Lispector said: "Now I want to photograph perfume," no, she did not *say* that, she *wrote* it. I am going to have to photograph perfume, difference. I am going to have to draw the outside of the outside from the point of view of the outside of the inside, and make the outside that is only out believe that the in is inside, what's more I'll have to deal with the word *interior* which is so often treated with scorn. Are we not all mad? Why, I ask myself, must I demonstrate today, in our times, that trees grow? Or rather: why must the tree prove that it grows? But also, when I hear certain discourses, and discourses are often our enemies: it is urgently necessary to prove that the tree grows, that there is difference, and at the same time I do not know how to go about proving with words, saying with words something that is the wordless music of *jouissance*.[3] I will nonetheless attempt to paint with words the cave I have been living in since I began thinking about this conference.

Before the conference, I also asked myself about the layout of the scene, his, that is to say yours and mine, and everything became terribly loaded, left right, above below, the armchair the seat. I said to myself: "I am afraid of you," "I am playing with you," this is no longer entirely true. It is very difficult because "*you*" is all of you now, whereas when I thought, when I wrote, "you" [*toi*] was *him*.[4] I said to him: you are extremely familiar to me. I know you all the way to what is unknown to you about yourself. (I am beginning to say dangerous things, but it is impossible to do otherwise.) I have read you, I read you (I am speaking to you [*toi*], even if I am speaking in this direction, before me) and I see you in your texts, I see you walk step by step, with an Indian step in your texts (as an Indian walks, with a wild step, I mean an animal's step, all ears) and, walking silently, you look in every direction. And you foresee. (Allow me to say "*tu*," even if I am turned toward *vous*.) Perhaps "you foresee" is your path, your forepath,[5] you advance in foresight and in prevision.

With *circumspection*. You advance: by circles, by circling. Playing with peril.[6]

I know you, here is the *born-man*, I said to myself, it is obvious, I said to myself. I mean: the man with a line of descent, here is the son, son of the mother, here is the father son, father of sons, father of fiction-daughter . . .

I said: "He is a man." Is this the truth? Which truth?

He is man with specifications. With nuances. How to paint a portrait of the sexual difference of the sexed soul? With colors, shades, sounds, signifiers. Man in maturity, already aware of the networks of identifications always trembling and always exchanged between men and women and . . . , and between the stages in masculine maturation, keeping within himself the theme of masculine rivalry, of power—but this theme played less vigorously, softened—, having understood from his own experience the fragility of the other man, I mean the other son, that is, himself, therefore having bent back some of the rigidity as would a maternal woman. The mother in him is an acquisition. The son made him tremble. He is man plus mother. He is *homme mère*, thus blind.[7] He is child. He is overchild [*surenfant*]: child of his children. But in the first place, to begin before you [*toi*] who are here: *here is the circumcised one*, and in saying this I am only following you.[8] I am revealing nothing to you [the audience], because this is inscribed almost as a "proper name" in all his texts, he who I usually call "Derrida" when he is not there.

Here is the circumcised one: this is what came to me through so many extraordinary texts, all those texts which are apparently philosophical, really philosophical, philosophical in truth, and which at the same time, for me, are in the first place an immense story at once groping in the dark and finding nearly, which are, in the end the most perilous, the most courageous, the most mad autobiographical or biographical enterprise of these times, of this era. I am doing nothing more than seeing what he shows and reading what he reads: *Here is the circumcised one*, this is what came, with "cis," with "si," and "ci"[9] and circumspection.

I have had, in my hands—because J.D., you, gave it to me recently—an extraordinary text with an extraordinary title: *Circonfession* . . .[10] I let it resonate: *cirque* [circus], *con* [cunt], *fesse* [buttock], *sion* [zion], *si on* [if one], *sillon* [furrow], *si on t'oublie ô sion* [if we forget you oh zion], signifiers are his thing. If there is something that makes itself heard, makes itself seen and at the same time hides in this text, it is the incalculable importance in the text, in the time, in the destiny, in the progeny, in the combats, in the hope called Jacques Derrida

of this having-been-(circumcised) and this circumcised-being,

an importance with unheard-of echoes, the fascinating importance of this act committed on the body of the newborn who is not yet and already himself, of this additional removal, of this stripping off[11] dedicated to a little-known god, of this uncapping, of this rape, and all of this before himself and on himself, of this letter carved before he knew how to read—it is indeed this circumcised being. I must add that as I speak I will be obliged to do what Derrida always does: to retract, otherwise, displace, push to the side, what was just said. The word *circumcised* also.

You are circumcised, I said, thus I begin with the body; I could have begun otherwise. This body, your body, because your text is constantly of the body, is *signed*, it is *signed* in a thousand ways, it is constantly raising the question of the signature, it is a text signed in blood.[12] But you will ask me: "Is this story of circumcised-being a trait of masculinity? Are all men circumcised?" Perhaps. I do not know. In any case, for Jacques, masculinity—no, not masculinity: he, the one to whom this was done, this attempt to engrave him before he knew his name, goes off on the path that leads him toward death, and then well beyond, of course, starting from the scene of circumcision. The path leads through there, through something that is—I do not want to say it simply—"the missing membrane as an addition." The (no)-more-prepuce.[13] This is a theme of infinite richness, not only for our imaginations or our experiences but above all for what Jacques has done with this little piece of missing skin, stretching it like Saint Augustine's sky-skin of which you speak, transforming it (the membrane) into a sort of immense manuscript. With this lacking membrane, something that (I am speaking about us at the same time) is the wound, a wound from long ago.

A wound inflicted by who? This is a question that runs through this text *Circumfession*—which is his response, his story, perhaps his myth—and arrives here: the mother. With circumcision appears, enters, having always been there of course, the mark of the mother on the son. The mother who cuts? It is the mother who saws, the mother/saw. The mother circumscribes—and I ask myself: are (all) men at the mercy of the mother/saw?[14] Perhaps. In any case, the mother-son scene says a good part of what, to my eyes, occupies the left-hand scene (of the one who is to my left today), of sexual difference. We know variations on this complex scene: the son's hate of the mother, and, conversely, the alliance, the mother-son ring, and for him, you, something infinitely knotted, woven and utterly moving, which is on the order of love (it was also my intention to speak of love today), which cannot be reduced simply to saying mother and son, but to a set of decisive, gripping situations, situations of the passions, which is to say of suffering, of the separation of inseparables, of forgetting and unforgetting, beginning with this one: his mother does not read him. It is he who confides this in us, or simply tells us (he whom his mother does not read).

To return to this story of circumcision, I am interested in it insofar as I am not circumcised, but I know that he could tell me that perhaps I am; I see here an infinite source of meditation, of research, of pain, also of joy. What if we were all a little bit signed without consciously knowing it? and all stretched between wound and pleasure [*plaie et plaisir*]? All a little bit opened by—the other? A meditation on the question of loss and mourning that plows such a large region in Jacques' texts, the question of how to lose what one has already lost, how to be lucky enough to lose what one has already lost, how to have (still, always) more to lose (in other words, how to have having, because having is to lose, having is pregnant with loss). Because in this scene of deprepuceflowering[15] (you will notice that I am getting closer to the flea [*puce*]), one could say, one could affirm that the circumcised one (is) (profits from being) uncircumcisable. But knowing that I am in derridian territory, as soon as I have said that, I expect to soon be able to say, once I have gone around the ring, the opposite. But all the same, he is circumcised. I can hold to this reality in the flesh.

The circumcised one is explicitly different. He therefore "feels different." Different from before. And from the "others." Perhaps he is not different, if all men are "circumcised," but nonetheless that is how it begins: as different. And I suppose, because I have a circumcised brother, that effectively one/he/you feel(s) different, he feels, you feel different from. But different *in spite of* himself. Or without choice.[16]

And us? It is through difference that a woman relates to herself.[17] When one speaks of sexual difference in society, that is, at war, the person who bears difference as a burden, as a question, is very often the woman. A woman enters *on stage* as having that strange difference she can only describe in this differential space where she will encounter you. Where does feeling the difference begin? Where does our feeling the difference begin?

The circumcised one will thus have been circumcised in the first place in spite of himself. This "in spite of" is part of the tension (of this text) called *Circumfession*. Circumcised different. Without having been asked his opinion. Without him being able to do anything. Without you being able to do anything. First. Before him. As a circumcised one, he is the subject of a book, the Bible. It is by the stroke of a Book that he begins to belong to this rich and complicated universe of the circumcised and the non-circumcised. Thus: *it is written*. Circumcised by bookstroke. Cut back. The limit between me and the other is carved in the body itself. What makes the difference, that is, the cut of union, is carved in the very flesh of this I. The other bites me, it is written. Or else it is the I that bites (himself). Henceforth the other will be legible in this body (but the other who?).

And for us (women), is it written? What could I find as an equivalent? What blow? Nothing, in my opinion, that is so antique, no act as old as this in our existence, nothing so antecedent. Woman-difference is localized, lodged, often even hidden from ourselves, in the body, and I think that *it is not written*, not with a knife, not with a stylus, not with the teeth. It is flesh-mystery without tragedy. And if there is a trace, and if there is a scene, it is not before, it is later, tomorrow, "when I will be big," it is to be imagined. There is an oral narrative, beginning with the story we are told, for example the announcement of having periods. The only sort of memory of the body I can find, which is obviously very different from the impossible "memory" of circumcision, would be situated there, in the forewarning, a mystery of the order of the flesh. We invest in the promised rite of our own body. Here too it will concern the loss of blood, but tomorrow, and the loss of this blood is lived as a gain. As a wedding with oneself.

Circumcision remains 1) *what you did not "see,"* what you did not "live," what was given to you and which you could not receive, what, before being you, you only underwent, felt, before being Derrida or J.D.; or Elie, because in the end you learn and you tell us that not only are you a great number of signs, of denominations, but also this one, *Elie,*[18] a Jewish name, given on the occasion of what was taken from you, this name that belongs to you and does not belong to you or at least is yours and is not inscribed (it cannot be seen anywhere) and in addition gives you this extraordinary chance of giving you in French two *e*'s, two feminine marks to add to the dowry of signifiers that is yours, Elie, *et lie, et lit, l, i, elle y . . .*[19] What luck you have! To begin with *el elle aile . . .*[20] (secretly).

. . .

Another thing, since I am on the side of the body: this text is full of bodily expressions, excretions, secretions, effusions. I think that Derrida is at once so well-read and so un-read, so loved and so aggressed because he is one of the rare "men," or perhaps the only one, to risk his active body in the text. A body movement on the order of circling around inscribes and is inscribed in *Circumfession*. You yourself circle around this real and metaphorical penis, this blinded, wounded, healed, resuscitated, etc, penis, you circle around this sex, and at the same time your eye, our eye circles back on itself feeling faint.

What would "a woman" do where for you there is penis? What is there for us, for me? Insofar as I am a woman, what I feel in writing, in reading, is that there is *interior*. No organ. But the earth, which trembles. The night, which pants. If I work with body and text, I work (from) the interior. But "my sex" is this interior earth we listen to. If there is an organ, it is the imagined, felt organ that serves as a sex: *the heart*. But, as I have said elsewhere, the heart is the most mysterious pleasure organ, the sublime sex common to the two "sexes."

For Elie, the textual scene is erotic, and immediately loaded with sexual scenes. A sensual sexuality is at work, without detours, causing pleasure and thought. In a certain sense your text "has a one-track mind." I mean it can only think with the force and the help of that track. Can only think of/while spilling out. Of/while sucking its own blood. Your text bleeds. Licks the wound. Circumfesses, avows savoring its losses.

On the other hand, on the other side, when it is written, as soon as it gives itself over to being read, sexuality is displaced into the text, "reconfigured," sublimated. Eroticism is cardiac. *Jouissance* is almost always of the sublime body. Or the whole body—as if pensive.

Because the body-that-has-sexual-pleasure, the sexual organ, is not only in the body, but in the cardiac world, in the cardiac earth, the inner surfaces of the sky and the night, in the music that is the song of the flesh. Folk tales say: it is women who sing. A man who sings is a being invaded by women.

Appearances are deceptive. We believe that women cry and that men are dry. But you, the man, can only think of crying.

▦ ▦ ▦

Who are your others, in your texts? Who do you say you read? Who do you feed on? Who do you play with? There is the series: Husserl, Heidegger, Genet, Hegel, Celan, Blanchot, Freud, P.S., etc., thus far apparently masculine. And no women? And no "women," which does not mean there are no women in the text. Because you have voices. There are, as we know, women's voices in you, you are a ventriloquist. There is cas/Cendre,[21] for example.

There is the indecipherable chorus, heart of two hearts, voice of two voices, but of a single music, of *The Post Card*, there is the inseparable agreement—in the—disagreement that speaks so strangely with a single voice it seems. As if in mourning there was only one voice for two. As in the last instant of the act of love.

▦ ▦ ▦

A moment ago I said: I "know" you, I "see" you, because I think I do. And I expect you to respond: "it is not so simple." The not so simple is what you are. It is what you have given to the thinking, speaking century, this attitude on alert: *notsosimplicity*. Such a simple step. Not so simple.[22]

To begin with I was afraid. I am also afraid because with you I do not have the extraordinary freedom that the dead give us.

I am afraid because you are living and what is more, a living being who detests death.

I am afraid that in speaking I will do what we always do when we speak; I am afraid of killing a little bit. As soon as you speak about a living person, you kill him a bit, you alive him a bit, you give him a bit of life, but you take some away as well.

I am afraid also because in nearly all your traits you are the opposite of what you are.

You are in a cross. As a Jew you are indeed crossed. If you are Jewish, it's where you are non-Jewish, if you are innocent, it's where you are guilty, if you are guilty, innocent. If you are certain, it is because you are so uncertain. So happy so sad simultaneously. So human that where you are so much a "man," we can doubt whether you really are one. And the cross, shining, stars.[23] And there you are sliding, passing, without stopping, without edge [*arête*]. One cannot seize a single trait. One cannot begrudge you for it. And that is why so often people begrudge you [*on t'en veut*]. Which is to say they want some of you.[24] Why? Because you are the little boy who goes off together with her, the earth (Esther) along the trail of the *Petit Bois* (which I know, I took it together with my father), and you add that you always made a fuss with her, you cried with her, to be with her, and then you were supposed to be ill as well to stay with her. You say quite correctly that you are there for no one, but we see you pass. This is why people begrudge you.

###

There are unsaid, taboo things [*de l'interdit*] between us.

Do not kill me. Do not kill.

The taboo is silent (thus even more taboo).

Between us, where is the truth? It is between us. And it is afraid. I am afraid and I know you are afraid. Where can I grab hold of you since you are immediately the opposite or the other? If I grab you I will miss you.

I said: I know you, which is only a belief, in order to begin to speak; but what is disturbing is that I don't know myself. How different he is from me, I think to myself. But I can only say this from within a sense of resemblance (to myself or to you). Difference always operates between an us as an (im)possibility of resemblance. I notice the differences that compose "difference" in the exchange of resemblances. Moreover difference is in the exchange. Moreover it moves—without stopping—from the one to the other. And it lives off the two. It is our incalculable resultant.

I can speak of him, of you, of her, of a she,[25] I cannot speak about "myself."

###

Apparently the child who saw that the emperor was naked was a girl. This is a rumor I heard. What I know: little girls, in folk tales as well as in life, are surprised by the phallocratic destiny of little boys. And which is the little boy who escapes from this stiffening and this murkiness? The poet. He sees through the opacity. Because he lives in the world-beyond-reality. Let us call it: the land of Truth. The Truth does not exist in reality. It is our sublime illusion. In reality.

All little sisters have sensed one day their brothers hardening and no longer forgiving. In truth . . . The truth is in the text between us. In the text that is woven between the two. But if someone were to ask me, as they do in folk tales, if I wanted to have/be a man's body to try it out, I would say "of course." I would be fascinated to know the world with another body, to be able to really work on sexual difference from one side and from the other, to know the air, the stones, the earth with other muscles, to know the mysterious masculine orgasm, yes, I would like to know this voyage, and everything that accompanies it, and which I can see at the moment to my left, which I sense, but which I do not know, and taste a certain kind of anxiety, of trembling, insurrection, depression, resurrection, rooting in the center of the body. But I will never know it. I could get close, very close, enter into zones governed by the heart where I can guess at nearly-you. I could go toward transfiguration. Because by dint of listening-to/living a you, or of reading a book by this one or someone else, by dint of slipping, in passing, inside a thought, and of letting myself read—I mean be read—it sometimes happens, when there are affinities, that on the inner surfaces of the soul is produced a sort of imitation in relief. There is some of you in me, at least I believe so—this is what I call "knowledge"—but.

But I will never pass over to the other side no matter how good the approximation is. Moreover, as I already said, it is in proximity that the contours of difference are drawn finely and clearly.

("S.D."—is not a region, nor a thing, nor a precise space between two; it is movement itself, reflection, the reflexive *Se*,[26] the negative goddess without negativity, the ungraspable that touches me, that, coming from what is closest to me, gives me in a flash the impossible me-other, makes the you-that-I-am appear, in the contact with the other.)

And us? The woman-body, for me, is the place *from where*, the soft place from where[27] girls or boys, humans, descendants are born, this place "below the belt," which is like two hands, like tomorrow,[28] and has more than one memory, a memory of what has taken place, a memory of what will take place. Not a phantom memory, but transmitted, inherited; I am thinking of women who have not had children themselves, but have the child written nonetheless in their flesh, from woman to mother to grandmother, from mother to daughter to granddaughter.

In saying all I have said, I have cheated, in spite of myself, without intending to. I spoke as if the characters of this scene were: a woman, a man, obviously. Such a scene with such characters is no doubt possible, there could be a man who is a man-without-any-doubt, a woman who is a woman-without-any-doubt. But I know from experience (I only know anything from experience, that is, after errors) that very often a "woman" is not a woman nor a "man" a man, that very often a "woman," a "man" is an ensemble of x elements. I know a woman who is at second glance an ensemble of five little boys and one little girl. As for the following glances . . .

I do not know what my ensemble is. Who are I? Do I claim that my are-I is predominantly woman? I have a disturbing feeling when speaking in the direction of these ensembles. It seems to me that in the social-political scene today women more than men are ensembles that are occupied, populated, naturalized, grafted by a certain number of shares of otherness, and that men for the most part are occupied by predominantly masculine elements. Our interior identifications are innumerable: grandfather, granddaughter, brother (without counting the vegetable, animal, chemical, phonic, astral elements . . .), but if one could calculate the sum of these ensembles it would give some odd things; society is composed in appearance of half men and half women, more or less, and in reality of a majority of so-called masculine elements. But in truth, that is, in secret, it is quite different.

But sometimes when I speak with Jacques, or when I listen to him, I think very simple things (because he is the one who is wary of the danger of simplicity): he is truly a man, and I am truly a woman. All you have to do is look, all you have to do is listen, I think, it must at least be a little true. In the moment I think "it's obvious," I remember what he reminds us of incessantly, as do I in my own way: that we are blind, that it is only ever a question of our blind person's point of view, that we are blind people who paint our own portraits, with bold, dangerously confident strokes, and that *wisdom* begins with knowing that we cannot stop ourselves, being blind, from believing we are what we are while knowing that we know nothing of what we are, which Shakespeare had already told us.

These three days of the conference have given us hundreds of examples of this; I think that no one here could be resolved into their simple appearance, and that hundreds of times we have heard a woman composed of uncle, grandnephew, big brother, etc., and at the same time we make do with the appearance.

⸭ ⸭ ⸭

You and I, he and I, we "write." "In addition," we write ourselves—we invent ourselves. I mean: I invent myself, you invent yourself . . . [29]

Fortunately there are the texts. That is where "S.D." leaves traces that last long enough for us to have the time to note them, time we do not have in the quick of reality. Language knows what we do not know (we do not know who-we are-I[30] nor what we say), and especially written language, which goes at the slow speed of writing.

What we do not know about ourselves—we write it, in our language: there it is, it is ready to be read. If only we could read our own writing [*nous lire*]!

The way we do something completely differently, the way we passionately love the same person—Language—differently: this too can be seen by reading our texts.

I will evoke various positions of the body-in-writing. For me, in the beginning, there is nothing. I begin without words and with body. It is a letting myself go to the bottom, letting myself sink to the bottom of now, a collecting together of the soul. Let us wait. This requires an unconscious, unformulated belief in a force, in a materiality that will come, that will manifest itself, an underground sea, a current that is always there, that will rise and carry me.

When I begin to "write," I do not write, I snuggle up, I become an ear, I follow a rhythm.

I do not know your inaugural state, when you are at home without witness. I see you afterward in the book beginning with the stroke of a word. "Someone" sends you a word. You catch it. What strikes me in his writing is the *taste of the word*. Your tongue has a good ear for the most distant echoes, the most ancient murmurs of the word.

I say *the* word. *A* word. There are poets who use *words* where we least expect it, *all words*. But for him, it is *one* word that suddenly enters, becomes powerful and carries him away. Becomes precious, having been precious in the first place, of course. The word that leads him, and that he will lead all the way to the apocalypse, is always a word that promises to be a mouthful, that had a close call, and that announces one hell of a voyage.[31] *A word* is the first motor.

To which is subsequently added the pleasure taken with syntax, that is, with the notsosimplicity of language. One would think that it dances only for him. I do not forget that I am speaking about a "philosopher," and yet what makes philosophy dance is indeed this passion, this avidity, this taste for the playfulness of language, this Poetry. Sexual and textual oscillation (it is the same thing) is what enchants him. What gives him his mocking air (*moqueur*. I mean "heart-word" [*mot-cœur*], of course). Jumping on the word, making meaning burst out and fail, fearing danger, laughing at all self-confidence . . .

But for me, in the dark, not a word to begin with, only the turmoil [*émoi*] and the music . . .

. . .

Translated by Eric Prenowitz

2

THE
ORIGINS:
ALGERIA
AND
GERMANY

Hélène Cixous was born in Algeria in 1937 to a Jewish family of mixed origins: her father belonged to a Sephardic family, rooted in Algeria, most likely, since the age of the expulsion of the Jews from Spain and Portugal at the end of the fiftienth century, while her mother's Ashkenazic ancestors came from Central Europe. Because Algeria was a French colony at the time of the Second World War, Cixous's family suffered from the antisemitic laws imposed in France by the Nazi regime: as Jews, they were not only deprived of their French nationality but Georges Cixous, Hélène's father, was also forbidden to practice medicine. The lung disease from which he already suffered worsened because of exhaustion until he died from it, shortly after the end of the war. Eve, Hélène's mother, then trained as a midwife and worked hard to provide for her children. It was a difficult time for the family: the Algerian fight for independence from France had begun at the end of the Second World War, and the widow and her children were considered "foreigners" by both sides, French colonizers and Arab resistants. This double experience of dispossession and exclusion, embodied by the father's death—sensed as an abandonment by the child—deeply marked Hélène Cixous, and became one of the most powerful driving forces of her work and life. Refusing to adhere to any fixed identity ("woman," "feminist," "Jewish . . . "), she committed herself to a stance against all forms of exclusion and abuse, not only—but particularly—those due to sexism and racism.

Some critics have said that Cixous only began to talk openly about Algeria and her experience of colonization late in her career, mainly since the nineties, and especially with the publication of *The Reveries of the Wild Woman* (2000). In fact, she has referred constantly to Algeria and to her origins since the very outset of her literary work and, more precisely, since her first novel, *Dedans* (1969). It is true, though, that in 1997 the publication of four texts on her Algerian childhood—two of which were included in *Stigmata: Escaping Texts* (1998)[1]—marked a sort of burst of reminiscences. The longest of these works was a book about her father (*OR: Les Lettres de mon père*), where the narrator finds a stack of letters written by her father while he was engaged to her mother. This fiction, however, does not reproduce—or invent—said correspondence, but focuses on the dilemma of the daughter: will she open the box and read the letters, at the risk of discovering a *new* father, different from the idealized figure she has dreamed all these years long, since his death? Or will she let the letters sleep and continue to adore the father she has remembered and recreated in her imagination since her childhood? This dilemma is close to one presented by Cixous in a recent work, *Si près* (2007), and also in the third text of this section, "Letter-Beings and Time," which is an unpublished lecture she gave at the University at Albany, State University of New York, also in 2007. In these two texts the writer considers the possibility of traveling to Algeria after a thirty-year absence, but she is prevented from returning there by the idea that the *real* contemporary Algeria may not fit the one she remembers, misses, and dreams about. However, this disjunction between imagination and reality, or between fiction and fact, is not one. Both oppositions turn out to be only apparent, because, for the author, there is no border between literature and reality.

The first text of part 2 is a "poetic novella" entitled *A Real Garden*. It was published in 1971, and is therefore one of the earliest Cixousian works in which she speaks of her origins and childhood, but in such a poetic and oneiric mode that it makes it difficult for the reader to identify the story with the author's life. As in *Dedans* and many other later texts, Cixous uses the image of the garden to express a feeling of belonging—or the impossibility of it. The garden is usually a metaphor for paradise—which is always lost or unattainable—and the metaphorical character of this particular garden is emphasized by the fact that it is "the only one." Being unique, it does not have a name, like the narrator; which signifies that neither of them belongs to anybody. The voice that speaks (in the masculine, rare in later Cixous's texts) says that he does not remember anything save the garden, not even his own name. This absence of a name indicates a lack of origins, and his total solitude, although his navel marks a bond he once had with another being. His loneliness also comes from a feeling of exclusion due to his rejection by the other inhabitants of the garden. In this small world there are nursemaids, the children they look after, and garden keepers. But the narrator does not fit in any of these categories, and he is despised and even aggressed by the others because he lacks a fixed identity and does not belong to a community. Outside the garden there is a war (they hear the bombs falling)—and in this sense it can be considered a refuge—but another war is about to happen inside. The first physical attack the narrator endures is precisely addressed to his navel, the symbol of his origins: one nurse pricks him in the navel with an umbrella, saying that there is "trash" in her way. This scene translates, in a nightmarish way, the first experiences of exclusion lived by the author: before even knowing what Jewish meant—and that she was "a Jew"—she received the first blows of the antisemitism so widely spread among the French community in Algeria.

The strong sentiment of inadequacy felt by the narrator is also represented by his myopia. Hélène Cixous has written extensively on myopia, and more widely on the gaze, especially in "Savoir" (included in *Veils*, a book written with Jacques Derrida, published in 1998). We usually think of shortsightedness as a physical handicap, or even, in a figured sense, as a moral fault. In *A Real Garden*, because of his myopia, the narrator falls into the trap of a practical joke prepared by the nurses and garden keepers. In an attempt to drive back their contempt and aggression, he had earlier told them that his father would come to fetch him. He was well aware that "'father' was a metaphor," but he felt so lonely that he began "to desire and to believe. Then to pray" (for the father's return). So when his enemies announce that his father has come to the garden, he swallows the lie and runs to embrace him, but instead finds himself falling between the thighs of a nurse. This cruel hoax is based on his shortsightedness (the author explains elsewhere other agonizing anecdotes provoked by tricks that myopia played on her during childhood). Nevertheless, myopia, in a typical Cixousian use of metaphor, also represents another, more unusual and subtle way to see. The narrator of *A Real Garden*, for instance, sees better "with [his] fingers" than with his eyes; relating sight to the sense of touch, Cixous describes a gaze whose appropriation, and domination over, the watched object she shies away from. We shall see another interesting example of this relationship between sight and touch in part 3 ("Love (and) the Other") with the excerpt from *Limonade tout était si infini.*

At the end of *A Real Garden* the narrator is "pushed back" by the others' aggression—first to the "animal kingdom" and ultimately "to the indefinable." This process can be read as a total deprivation of identity, to the point where the narrator even loses his humanity, but, in a typically Cixousian reversion, it also allows him to identify with nature and with the earth, which is a source of true "happiness." Instead of needing to define himself through a static identity, or needing to find himself a community in which to feel safe, the narrator discovers and learns to appreciate his animal and even mineral identifications (let's not forget Cixous's definition of identity as "ensembles" in "Tales of Sexual Difference," discussed in part 1). At the end of the novella, a bomb falls in the garden, and the speaking voice realizes that "I was the garden, I was inside, I was made of priceless diamonds and I had no name." His loneliness, as painful as it is, has prompted him to reflect upon his origins and to value them without allowing them to become a barrier to freedom and happiness.

The second text is an excerpt of *Osnabrück,* a fiction published in 1999. As *OR* was a book focused on the father, *Osnabrück*—the name of the German town from which Hélène Cixous's maternal line comes—is devoted to the mother. The difference between them is clear: the father exists only in the narrator's imagination and memory, but her mother is still alive and leading an independent life. Hélène Cixous has explained that, shortly before beginning to write this fiction, she had proclaimed that she would never write *on* her mother, because it would seemingly be violence inflicted upon her. However, as other books that she "would never write," *Osnabrück* imposed itself. *Osnabrück* deals with a trip to this town, which is, in fact, a recall of the mother's origins, entangled with the events that shook Europe in the twentieth century. Hélène Cixous's maternal family suffered from the Nazi persecution, and her mother, Eve, only escaped genocide because she had already married and moved to Algeria where her husband lived. For her daughter, Eve has always been "for life"; she embodies the will to live and the power of survival above and beyond all misfortunes. The fact that she chose to be a midwife—whereas her husband was a doctor and thus always in contact with death—also confirms her choice "for life." Eve is turned toward the future, while her daughter looks at the past and at the beloved who are dead. This opposition can be represented by the image of a tie: while the writer thinks that the living must keep a link with those departed, maintained through memories, dreams, and, above all, writing, her mother devotes herself to cutting cords. The sentence in German that opens this fragment: "MUTTER, KANN ICH TRENNEN"—Mother, "*may I unstitch it*,"[2] translates the narrator herself—refers to sewing, but it has also a metaphorical sense: "Mother may I separate?" that is to say, may I lead my life without cutting the thread? (We will read in part 4, "The Animal," an excerpt from *Messie* that deals precisely with this same question: how to separate oneself from the "mother"—in the broad sense of a person to whom one feels attached—without cutting the affective link.)

The problem involved in the mother's attachment to life is that she has reached a "posthumous life" because she has attained old age and survived all her contemporaries. Written in italics, we can hear the mother's voice describing in a dispassionate tone the effects of old age upon her. She feels separated from herself, as if "*the agreement with oneself*" was unstitched, or as if another person inhabited her body. "*I'm living now with another who has my keys*," says the old woman, referring to the fact that she is losing her memory and keeps forgetting her keys in the lock, or forgetting that she has already verified whether she has locked the door or not, or sometimes not even knowing what she is doing in front of her door ... This uninvited guest is death itself, slowly beginning its (needle)work. One of the worst effects of growing old—which is not "interesting" at all, says down-to-earth Eve—is losing her words, the words she "*desire*[s]" and "*call*[s] *for*," replaced by the single word, "*Word*"; that is why "*Word*" (in French: *Mot*) becomes the nickname of Death (*Mort*). This loss of words is not a minor annoyance, because for Hélène Cixous words are like animated beings or like animals (she coined thus the word *animot(s)*, a concept also developed by Derrida).[3] If we look closely at words, at their history, at the ambiguity of their signifiers, they can give us insights to our unconscious. Loosening the tie that links us to words means therefore losing one's deep self. Or, expressed in Eve's words: "*as soon as I sew the stitch unstitches itself I fear my undoing.*"

Despite her pragmatistic approach—"*knowing I have no chance of victory, all hope is to delay my defeat*"—the reflection on time and death that constitutes the mother's monologue ("*it takes time to understand the law* [of time]," she states) cannot be qualified as morbid or pessimistic. The conclusion of it is that "*there is no end, only beginnings of time, with time one discovers that everything happens to us and everything comes back to us all at once."* We must therefore cultivate memories in order to keep the dead alive by not forgetting anything or anybody and not to cut the tie that links us with the past—through our origins—and with the future—to the point of going past such chronological opposition and overcoming death. Literature is especially apt to do so, as reading and writing place us in a universal and timeless lineage of lovers, as Cixous would say. In fact, she rejoins, in this ambitious purpose, other writers she admires, Marcel Proust above all. But we could also relate this story to Shakespeare: comedy blends with drama, especially in the scene at the funeral parlor—which appears to be a dream working as an exorcism (as dreaming usually does) of the mother's death—and in the final dialogue in the kitchen. (We may add that in Cixous's fiction the mother is often found in a domestic environment or doing house-work, which does not mean that what she does or says is less important than other characters' actions and words; on the contrary, as we can see in this text, household activities become powerful metaphors.) Its last scene (which also closes the book) is full of humor, and also of pain: tears fall from the narrator's eyes, but she attributes them to the fact that she is peeling onions. We also learn that *trennen*, the German word for "unstitch" or "separate," is close to *Tränen*, meaning "tears": as is frequent in Cixous's world, signifiers offer us lessons of life.

Moreover, the philosophical implications of this story, which may seem anecdotal or purely autobiographical, allow us to consider the text not only as "fiction" but even as "philosophical fiction," the way Cixous has qualified some of her work. This is the case of the last excerpt of this section, "Letter-Beings and Time" (2007). This text is very close to *Si près*, a book-length fiction published the same year, in which the author talks about a trip to Algeria, which she has not visited for thirty years. But, as the title indicates ("Les lettres et le temps" in the original French), what is at stake here is more than a nostalgic visit to the motherland. Peggy Kamuf translated "lettres" (letters) by "letter-beings" because the author plays with the homophony between *lettre* and *l'être* (the being) in French. "Letter" is a key word in Cixous's uni-verse: in *OR: Les lettres de mon père*, the book devoted to her father, the writer herself defines the letter as a "sign" and a "metaphor." *Or* means "gold" in French, as well as a conjunction that could be translated as "however," but it is also formed by two letters belonging to the father's name (Ge*or*ges). These two letters are also present in *Or*an, Hélène

Cixous's home town, and in the name of Zohra Drif, a fellow student in the *lycée* Fromentin of Algiers. In 1998 Cixous published a short text entitled "Letter to Zohra Drif,"[4] first in English and the year after in French. In it she addressed an "open letter" to this woman—who distinguished herself after college by her brave participation in the fight for Algeria's independence—telling her to what extent she, Hélène Cixous herself, was also a victim of the others' "hostility" in Algeria. But the fact that they were both victims of sly rejection and contempt did not bring them closer together, because there were two "different combined hostilities, one addressed to the neitherthis northat being, Judaic, exdeFrancified reFrenchified, which was my image seen from the French Fromentin point of view, the other turned against the Arab Muslim being" who was Zohra. This feeling of absolute solitude and inadequateness—already perceived in the first text of part 2, *A Real Garden*—is what made the writer think that she had never belonged to Algeria, neither had Algeria ever been *hers*. Even uttering the statement "I was born in Algeria," which is a fact, still provokes within her "a sensation of contraband, and even a hint of novels, something that resembles a genre, as if this sentence were a quotation, the beginning of an autobiography." We can recognize here (by the concept of "quotation") the feeling of being inhabited by another person expressed in the previous text and, above all, the idea that "an autobiography" is "counterfeit" instead of the general belief that it is more *true* than fiction.

The author herself compares this sensation of nonbelonging to Algeria with the totally different relationship she has with her mother's origins: "Just as Osnabrück, no matter how disappeared forever it may be, seems to me to belong solidly to the Jonas family, just as the signature Jonas of Osnabrück seems natural to me, so with everything connected to the being Algeria, I am timid." This statement demonstrates that Algeria represents, for Hélène Cixous, more of an "allegory" than a reality: "I recognize that for thirty-five years an *Allegory* has taken the place of Algeria in my head." An allegory can be defined as "the expression by means of symbolic fictional figures and actions of truths or generalizations about human existence." Moreover—which is important to the writer—the word begins with the same letters as Algeria and also contains the syllable *or* and the French verb *aller*, to go (pronounced "allé," the first part of the French word *allégorie*). This is relevant because the dilemma of this text's narrator, as well as that of the narrator in *Si près*, is whether to go or not go to Algeria: "It is now thirty-five years that I have not wanted to go to Algeria, I say to myself, I never thought of going there, I always thought of not going there, I wanted rather not-to-go-to Algeria ..." The most important thing is avoiding "to go there the wrong way;" rather, the good way would be "to go there as in a dream [...] To go there as *a dream* [...] with the force but the impunity, and even the immunity of a letter." Or, rather, of a letter-being, because this allegory, this imaginary Algeria is "a fiction that I invent and of which I am the invention," says the narrator, adding: "I would not swear as to my authenticity." Algeria merges thus with the narrator's being: *A Real Garden*—which we can consider another allegory—ended with the identification of the narrator and the garden; "Letter-Beings and Time" gives us the key to what Cixous called "my algeriance," which is "a vast set of rather disparate reflections sprung up around the notions of country, native country, original country, names of countries and around this word *country* ..." Therefore, while deconstructing such concepts as truth or authenticity, Hélène Cixous is also questioning the idea of origins and particularly the separation between *reality* and *fiction*, which are not incompatible opposites, but instead the very substance of literature.

4

A REAL GARDEN
(1971)

to Omi

I went in unsuspectingly, it was a real garden; right from the gate one could see that the earth existed. Then the gate gently closed itself and one was in the garden. Outside and quite far away, people were going to war. Bombs were falling and shaking the canvas of the tent. They hadn't called it the sky for a long time because from down here you could see that beyond the walls it was being torn to shreds. The earth smelled good.

I had a name. The city had a name, and the whole world had one except the garden which was just called the garden because it was the only one. Since nobody called me, my name wasn't used any more. For a while, a few years, I said it aloud some days, just in case things changed and people began to speak to each other again. To tell the truth I didn't believe this but a vague sort of loyalty went on dictating its laws to me. So I never out loud admitted that I was happy to have gone into the garden precisely because it didn't have a name and except for the coleopteran, the lepidopteran, the keepers of the paths, the nursemaids and the children, I was alone.

I hadn't always been alone, I must have been with someone, maybe inside even, since I had a navel in the middle of my belly, with your bare eyes you could see this; but maybe it wasn't a navel, I wasn't so sure about that any more since the day a nursemaid went past me and said that the keepers shouldn't leave such trash lying around, and she jabbed the tip of her umbrella into the eye of my navel as she spoke, and she poked little with twisty prods all over me; this hurt physically and mentally; I kept a piercing little pain in my thingummy, and especially an unbearable doubt that infected my whole universe in the end from right to left and from bottom to top, as well as the network of my thoughts all through time.

Since I didn't remember having been anywhere else, what was outside, or what was behind me when I entered the garden, and since, aside from the gate's creak which I could conjure up whenever I felt like it, I could hear nothing behind me, nothing at all except from time to time the bombs and the maids, except the little exhalations of the earth, I began to fear the worst: in a world where they could treat me like this, anything could happen. I no longer dared remember I'd had a name, fearing it might come back to me and might be a name like trash or another of those names that would again diminish me. I no longer dared think of myself or of the maids, I kept seeing the umbrella which swelled up as it came down over me; and I wanted to hide but I couldn't move fast enough, then it was too late, and I heard the maid. If it hadn't been for the umbrella, I might have thought she was speaking of someone else, but it was really me she was talking about, and I had to go on listening right to the end, since it was as if I was nailed to the ground. One more detail to show the horror of my situation, this nurse stood straight up over me so that her white mass filled my entire field of vision and I got an eyeful of her milky opacity.

To this circumstance I attribute the aggravation of my myopia, but maybe I'm wrong; I've never been able to see people clearly. It's a selective myopia: I can make out lines, perspectives, objects in space or isolated, 20/20—and I have photographic vision for plants and insects. It's people I see badly, I mean the human beings, although I'm able to distinguish between the maids in white, the keepers in blue and the clumps of children who are smaller than the whites and the blues, and whose colors are much brighter and more varied.

To come to the point, I began to doubt so sadly that I started to regret having forgotten my name, then as I could see less and less, I started to think of the future, finally since nobody called me anymore and not even "trash," nothing at all, I started to feel lonely. I started thinking about the bombs, about outside, about what must have been behind me when I was standing in front of the gate to the garden; I started to desire and to believe. Then to pray. Not knowing any prayers, I invented one. It was a simple prayer, and to reinforce it, sometimes I made sacrifices, the way I saw the children doing: I made a little heap of cricket legs and butterfly wings which I arranged in the shape of flowers, with stamen legs and petal wings, and I prayed: "Come, come, come and find me find me mister grace please come come." Sometimes I sucked on a cricket as I was praying, and that calmed me. Vanitas. Zero!

One day a keeper going by says to his co-worker (they kept everything and kept one another too): "Do me a favor and get that thing out of here!" I felt less pain than for the nurse, first of all because it wasn't the first time they'd shown they despised me, next because I know from experience that the keepers' language is pretty basic. If I was a "that," it meant nothing, I could be anything. Furthermore they hadn't touched me nor moved me, so maybe it wasn't me they were talking about.

All the same in my heart of hearts I forced myself to acknowledge the regressive process. Once I was still on the edge of the animal kingdom, now I was being pushed back to the indefinable. I could have proved my existence and my worth had I felt like it, and maybe I would have done so, either by speaking up loud and clear or by penning a letter of protest, which tempted me but also bothered me because I didn't know how to sign, but in any case I didn't need to ponder this long for I soon noticed that I was not a direct object of disgust merely the pretext for bickering between two beings who'd probably never cast so much as a glance in my direction. Not daring to light into each other with their sticks for fear of hurting themselves, the garden's keepers took to psychological maneuvers; I was just a pawn on their chessboard. Every day it was: "get that out of here or I'll make mincemeat of you" which at the beginning scared me then little by little left me cold, finally, on the verge of indifference, gave me the idea of getting back at them by letting them think they were coming for me soon, which would deprive them of me as an intermediary. I had the pleasure of telling them this to their two faces and seeing them at long last look at me. I must emphasize that I'd been preparing my offensive for some days and each of my words was weighed and linked to the others in a calculated mixture of irony and of nonchalance. I declared: "Rest assured, Gentle Keepers, that henceforth I shall take care not to show myself to you outside your on-duty hours, for any professional reason whatsoever even should it appear to me urgent. Rest assured that I myself shall get that out of here, and that I should never ever have allowed myself to linger had my father not been supposed to come for me soon." Had they begged me to stay, I'd have departed without haste. But they didn't have the time, and I didn't either. A flock of white maids fluttered and peeped between us, pursued by a swarm of chirping, whistling children, throwing stones at them. They could have recruited me, I'd have rejoiced and picked up the nearest stones; but they didn't acknowledge me. I was going to feel sad, when the two keepers began shouting, waving their four arms in all directions: "There he is! There he is!" Meanwhile my declaration had impressed me as much as them: when I told them my father was coming I didn't believe it. "Father" was a metaphor. But I said it with so many rich words they took my declaration literally and they started to keep a watch out, not only on the garden and one another but also on the surroundings. By dint of keeping their eyes peeled, they ended up believing they saw him coming. Where, over here, no over here, no over there no over here, here here here, everywhere in short. Whence the swiveling of trunks, arms, and the vagueness of their information.

In any case they thought they saw him. I believed it my duty to believe them. I couldn't trust my eyes since the space beyond my out-stretched hands looked like a sheet of fresh plaster. I wasn't even sure that it was the nursemaids I'd heard go by, since all I'd managed to see were some faceless white eggs rolling along two yards away. They were more and more convinced: there he is, they shouted. My own convic-tion grew firmer; I was ready. "I'll do my best," I say. By dint of believ-ing I began to see, poorly but better. Your father is waiting for you, go quick, go quick they shouted sure of themselves. Out of prudence and obedience I began to run, and while I ran I had time to think that if my father was waiting for me, it wasn't because I'd said it but rather I'd said it because I'd felt him coming. I ran for a long time because I didn't see well. But as I was full of confidence, I let myself be led by instinct. I went by a bench full of maids. They were clapping and say-ing: go, there he is, you can see him, it's him over there sitting on the slope, it's him!!! I didn't see but I believed the maids. Plus there was a little black on the white.

I reached the slope; borne along by eagerness, hope, belief, fatigue, curiosity, I flung myself down, arms wide open and eyes too. I was flat on my stomach on the slope which wasn't white but ochre, close up.

To find him I started to crawl, arms flung wide so as to cover the greatest possible surface. I was a bit upset with him for not coming to meet me but he must have been upset I was taking so long. I was so busy with my crawling that I didn't hear the silence right to the end. Also I took a certain pleasure in feeling the earth rub against my stomach and my organs.

Finally I saw the black close up, I jumped on it pushed by every cell of my body with all the force of my innocence and I squeezed the fat black-covered knees of a strange nursemaid. "I've got him!" she cried, opening her thighs and I fell inside.

A big laugh rocked the earth. They all laughed hard. I felt a sudden chagrin. I should so have liked the maids to cuddle me. If I was them I would have. The one I was underneath laughed so fatly that she crackled and farted from everywhere. She was a big fat nursemaid.

I felt really sorry for myself.

Between the thighs there was nothing. I believed I saw a white bone, but I didn't believe any more. Besides nothing mattered to me, I couldn't complain even, I was fine even, and in a while I was better. Under the knees I could see the graininess of the earth and I felt I was in a familiar place.

Me too I wanted to laugh to be like them, but it didn't happen. So I listened to them all. A long laugh. Now and then a bomb, but maybe this was the war's laughter.

The next day it was still laughing. Habit. Rest, Earth. Rest, Earth. Rest. Fewer ideas. No time at all. Except the earth's time. No more feelings, except one: I hate the maids.

From time to time some distractions like listening to the bombs, peeping between the maids' thighs, or better, when there was a chance to steal a child from them cut off one paw before giving it back, or make a curious little three-year-old girl eat a snail. That's good for a laugh.

And an occupation: reflect upon my origins since no father for me, no anybody, on the contrary everybody against me. Unless my destiny be the proof of the existence of the father, but that I won't know till the end.

In the beginning, I didn't know it was the beginning, I'd never seen him, didn't want to see him. He had put me there, a keeper told me so, therefore I wasn't unaware of it, but this knowledge was just the condensation of words from the side of other people's mouths. In my opinion, the garden and I were more closely connected than the keeper and I. At times I was even sure the garden and I were made of the same substance, sand and earth rubbed my bones, mosses, ferns violets and strelitzia sprouted from my skin, stretched out my limbs. In springtime I let the caterpillars stride over me, in rusty soft processions and when they made moving rings around my spread fingers, my skin had the stiffness of bark. I liked the sand a lot more than my own skin. One day I fell, I had my hands full of sand I didn't want to let go of. Crazy, the keepers would say, whereas, sand, there was more of it than all the hands of all the men of all the earth could use; but I loved it. Is it that people let go of what they love because there are other objects? And who'd have given me back the same handful? Who'd have reassured me I'd have the same sensation of complete and utter happiness with other grains? Don't they know happiness is composed precisely of the unique conjunction of thousands of irreplaceable grains, cupped in a single hand, so that one doesn't know who does the hugging, whether it's the hand or the sand? That's why I was so careful not to lose the happiness I'd achieved at the end of a long day of groping, during which I had taken, weighed, shaken, thrown back dozens of handfuls of grains of which only the last had given me with the same feeling of joy. That's why I fell with a brutal and mineral speed, and slammed into the ground in three different spots, with the right parietal bone (because I tried to raise my head), with my elbows pointed forward, with my hands clasped over my stomach, and with my knees. From the shock, one of my knees, the right one, split; once I was flat on my right side, I must have slept a while, for I remember very well the sun in my back when my knee gave way, and the sun was shining into my left eye at a 45 degree angle to the earth when I saw it next. During my absence, I kept hold of my sand. This could have been on purpose or not, but I never let go when I love. It was late: I felt I ought to get up. I had to go on living. I looked myself over. I saw myself rather poorly. I see people poorly whereas I perceive differences of caliber, edge, shine, weight, between two or three grains of sand. I saw myself poorly, but I was used to moving and touching myself, I knew how to recognize myself. With my fingers I even saw myself well. I was having trouble moving. I was tired, I didn't rule out a touch of laziness, finally some kind of sticky stuff had come out of my knee and for the time being I was sticking to the ground. The blood kept me from moving and thinking. I trickled a little of my sand on it and the rest on my leg. The earth smelled good. A few ants were stuck in the blood on my leg but they still waved their antennae, I munched four or five of them. Four or five bombs tumbled by mistake into the garden.

Everyone shouted: "There they are! There they are!" Each in turn.

The maids ran the fastest. They ran over me so fast I didn't have time to look between the thighs: at this speed I saw only an enormous thigh with a hundred feet. The keepers were running, got embarrassed, stopped, ran. I felt them go by, especially those who were running looking over their shoulders and giving me a jab in the knee, which shook off the sand. Finally the whole world went by except me. A second later a bomb fell on top of what I thought was my navel. I leaped. In the old days I'd have been scared. But now I knew it was me the garden. I was the garden, I was inside, I was made of priceless diamonds and I had no name. Earth, Earth, I cried.

Translated by Beverley Bie Brahic

5
OSNABRÜCK
(1999)

MUTTER, KANN ICH TRENNEN, when I was little that's what I used to say to Omi as soon as I had finished stitching a square of fabric, *may I unstitch it* this comes back to me in the morning, I didn't sew very well, no sooner stitched than unstitched, says my mother while chopping onions we were standing in the kitchen where we have never sat down in our lives, and now as soon as I get up I see myself going into Omi's bedroom in Osnabrück every morning. *Trennen*, that means to undo, unstitch. Rip out the thread.

—It means to separate, I was thinking.

Mother may I separate? Can I?

You permit me, do you permit me mother separation?

Mutter, Kann ich trennen, my mother used to ask her mother when she was little. There's the sentence. I say to myself. Something in the sentence added to the chopped onion made tears come to my eyes . . .

Tears: *Tränen*.

Mother may I, can I separate?

Repairing then separating, repairing in order to separate may I Mother, can I separate

Do you permit me? Is it possible?

—Let me do it says my mother, unlike you it doesn't make me cry. *Trennen* that means to *unstitch*.

—What a sentence, what a verb, what a word, I say blinded by a gush of tears.

—Which word?

—*Trennen.* So many meanings!

—*Tränen?* No. *Trennen.*

I took my mother's sentence to her mother and I began to open it. To open the seam, one has to tug very hard on the two edges of the fabric so as to loosen the thread and make it easy to see the seam. It's done, mother, and now can I undo? To do it well one has to separate the lips of the seam. I tugged. Then I began to cut. That's what my mother had always wanted to be able to do: to open what is closed, once finished to undo everything and leave. But one can't *Trennen* without the approval of *Mutter,* one has to get her consent, do you agree to grant me separation mama, one must agree about the unstitching, reach an understanding to end the tie, may I cut now I asked myself.

The moment to cut is here. But not the possibility. I cannot separate myself from mama myself I thought. I cannot separate myself

—*This is it she thought all at once it's beginning, for years it had not begun, for years I went to visit so many people in the hospital, then to their bedrooms, then to the hospital, then to the retirement home, I accompanied my sister-in-law to the hospital, then another sister-in-law to another hospital, then the friend of my husband's who had betrayed first my husband then me then the years swept away the traces of the betrayal, and all that was left was a man who had totally lost his mind, whom I accompanied to a very good hospital, my husband left fifty years ago, is it worth the trouble of remaining such a long time after time, for years I visited all the friends who never visited me, I have been faithful to the women friends who turned their backs on me fifty years ago and then thirty years ago called me to come keep them company in the hospital or in the retirement home, and we got together again after a twenty-year interruption as if there had never been an interruption, when one is thirty one has no idea of time one believes that what is finished is done with, fifty years later we realize that time is our captain on board, nothing resists it, we love, we hate, we suffer, we think we are ourselves, we think that we desire and decide and detest the people we detest and who detest us, but from time we come and to time we return, it takes time to understand the law, there is no end, only beginnings of time, with time one discovers that everything happens to us and everything comes back to us all at once. Things that do not happen for years and years until we begin to wonder if they will ever happen, in our lifetimes, happen all at once just the same.*

This is it words are leaving, especially the French ones the foreigners one by one get back on the train. Yesterday I looked everywhere for une brouette, *a wheelbarrow, and I didn't find it.*

This is it it's beginning, the effort. It's coming, it's happening. This old age. And to say it is myself would not be true. I'm living now with another who has my keys. She's the one who slows me down, who gropes at my keyhole, she drags my feet a little in the hallway when no one sees me, what I've stitched she unstitches, Mutter mutter kann ich trennen, *who lies down sadly in my bed, who takes the elevator and distracted right away goes back up to check distracted that she has indeed locked my front door but once in front of the door no longer knowing what drove her to go back up when she meant to go down to do errands, go to the bank, to the pharmacy, buy a bathing suit, takes the elevator again and goes down to the lobby of the building where she suddenly stops having remembered that she forgot to lock the door, she has just enough time to take the elevator again that goes back up and once up there to confirm that she did indeed lock the door it's not interesting to grow old, Madeleine called me five minutes after having called me because she forgot that she had just called me, Lucienne can't go out any longer dizziness holds her back, Mireille's knee has seized up, life creaks it's better to leave, Mr. Frengé called me he's alone now he would like to go out, I like to have company but not a lover thinks the other, that sort of exploit is finished.*

What saddens me is a shame I shouldn't feel, that's what saddens me this little shame that makes my heart itch, this little scab that I'm ashamed of having, I'm ashamed of my foreign little shame, which scratches my heart and chews at my soul thus, here she is, the final sister, my promised decline a depressing combat, I engage in it feebly and knowing I have no chance of victory, all hope is to delay my defeat. Here now all the streets are steep and every scene exacts a high price, I wonder who makes me pay a tax for every step, bills me for every hour in truth I know her, I am getting to know her, it's you death who are accompanying me, I hear your whistled advice, I've got you under my skull, you whisper to me stagger me steal me from myself, you surprise me, it hadn't occurred to me that you would inhabit me long before the finale.

I'm haunted, ashamed, mortified, I've got death, I caught it I don't dare say to my daughter what I am so afraid to hear myself confess,

it is there and yet "it will come" as they say, well she has already come, you know, she lives on the third floor where in spite of myself I hide her and she is hidden from me, I don't dare tell you the tricks she plays on me, it's pure nastiness, the strings stretched across the hallway to make me stumble and I'm the one who helps her and gives her a hand to stretch them across my own hallway, I take orders from death, I pass over to the enemy and I am the enemy, it's miserable to be oneself two to mistreat oneself, to push oneself in the stairs, to make oneself fall, to unstitch the agreement with oneself.

It would be one thing if I could think about it and talk about it, if I could dignify the blasted thing, but as soon as I lift up my brain a little at the cost of a great effort that sets my nerves on edge, to try to construct a sentence of words, everything escapes me, the words especially the words, the devils, one would almost think they were soldiers of death, they taunt me especially in the French language skip around my forehead, they flutter in dispersed formation at a tiny distance from my eyelids and I don't see them, they melt, they slip away, yesterday I wanted to say tarragon, *I looked for it in vain and finally I bought some* dragon, *and the proof that they are devils and the messengers of death is that all the words I desire, call for, pray for, want, flee from me when it's their turn, all I have to do is direct the prayer of my thought toward one of them for it to withdraw at a leap into the background, all of them, yes, except the word* Word *itself. This goes quite far: the word* Word *now comes in the place of every other word, as soon as I want to say one or the other, death, for She is the author of all my holes, tears it out of my flesh of words, presto, each time it's the gesture of a molar-puller, and in the place of the one that's disappeared, is displayed as a hole-plugging stand-in the word* Word. *The word* Word [Mot] *horrifies me, it's the damned proof and one day I'll go so far as to suspect it of being the surreptitious nickname of Death* [Mort], *all the same it's really too funny this replacement of letters by their envelope. Yesterday I was looking everywhere for* shallot *until I thought I shall not be defeated and decided to take the elevator to go to the supermarket to find the thing of the word, but once in the street I didn't go to the supermarket instead of that I went back to the house because I had forgotten in the elevator what I had forgotten in the house. Not only do you lose your strength but you have to expend twice as much. I'm even afraid to think every time I think the word leaves, the more I think the more words get used up, as soon as I sew the stitch unstitches itself I fear my undoing.*

—You notice all the same, says my mother, that I am still good at certain syllables, today I managed to take "surreptitious," as well as "fascinate," I even said "the surreptitious fascinates me" at my age that's still not bad and without doing gymnastics. And still another word . . .

—This is it, this time it has really begun, she says to me with eyelids lowered over chaste eyes. What? I say. Age, she says. Are you sure? I say. There are signs, she says. What signs? I say. —If there's something that falls I wonder if I have to pick it up. I feel my strength leaving me. I am slowing down. For some time now. Little by little. I feel my bicycle has gone totally flat. As for the horse, a long time ago I gave up its exploits.

"Fuchsia!" she says.

Everyone leaves, everyone has left. These places yesterday populated and bustling are deserted and depressing like cities emptied out by war. People lived here yesterday. The world is an immense han- from which friends have fled: it looks like the scene of an amnesia. One can't evoke anything any longer. Time is razed. How strange it is posthumous life, the world is without. My thinking is disarticulating. I'm looking for "the place from which trains leave." I initiate a gesture I forget the goal, I go astr- on the way, there's no direction any more, something urgent escapes me. The children! Ha! they don't let themselves be suppressed Hélène Pierre. But they are so discreet and disarmed. I might forget to feed them. But I don't forget. They are too well-behaved and patient. They meow unhurriedly while waiting for life. Some milk! Where does one find milk in a country that's been totally pillaged? Before death there was some of every- thing but that's become unimaginable. I'm looking for a little bit of milk for a baby's bottle: that's my goal which occupies the space of my thoughts and my whole future. And now I'm looking for onion in German.

FUNERAL PARLOR

It had happened. She was dead.

We were sitting Eve and I on two chairs in front of the narrow, stingy counter. She, she is behind, in the little room just off to the side, invisible without light, never again. She is my letter that is going to be picked up and expedited. I cannot take it back.

The manager was talking. He was trying to push us. He maintained that with a single embalming operation one didn't get very far. With a second the body held up longer. We were not answering. He of course found us to be miserly. Eve was thinking: why would one want to maintain a dead body for a longer time. She was thinking: it's out of the question to spend more for a scheme. I was reading her thoughts. I was thinking: the body is going to decompose, it is going to detach itself, it is going to take refuge in dust. Intermediate time. We were tired on the defensive. The future absence of mama was mounting, what was going to explode would bury me and I could do nothing about it. Soon I could no longer speak to her ever again. I will have a mouth full of absence. I end up telling her the truth. I could always tell her everything. "Mama,—I begged—I am dreaming that you are dead." Ach! Eve exclaimed. So there, I had struck her. She wasn't expecting that. Then she got hold of herself again. If there is a moment when I need her, this is certainly it. "I have not yet departed," she asserted.

Suddenly the man said: "Don't you want to see her a last time? Because, after, we close."

Then everything awoke in my sleeping and absent heart, suffering rose up howling. See her! The last time! Before after! Mama! —Yes, says Eve, we want to. Yes.

We took a step into the penumbral light of the shop. We were going to look for mama. Giant, violent thoughts were rioting in my chest. If I saw her, my mama, I am going *to want* to take her in my arms, how not to want to kiss her, hug her, caress her face, say her name, press her within me try to surround her tears were gushing still now they are flowing so hard that I am holding the notebook two feet away from me, I would take her in my arms I would lose her saying her name, the cat cries with fright upon seeing me howl everything cries I am dying from death, the heart descends slowly into the chasm, but then—I feared this—if I lost her in this last embrace, if she was taken from me, if, in place of mama, she were cold, if she escapes me in my very arms beneath my lips, if the ultimate and atrocious happiness of having her were changed for me into someone departed, someone icy someone else who is irredeemable, if I touched death if I were absolutely thrown into the brutal obviousness of her absence, if it wasn't mama, the one I call and adore, it this proposed promised last time, this moment of madly desired happiness was going to stopper the gaping and vague anguish that is blowing in me, I know it takes only a brief careless act, an error, a second, for the hundreds of richly illuminated volumes of a long loving life to be struck down. I have everything to lose.

I took a step. One couldn't refuse. Eve came forward. I followed her crazed almost destroyed. It was a long time since the salesman had been trying to get us to buy a more expensive emblaming and when I let my mother argue. Now everything that had been suspended behind the counter was going to happen, I was expecting to be shattered. And in the immense whirlwind of terror that tossed me around there thrashed like a broken bird the demented desire, the passion of mama, a minute of love, I would give the book to hold her a minute more in my arms and reheat my soul on the warmth of mama.

I followed Eve behind the curtain. Fortunately she was with me, Eve after-like-before, otherwise I would already be mad.

—I WOULD LIKE SO MUCH TO GO ONE MORE TIME TO OSNABRÜCK dreamed my mother, I would like so much to take the train in that-place-from-which-trains-leave one more time and go see one more time Osnabrück Osnabrück Osnabrück.

—I should go once to Osnabrück with mama to Osnabrück where I have never gone, I should, I should find the time the desire the station I thought and I tried to want to go there for her birthday.

—*Zwiebeln!* That's it!

—Mama!

I let out a slight, soft cry in the kitchen I held it back a little and then I exclaimed gently so as not to alarm us her and me, being all the same the older one.

—Mama! she exclaimed surprising herself.

—What if we went to Osnabrück? I said hastily.

Right away a force that I had not seen pushed me toward her. I bent my head above hers. For a brief moment we saw our two mouths very close up, and that there was a chance they would touch each other, and veering off just in time, we kissed with our noses, I touched her nose with the end of my nose and we rubbed noses.

—Mydaughter! she drew back her somewhat delighted face. To Osnabrück? We will go?

—Yes, I said. We will go. We will go to Osnabrück where I have never wanted to go. It is time.

—I did not say "There is time." We will go in the next book, I thought.

Osnabrück where there are no more Jews.

—One gets the train *at the Gare de l'Est* and one travels all night, said my mother, the words were coming back, her dead were getting ready to come meet us, her eyes were shining.

I ought to have been happy.

I cannot write this book. Neither begin nor end. Not yet.

Here we are both of us in the kitchen with Omi our mother in the story, Eve peels onions and I shed a torrent of tears.

Translated by Peggy Kamuf

6

LETTER-BEINGS AND TIME
(2007)

. . .

Let her
letter go

But it is not of these letters that I wished to speak. I wished to speak
of the letter that I have been (following) as if in a dream ever since I
sent it, a morning in April at least twenty years ago, and maybe fifty,
ahead of myself, ahead of time, above the waters of the Deluge, which
I sent, in the place of my eyes, to see if by chance the land my mother,
I mean Algeria, might not have resuscitated, I wished to speak of the
letter to which I had spoken one day, as one goes and talks to a letter in
the place of the addressee, by way of transference, by way of hypallage.
The letter to Zohra Drif. As the young Balzac will have written to his
letter, in the place of Mme de Berny, as he will have written a letter to
his letter, like this: "Go my letter! appear with all the morning's graces,
the companions of the dew, etc . . .

How many things I have to say! I will begin by asking forgiveness
for . . .

. . ."

Me too, a long time ago, I put a letter in the place of Algeria, the
one that I love. How many things I had to say!

It is now thirty-five years that I have not wanted to go to Algeria, I
say to myself, I never thought of going there, I always thought of not
going there, I wanted rather not-to-go-to Algeria, each time that I could
go to Algeria it didn't happen finally, there are countries where I end up

always not going, I don't do anything for this, on the one hand I have my reasons, on the other hand there are the circumstances, for Algeria it is not that I didn't want ever again to go there again, I wanted rather to go there for sure, better not to go there than to go there the wrong way, I couldn't go there any old way, it is much too dangerous, I have always taken care to retain the hypothesis that admits as probable a trip to Algeria, but I have always simultaneously admitted the contrary hypothesis: it is possible that I will never manage to go to Algeria. In reality. In the (first) case I would retain what I call "my algeriance," a vast set of rather disparate reflections sprung up around the notions of country, native country, original country, names of countries and around this word *country,* that is *pays,* which burrows down into the mental wax and spreads in the heart of the one who says it *la paix et la pagaille,* peace and chaos, the one like the other. If a country is recognized for what it sows, then Algeria is a great country I said to myself. I didn't want to go to Algeria and thus I preserved intact the ideal beauty of the Jardin d'Essais, as it was invented by my father in a first moment than reinvented in another part with my friend Jacques Derrida, I hoped not to go to Algeria long enough, and thus to keep the Jardin d'Essais like a reedition of Paradise on earth, and like a personal, unique and destinal paradise as this Jardin of literary Essays attempted by the one and by the other.

Algeria. To go there as in a dream, that would be the ideal I said to myself. To go there as *a dream,* I dreamed. To go there in such a magic, such an intense powerful, light, fleeing, total fashion that I would have been there even while being as if I was not there myself but another, with the force but the impunity, and even the immunity of a letter. If I could have sent myself there, sent it to myself. Letter-being. It's like for the letter to Zohra Drif that I had had the idea and the need to write. I had thought to write a letter to Z.D. in 1960, perhaps it was in 1958. For the first time. Finally I didn't write it. I didn't really think it either. I had as it were felt the light touch of a letter pass over me. It was clear but vague, that's it, it was the beginning of an impulse, one goes and then, no, but it would have been written clearly to Zohra, it's me in the gathering of the circle who lacked precision, I had the desire, the quivering wings, the letter fluttered at my window, not very far not so close, creature of the morning's dawn, then I rose and I thought I'd perhaps dreamed it. I will write a letter, it will be impossible, dear Zohra I am writing to you, from which moral political ethical philosophical viewpoint I have no idea, I have always dreamed of blowing up trains and walls if you do it I have no doubt of being happy because the inadmissible thing is admissible the blood that you speak is the same in my language, next the ideal would be to blow up the separations I wanted to tell you but my voice was separated from me it would have been necessary to begin a sentence by *we* I don't doubt the impossible, what I have most despaired of you are doing, I am on the left side of your dream, you realize almost all the irreparable desires that it made me so sad to have for nothing, if I am not you are

next I will reread this letter, it will be crossed out everywhere, I will have to block out almost all the words, that is, the words were blocking out their meaning to me, I will cleave them, I will zap them with a Z, I will leap a fence, I'll take a breath, I'll not zadvance, what do I have in common with Zohra except the silent weight of fits of zanger in the classroom, I will open the door we can blow up the door, everything impossible will be easy, I will write: I am amazed I see the just person, which I will never be, I see the resemblance to you, I am not against blows from a golden lance and the exultations of bombs

while I was living *in the letter*, sometimes in my place, sometimes in the place of Zohra at least the one whom I imagined to be Zohra, a happiness took hold of me, that I had and have never known elsewhere. It was a happiness of relief. The contents of this happiness was triumphant. I can thus enjoy a happiness that is not mine, I can be in the freedom of someone other, I can be free because of an other liberty that Z takes for me.

The letter is a tangle. No one can untangle what I think from what I think. Violence, justice revolt, courage, right, everything is all tangled up.

What is certain it that it stayed with me. A letter that I did not write. There are dozens of letters that I did not finally write to my beloved, that I was going to write, that I wrote passionately during the night, I signed with fire, I got up, the letter returned to the other world. They did not stay with me. I realize today that the letter to Z.D. is the only one to have reached the ineffaceable.

The idea occurs to me at this very instant, May 8, 2006, that perhaps the decision to go to Algiers was taken already with this letter and by all the innumerable, imperceptible circumstances, gestures, consequences contained in this sheet of paper, under the name of Z.D., perhaps this letter that has stayed with me has mingled itself with me, its totally invisible phantom atoms have spread into those regions about which we know nothing where our future events foment, so that the decision taking shape slowly, being secreted for decades, will naturally have the slow irresistible force of an accumulated seism that has been stewing for a thousand years.

The fact remains that no one today could say if I wrote *the letter* to Z.D. in the end or if I did not write it in the end. I put *time* into it. That makes any evaluation difficult. With time the letter will not have failed to change, and often. In the beginning it was an impulse, but a tenacious, seductive one. I saw myself writing in five minutes an enthusiastic spontaneous letter. Rapid. Because of its improvised character, I would not weigh my words. The idea that it would be a total surprise for Zohra did not embarrass me, between us there was none of those virtual spaces in which letters might appear, moreover the idea that we knew each other only superficially had no weight, my impetus, my soul's passion swept aside these considerations. I could thereupon surmise that Zohra on her side could not have the least idea of what was stirring within me, since 1951 on the one hand and since forever likewise. It was objectively impossible that she had the least intimation of my Algerian turmoil. All these ideas that might have cut off my impetus were dispersed by the breath that animated me in the blink of an eye. What prevented me from writing this letter, which, to summarize, was a burst of laughter, a jubilation rather than an argued missive, was the question of the address. I was nineteen years old perhaps I was no longer in Algeria, but to say I was in Paris would be exaggerated, I was in a state of mist, but in the corridors of Paris. Everything solid, brilliant, bleeding, sparkling, breathing, carnal was in Algiers, in Paris I floated in a gaseous state, I dragged through the dust, I didn't breathe. The sky? Terrible. So even the sky can be sullied by the soot of a country even the clouds suffered from a lack of lightness. To come back to Algiers, to Zohra, to the letter, I didn't have the address of Z. Not-to-have-the-address of the person to whom I wanted at all costs to write was as if I were still in Algeria wanting at all costs to speak to, touch, find I knew exactly what and whom, but I didn't know how, *where*, to reach her, the telephones were always cut off, the iron gates raised in an exaggerated way up to the first floor without handle, without doorbells, the street names unknown, and it began again. If only I had been able to write to Z.D. in care of the Lycée Fromentin where we had been in the same class three years before the letter. But that was not to be done. The letter would not be transmitted. I would not be advised. I would fall into the category of one of those destinerrances whose tragic models I have seen to my sorrow, before finding them gathered malevolent identified as the very fate of humanity, under the appellation invented by my friend J.D., all the letters that are supposed to have arrived, and with which Shakespeare, Balzac, Stendhal make literature weep, those promises of life, which do not fail to get lost and which are transformed into messages of death, they are veritable bombs. The lycée was not my friend, it was Zohra's enemy, it was neither a post office, nor a home, our French extheater antiZohra on the one hand anti-me on the other. The hypothesis that I could write to the Prison. "Z.D. Prison"—which one?—seemed to me a version of the letter addressed in care of the Lycée. I saw everywhere hostility, rejection, scorn that would greet on the one hand a request signed by the one who I then was from the point of the enemy, on the other hand the addressee considered otherwise but from the same point of view. Two different combined hostilities, one addressed to the neitherthis northat being, judaic, exdeFrancified reFrenchified, which was my image seen from the French Fromentin point of view, the other turned against the Arab Muslim being, ex-boarding student at the Lycée Fromentin from there passed over from one day to the next into the recesses of the Casbah that she leaves with a basket full of fatality—there was no chance. Logically. I wanted my letter to arrive, or rather, I wanted it not to be stopped on its way. I couldn't address it except to "Zohra Drif, Algeria."

If I had had the address of Z.D. in prison, what would have happened? I don't remember exactly what I would have written mentally. I do remember my state of mind: I was under an enchanted spell, I believe. Finally, I said to myself, this letter that I couldn't send anywhere has nevertheless left unbeknownst to me. No one escapes the principle of destinerrancy. I never thought about it again. Later I wrote "Letter to Zohra Drif." I can still see myself writing this text very quickly, I was happy enough with it, it came to me as if dictated, as happens to those who lead a life in the world to be written, I wanted to express something of the mysterious Detour that has always been inflicted on me, originary malediction weighing on my relation to this native land that has never been my country except in literary utterances, and I heard being dictated to me this "Letter to Z.D" metaphor of my Algerian countertemporaneity. And right away this "Letter" was published in French and immediately after in American. I thought I had found the means of translating the famous Detour into the two languages to which I confide my uncertain, divided human condition, and more precisely the languages where I lay down as in cradles or hospital beds my severed being. For I am severed from Algeria, exrooted from Algeria, and reattached for life to the French language. At that time the name of Zohra had distanced itself from Zohra. When I titled this text "Letter to Zohra Drif," the name of Z had a range that had gone beyond Z to come closer to a certain Algeria for which I was not nostalgic that I loved because it was not mine, because it was she because it was not me, because she was another, because finally time separated us, I was not in Algeria she was not in me, she was not in prison, I could think of her. I didn't even know how to write her name. I didn't know where to put the H.

What seems to me the most important, I say to myself, is the Detour-returning effect of this text. There is a turn in the genre that resists analysis. The letter is a letter that is not supposed to be that [*l'être*], nor bound to be a letter and to whomever it may arrive to be received as a letter. Is it an open letter? If Z reads it, which cannot be completely excluded—if Zohra exists in reality, Zohra still lives—which I was able to verify—once Zohra read the "Letter to Zohra Drif" this singular literary exercise would instantly becomes an open letter to Zohra Drif I said to myself

All the same, if I declare: "in truth it is not to Z.D. that I had written this letter" I didn't write to the person of that name whom I had known earlier and never seen again. This "Letter" was of a genre whose character is unique. That from the viewpoint of literary convention it was an open-letter because published, I do not deny. But what does "open" mean? What interests me is the expression: one says "open" and not "public." Just because it's "open" does not mean it is not "closed." I had written a "letter" to someone who would never read it, I believed. There are letters whose destinerrant trajectory one believes can be calculated. Starting from the outline of this route one establishes a text at risk, a part of which remains knowingly incalculable. I had thus written this letter addressed to one of the characters of the person Z.D. without the intention of reaching the person, at least not in my lifetime, I say to myself. And this unstable but sincere certainty gave me pleasure of an exquisite nature, of the sort encountered only at the undecided frontier that is drawn and erased between the different regimes of reality and probability. Did I ever expect a response? Which response? Whereas conversely the "Letter to Zohra

Drif" was a response. Not that she, Z, wrote me a letter. As I see it, when we were at the Lycée Fromentin in the same class at opposed angles me in front to the left she in back to the right *she was a letter*, and I was *the other*, I had to be it [*j'avais à l'être*], I felt it, I wanted to respond, I was desperately looking for the way to respond. From birth, by my genealogy and by the catastrophic worldwide circumstances whose result and heir I was, I had been condemned on the one hand to be always the first to speak in front of the French from France so-called French and the French of Algeria so-called French, that is, 99 percent of the French present, the upshot being that I never hesitated. If there were French hence believers, I charged. In the Fromentin classroom as soon as a lesson began *I spoke first*. As soon as the teacher raised her voice, I had to speak. If the professor was doing Juno, I did Echo, the one in the first chapter who spoke faster than speech. I had to block the French authority. To the question how can one be born [*naître*] in Algeria without being there [*en être*] since the dawn, how can one be neither [*n'être*] from Algeria nor from France while being all the while in a counterfeit, a simulacrum of a country, in pseudonymity, in simulacrity, alone? To this question, I was condemned to respond with a strategy of velocity. I had to get free of France in the person of the teacher from France with a sentence that left her uncertain.

On the other hand I was condemned conversely *never to speak first* in front of those among whom I was born without being born from them, the said Arabs later the said Algerians, I would have been cross with myself if I had taken over the speech that was not mine but that should first have been theirs and to which access was constantly held behind bars, thus condemned always to speak first on the one hand and in the same place to listen to the speech that would come from the back of the class to the right and for which I was destined to be Echo, the one who left her body to keep only her voice, Echo the second. For example when everything about Zohra cried out: "*Ecquis adest?*" I saw clearly that her way of asking *if there was not someone here* was the expression of bitter doubt, ironic, no, it would not have been possible for her to say *is there someone* she expected that someone would respond no one and as for me all I could do was Echo, enraged shadow but too slight that I was, saying: *et adest*. It wasn't much, those cries. Is there not someone *here*? said Voice Z. —Here. That is what Voice H responds. Here. I cooed. Echooed. Voice Z: Whose cry? —Voice H: I. At the Lycée Fromentin we are good in Latin. A dead enough language. It's to be read. A repose is kept in secret by the dead. A peace forever young, a stunning beauty for having been plucked living out of wars. I am avid for Ovid, like everyone. *Carmen perpetuum.* The song is perpetual. We pass on. Suddenly we are exiled. The song continues. From afar we write open letters to the Far. "*Huc coeamus.*" Come let us reunite says the Letter. *Coeamus.* Unite us, I wanted to say.

In the end one writes: Nite us. It is so late, so far. Us. I fulfilled my mythological duty, I say to myself, with so much delay, remains only the echo of echo, but so faint, but as soon as possible. I had to dig a tunnel beneath destinies in order to pass along a little of the music of the errancies. As soon as possible and very late, I replied, plied, I said, sad, this time is not mine, no time is mine, there remain only a few shadows, my mother, and the books that know no age. "Whoever you are who touches this neither private nor public letter, deprived of address, may it at least be granted a place in your life. Tell yourself that it has not been included in the complete works of its author, but that it was as if torn from the tomb . . ." I had thought of adding these lines of postscript *sed quasi de funere rapta sui.* I changed my mind because of "the tomb." "As if torn from the tomb" calls for an explanation. One doesn't know whose tomb it is, one never knows to whom a tomb belongs, I thought, one never knows to whom a Letter belongs, I never knew, it has always seemed to me that I was born "as if torn from the tomb," I didn't want to have written a letter that ended with *tomb.*

On my left, the reasons to go to Algeria. On my right the reasons not to go. All of them, covered in fog, and beneath some of those indistinct layers of shifting pebbles, irregular polygons with sharp angles.

I advanced without knowing. As philosophy advises. At each step one sinks in, words pivot, beginning with the word Algeria. It's because: "I was born in Algeria." I hesitated. That's a fact. Should I file it on the right? Or on the left? Naturally, to each her own, there are millions of Algerias. That I was born in Algeria is a fact that is, from a certain point of view, indisputable. I will never deny being born-in-Algeria. All the same it suffices for me to say these words: "I was born in Algeria" to feel a slight ungluing of my being, like a sensation of contraband, and even a hint of novels, something that resembles a genre, as if this sentence were a quotation, the beginning of an autobiography. Just as Osnabrück, no matter how disappeared forever it may be, seems to me to belong solidly to the Jonas family, just as the signature Jonas of Osnabrück seems natural to me, so with everything connected to the being Algeria, I am timid. I just wrote "I was born in Algeria" and once again I felt that I didn't know what I was saying, what this sentence was saying to me, I don't know what it was thinking by saying "in Algeria" or borninAlgeria or what I thought of being born in without being of, being of nothingness, not being of Algeria, but with Algeria nonetheless. I felt this uncanny and exhilarating strangeness that has the gift of repeating itself, reigniting itself with each interrogation. I was astonished. Each time I make my declaration I astonish myself. Yet it is merely a fact and probable. And yet within me a slight incredulity arises. It is my status as specter that crosses my skull and with its light touch unglues all the modalities of believing.

Zohra as well was born in Algeria I say to myself. There is no doubt. And that is the difference between Z and me. Between my being born and me there is doubt.

Millions of complicated thoughts, an enormous quantity of memories for many screens, powerful and solemn legendary scenes that happened in a background between the venerable and eloquent monuments that raised their sphinxlike chests around the Place d'Armes, great deployments of war, I recognize that for thirty-five years an *Allegory* has taken the place of Algeria in my head. And even before the allegory was produced, I have no other memory except so profoundly planted in the folds of my flesh, so engraved in my personal grotto that it seems to me, as soon as I say this sentence, I am in the antiquity of a fiction that I invent and of which I am the invention. I forget myself. I would not swear as to my authenticity. For example I see all the people who live in France and give assurances as to being Algerian, and I don't see myself as one of their number. As soon as I say "from Algiers" there is danger. If I say France, it's less murky, I am outside. Algiers always is taking place in the subsoil, and I have always had to enter there because I have never been there, I have never *found* myself there, I have always had to *enter* there by crawling, either by going through the cracks in the shape of open mouths in the famous flesh-red rock as if I were a letter, or else by diminishing myself so as to slip between the bars.

I underwent the ordeal thousands of times and even every day when I went to the lycées, first to the lycée Lamoricière where the war's little Jews had just been reinjected after having been ejected from the land, exnationialized, excreted, legally execrated, then reinjected still all sticky into the Boîte Militaire with its walls padded in Catholicism, then to the lycée Stéphane Gsell that I never arrived at without having

gotten lost in the mountains of motionless fog among which the
Golden lance of Joan of Arc kept watch, then to the Lycée Fromentin
where from war's larva I passed without knowing into the subterranean
corridors that were going to lead me to literature, it could not have
been otherwise, I went from the abyss veiled with glassed-in margins, a
book in hand, where I soon noticed, in a corner of the classroom in the
back to the right the absolutely exact face of the one that I would never
be on my side and in which I recognized in a second under the name
of Zohra Drif the inversely symmetrical being from me. And it was
beginning from point Z that I could begin at the Lycée Fromentin to
crystallize in a less delirious fashion and in the open air my being of the
other side. After having been buried during my very long childhoods in
the underground corridors beneath the Algeria of France, for I can say
retrospectively that I was born beneath this Algeria of France, I always
knew that I had the first pieces of knowledge that I was born destined
to the hole and the cellar, the premonition of which the innocent jubilation of my parents on earth forbid me from confessing for my first
three years. Nevertheless the light that I saw did not last long enough,
barely a year, for me to believe it was a natural phenomenon. I realize
quite well that my parents were able to believe they were in Algeria,
especially my father who was really born there and who since 1908 had
not ceased to progress in this belief of being-of and -in, raising himself
by degrees, in one of those ascending and harmonious academic arcs
that makes one believe one is going toward the universal Rose and that
it exists. Especially Eve my mother who having gotten herself out of the
German hell and when finding herself young and strong again in Oran
was able to believe being part of it. Whereas I from the beginning I saw
that they were dust and I saw them return to dust, trodden beneath the
soles of this supercountry where my father thought he had a place set
aside. Whereas I always knew that for roof I had the archway of a cellar
or a stairway. They rode bicycles on the land, they laughed I heard them,
I contemplated their radiance, they were going to be extinguished and
they didn't know it, I already had three hundred years' distance necessarily, the sun is going to set I thought with an anguish of worldwide
proportion. And it happened. At the lycées of the first General Marshall
Lamoricière up to the fourth General Marshall Bugeaud I always went
without illusion and without parents into battle against the Romans, in
the beginning I was on Hannibal's side, later I discovered that all wars
ended in dust, the greatest armies the greatest empires with millions of

sorrows slept in a few paragraphs in the History books, of the hundreds of millions of men and women who were born, there remains a number with zeros in the mouth of a pupil among the chewing gum and the caramel he himself is one of the zeros destined to be chewed up again after a little turn around the track, between the teeth of the next pupil. Already in the lycées the butcher's block is readied and the very name of the Lycée called Bugeaud, if you were paying attention, would have reminded the brief inhabitant of the fate of humanity. You think you are in an educational establishment, a nursemaid of children. In truth it is a monument to massacre. The children are seated on the bones. I will not let them cut my throat without having written my will, I thought.

. . .

Translated by Peggy Kamuf

3

LOVE (AND) THE OTHER

The question of alterity, of the relationship between the subject and the other is one of the principal threads in Hélène Cixous's work. Reflections on the other appear in most of her texts, from her most recent "fictions" back to her earliest writings, among which is "The Laugh of the Medusa" (1975). In all these creations the author never defines the notion of alterity—that would be against her way of thinking and of writing. She prefers to *perform* it through her writing, as we shall see in the pieces selected for part 3.

Cixous states in "The Laugh of the Medusa" that Western thought has always worked in oppositions, and suggests that this "logocentrism" is related to the "couple" of opposites that could lie under all other oppositions: the man woman couple. Since its origins, feminist theory denounced "woman" being always seen as "the Other of man" (as Simone de Beauvoir says in *The Second Sex*, 1949), instead of as an autonomous subject. "*The* woman" is what man is not, but at the same time she resembles him as his inverted reflection on the mirror. In "Sorties" (included in *The Newly Born Woman*, 1975) Cixous calls this the "paradox of alterity."[1] By this expression, she means that we usually conceive of the Other in relation to the Same: it is thus a "domesticated" other. Cixous exemplifies this through a comparison with colonial Algeria: "The other is there only to be appropriated, recaptured and destroyed as other. . . . Algeria was not France, but it was French." The opposition between *me* and the other also characterizes identity and difference, considering difference as what is eccentric (in the sense of "out of the center"), marginal, dangerous, but can be tamed through a violent appropiation of the other. This appropiation consists, primarily, of a singularization of *the* other. On the contrary, Cixous states, the other is always plural, and "no other is first"[2] amongst these others. This also implies the necessity and importance of acknowledging the singularity of every one of these multiple others.

The first text of part 3, from *Limonade tout était si infini* (1982), deals with this very paradox. In it, the author describes a scene where Franz Kafka (called F. in the text) greets a blind man (O.) in the German way, with a bow of his head—a gesture that the addressee would not be able to see because of his disability—but one he is able to perceive because F. accidentally grazes him with his hair. In her illuminating analysis, Peggy Kamuf notes that this story, as it is narrated by Cixous, reconciles two conceptions of the other: "the other in his singularity" and "the other as general concept."[3] Kafka accomplishes a "miracle," according to Cixous, because he respects the other, considering him in general (disregarding his particularities) and at the same time as a unique individual. As Gayatri Spivak has said, speaking of Cixous, "the only ethical relationship with the other" implies "the universalisation of singularity."[4]

Some of Cixous's early writings contain the suggestion that women might be more prone than men to the acceptance of difference. Therefore, women might, in turn, more easily allow the passage of the other "through them": a certain "permeability," a "non-exclusion" that men might find threatening ("Sorties"). It is, as the author ironically states, one of "the four powers of femininity": "the power to be the others that we are."[5] One of the ways Cixous has related women's capacity to embrace alterity is through maternity: women "know how to undergo detachment" because "to give birth does not mean to lose nor to enlarge herself" ("The Laugh of the Medusa"). This has led some critics, especially in the United States but also in France, to say that Cixous's thought is "essentialist," because it establishes essential—that is to say, fundamental but also precultural and unalterable—differences between the sexes. This interpretation of Cixous's discourse is, in fact, far from her thought, within which there is no place for a belief in *essence* or fixed identities. Alterity and difference go through our selves, men or women, and maternity is thus a "metaphor," specifies the writer. At the beginning of this excerpt from *Limonade tout était si infini*, we read that the three men who share this joyful experience feel "young, beautiful and womanly, because . . .

under the influence of cheerfulness the soul always reveals itself to be able to be a woman."

As said before, Hélène Cixous does not believe in fixed identities, and *woman* is only a label or a word, as is *blind*. We usually consider a blind person to be one who cannot see. But what does "to see" mean? asks the author. Does "see" refer exclusively to the capacity of distinguishing objects using the eyes? Or are we capable of perceiving reality by other means? Cixous deconstructs the traditional concept of vision throughout her work, but especially in her text "Savoir," included in the book *Veils* (with Jacques Derrida). In this episode of *Limonade tout était si infini,* she describes how the blind man, O., "stopped being blind in the very instant" when F. makes this "invisible gift" to him. O. is no more "a blind person" because F. has treated him "for the first time" as if his "disability" "concerned [him] solely." O. then has a supernatural vision of F.'s face, as if he is really *seeing* him, but he prefers to keep this secret to himself, in order not to break the magic. What has been broken instead is the "spell" that kept O. a prisoner of his blindness in the sight of others. The whole text is similar in tone to fairy tales, as are other writings of Cixous, the reason being that fairy tales, and childhood in general, do not rationalize—as is typical in adulthood—but only *translate* the unconscious's productions; in other words, they do not secern the unconscious from the rational but allow them, instead, to coexist, as they do in *real* life.

The "gift" F. gives to O. is like those gifts that fairy godmothers give to privileged children in fairy tales, but it is also a true gift in the Derridean sense. Jacques Derrida theorized about the concept of a gift, concluding that the true gift does not consist of a subject giving something to the addressee of the gift who then rewards the former with gratitude. A true gift, according to Derrida, takes place between two subjects who interrupt this "circularity" of exchange. Therefore, O. is grateful to F. for his gesture but does not thank him, because that would "annul" the gift. One cannot speak about this episode, yet it can be written—as writing has the power of keeping the secret even while apparently divulging it—because of the ambiguous nature of literature. We will return to this idea at the end of this introduction, referring to *Love Itself.*

Desire can be defined as the force that impels *me* to approach the other. However, desire—as many other drives and human behaviors—has been trapped in a "phallocentric logic" and thus based on inegality.

In his *Introduction to Narcissism* (1914), Freud developed the idea that men lose part of their narcissism or love of themselves when they address this love to an "object"—whereas women tend to preserve theirs. The only way for men to compensate for this loss is to "possess the beloved." Masculinity is traditionally structured by loss, states Cixous, following Freud, and therefore by an urgency to reappropriate. (Nevertheless, we shall keep in mind that, for Cixous, *man* and *woman* or *masculine* and *feminine* are not assimilated to biological essences, but to positions or identifications.) Since her early work, Hélène Cixous has been describing a new love, which is also called the "Other-Love" ("Sorties"). It is not based on the type of power relations in which one is always superior to the other, but instead on the "recognition of each other," beginning with the "intense and passionate work of knowing."

The second text of part 3, "Love of the Wolf"—originally published in French in 1994, then republished and enlarged as the first chapter of a book of the same title in 2003—is a poetic reflection on love based on several texts by Marina Tsvetaeva, who, herself, reads *The Captain's Daughter* by Pushkin.[6] Far from being an exercise in literary criticism in the usual sense of the term, Cixous here cultivates the art of "feli-citation," connected to *my* body and the other's body, but also to the "feline." *Messie* (see part 4), among other books by Cixous, shows us how the cat, for her, represents the cherished relation to the radically different other. The wolf, in Cixous's text, is a metaphor (through Pushkin, Tsvetaeva, and Little Red Riding Hood) for "the truth of love, its cruelty, its fangs, its claws, our aptitude for ferocity. Love is when you suddenly wake up as a cannibal . . . or else wake up destined for devourment." This "devourment" is much more than a metaphor, as its insistence on the most physical details of eating indicates: "As soon as we embrace, we salivate"; and "Love is always a little wol-f-ishy [*un peu-loup-che*]—a little peckish" (in French *peu loup-che* plays with the signifiers "wolf," "fishy," and "teddy bear," forming a real menagerie.)

But love consists of "wanting and being able to eat up and yet to stop at the boundary," since "real love is a don't-touch, yet still an almost-touching." It is a contact that is not really one, at least not in the sense of forcing one's self onto the other. The metaphor of fire, traditional in all literature on love, also makes an appearance in "Love of the Wolf": "That's what love is: falling into the jaws of fire." The one who loves wants to consume the object of her desire, but desists at the very last moment, holding back on the brink of the abyss. This stopping "at the boundary," however, is not without consequence, since it leaves *traces* and makes the other appear; it reveals the irreducible otherness of this other I love and would have liked to swallow to make him mine. Thus, the other's body remains intact of bites, but nonetheless it carries "traces of the gift."

Love is also in contact with death, more specifically with the death drive. The "world-of-two" that is love "depends for its survival on a single other person" since "it is on the basis of love that one recalls mortality." Fear of losing the beloved other but also of dying for the other—which Derrida terms the "double terror" of Augustine: "of surviving and not surviving"[7]—is one of the reasons why "*there is only trembling love.*"[8] With the wolf, Cixous adds dying *by* (that is, being killed by) the other, torn to pieces by his or her desire of appropriation. We should therefore be vigilant of predatory and self-destructive drives to avoid blindly giving in to them, which would result in the devastation of the universe created by love. In order to maintain our stance on the brink of the abyss, we must respect the other's integrity and the other's strangeness (or uncanniness, in the sense defined by Freud, which unites familiarity and unfamiliarity), rendered by the image of language: "*We speak to each other in a foreign tongue. . . . Indeed we understand each other . . . and it is a miracle, but the remains remain, the tongue in my mouth is not your tongue, I do not know how it moves in your mouth.*"[9]

In this fragment, the tongue as "language" becomes flesh organ by means of kissing. However, this is neither a transfiguration nor a metamorphosis: the two apparently incompatible meanings—the literal, or *corporeal,* and the *figurative*—coexist. Loving words are thus living words that can bite the text, escaping from the writer's will, and have physical effects on people, like the burn in the breast that provokes the "brand new word" of love for Tsvetaeva. The words of love are "bitten," because this bite is the sign, or the *signature,* on our body of "the other's appetite": of his or her desire to eat, which is the greatest "proof of love," but it is as well, due to the genitive's ambivalence, the signature of our own hunger for devouring and for being devoured. Love begins with a "secret" between two—and we must not forget the connection between "secret" and *sacred,* what is and must remain separated—which brings us once again to a question of language: "one begins speaking the language that no one else speaks—a language spoken only by two." The entry into the universe of desire betrays all others and is contrary to all sociability, as in the

European medieval model of such absolute and exclusive passion, the legend of Tristan and Isolde.

In this legend, passion is an *égarement* in the double meaning of "getting lost" (in the forest where Tristan and Isolde hide from the rage of King Mark and his knights) and "going mad" (the *Folies Tristan* describe how Tristan pretends to be a jester or a fool in order to come closer to the queen, to the point of appearing to be *égaré*, distracted, even in his own eyes). In such distraction, the lover can lose his or her own identity. When the wolf, because of his love of the lamb, abandons his inherent drive to devour, sacrificing "its very definition," Cixous asks, "Is it still a wolf?" It is possible that the wolf has "delupinized" to become a lamb in turn: "The wolf turns all white and starts quivering out of love of the lamb." However, "Love blackens the lamb" as the submissiveness of the wolf makes the lamb strong and perhaps even cruel. Nevertheless, we should not conclude that this is a symmetrical inversion of roles, one occupying the place of the other; the "gift" of love or the wolf's sacrifice—because "It is me my entire self that I give with the gift of love"—is impossible to return, as the author points out.

Love, as seen by Cixous in this text, deconstructs the dichotomy between the subject and the object of desire. Referring to "Little Red Riding Hood," the wolf we see lying in the grandmother's bed after having eaten her is at the same time himself *and* the grandmother, since "The truth of love is both-at-once." Thereby, desire upsets the traditional conception of the subject, allowing to reign in its stead an enriching but also terrible undecidability that concerns, in its process of destabilization, sexual difference: the wolf is "the he-she-wolf, double-wolf" (*le—la—loup, double-loup*)[10] and beyond the distinction between masculine/feminine, human/animal, me/you, and singular/plural.

This undecidability is also present in the last text of part 3, an excerpt from the book *Love Itself in the Letter Box* (2005). *Love Itself* describes a secret love between a man and a woman, the narrator of the story, which takes place in an apartment named after the street on which it is located in Paris: "Olivier de Serres." In a manner typical of Cixous's writing, this name—corresponding to a real street and, prior to that, a historical figure—carries multiple meanings, all of them related to love. *Serre* means "greenhouse" in French; this apartment is thus a refuge for the lovers, a closed world apart from the exterior one. The narrator calls it a "lair," a humid and somber "grotto," and a "temple"; so is the realm of love. *Serre* also means "claw"; when they enter Olivier de Serres, the lovers "fall" into the eagle's talons: they cease to be subjects but are instead subjected to "passion"— understood as intense love but also, in its etymological sense, as suffering, as in Christ's Passion. As for the first part of the name, Olivier refers to the olive tree, which symbolized both peace and immortality for the ancient Greeks. Olivier is also a character in one of the oldest literary works in French, the epic poem *The Song of Roland*, which is one of the intertexts of *Love Itself*. Cixous's book is, in fact, much more than a love story: it is also a "hymn to literature," as the author tells us at its very beginning. A hymn to the most cherished texts of Hélène Cixous: *A Passion in the Desert*, a novella by Balzac; all Stendhal's novels and autobiographical works; Antonin Artaud's correspondence; the work of Dostoevsky, Joyce, and Kafka; and *The Song of Roland* as well. In this medieval epic Olivier, Roland's best friend, represents a new model of chivalry, no longer based on virile and blind courage, but instead on fidelity and faith. Nevertheless, *Love Itself* deconstructs the notion of fidelity: as in many other cases, such as gratitude or hospitality— analyzed by Derrida throughout his work—when we need the assurance of fidelity it is because we have no faith in it, either because we fear infidelity or are about to commit it ourselves. Human faith is always "fractured" and "stuck back together," says the narrator of *Love Itself*.

Fidelity is also related to the accuracy of memory. The excerpt deals with these faithful and at the same time unfaithful remembrances of past events. The letters exchanged by the lovers for more than thirty years are witnesses to their story and render their love timeless. But the novel also questions chronology: the time reflected by the letters, the time of the events narrated, and the time of the narrator's writing are muddled. Memories are also split in two versions, those of each of the lovers, who often have different ones. And oblivion is as powerful as memory; Cixous speaks of "the Great Goddess of Forgetting," who acts in order to protect secrets that must be kept, for instance. Olivier de Serres is itself a secret garden, a spot privy to the lovers. When they enter this secluded place, they give away their names, not only because their relationship is clandestine and must be kept secret but also because names belong to the "exterior world" and are thus called "the exterror," as they lead to "the destruction of the burrow." The lovers lose their names and identities to be united under the only name present, Olivier de Serres, a "keyword" for love. To give a name to the other usually means appropriating this other, which is why the narrator says: "Between us never any name."

Yet the last episode of *Love Itself* deals with a secret, which the narrator betrays, related to a name. In a previous chapter ("One Time, Avenue de Choisy: Echo, my Love"), the narrator tells us how she thinks she heard her lover call her "my love," for the first and only time. It is hard for her to believe, because this possessive address is contrary to the respectful nature of their relationship. But she sees a "message" in this scene, it is like a letter he may or may not have addressed to her, and that she may or may not have received. This undecidability is at risk when, in the "Last Episode," the narrator searches for a confirmation of this memory, which she has kept for years like a precious secret. Asking him if he remembers, she can only expect a "catastrophe": she may have made the entire scene up, or he may have forgotten it. In any case, with her demand, she is going to destroy the ambiguity of the memory and thus its secret nature. Miraculously, as he responds to her inquiry for confirmation, a storm breaks out, and thunder prevents her from hearing his answer, if there was one. The "diluvian Speech" has replaced "our little human words." And the secret remains inviolate, thanks to the magical power of literature.

7

LEMONADE EVERYTHING WAS SO INFINITE (1982)

There were these three visions. Brief and ineffaceable as three flashes of eternity. None said. None knew. None forgot. And each had their intimation of immortality. Each had their own impression of the sacred.

But all ignored it. This became known, but later. By chance? So much later, long after them. Because each confided their vision to a memory that lived afterward. And each vision took a different path, until one day the three of them met in one person. But that's another story.

It is thus, then:

These three glimpses took place during the Saying-nothing, which is the ephemeral time, still virgin and susceptible like the unconscious, and is the time to receive visitations. Took place a little before the introduction was made. Said nothing. It is really thus.

They had traveled. The important thing was the arrival: to arrive together at the point of saying-nothing. That is what they wanted, each knew it: this is why the air in the room was so finely vibrant. Because they were so careful not to precede one another.

Were in the communion of fairies in labor around a cradle. Knowing the omnipotence of thought. Do mental calculations with knitted brows. In the process of giving birth to a destiny.

There was this discreet exaltation about the feeling of working together toward an oeuvre that most people totally fail to appreciate.

Because most people cannot even imagine that a first-time can be an oeuvre. And thus they meet like animals and do not realize that they crush the Encounter under their paws.

(—This is why this story is difficult to tell. Because the plot is so invisible—Each sentence must hold each of its words at the respectful distance of the encounter).

They came near (gently, with in the middle this intuition of a cradle). It is so rare and so gentle to say-nothing to begin with. There: this Saying-nothing together during the first moment was their first offering of friendship. Is the present par excellence: for it is the gift to each of nothing else than their own freedom to make use of them as they please. With silence admitted one another. Their future began . . . It all began under this delicate omen. This story too truly began then.

Because they had known how to grant one another this saying-nothing perfectly: There was not the slightest violence. None rushed. Without having passed the word on, each of their own accord: thus it all began by a rest.

Knew how to make no comment. But each felt richer with something impalpable and nameless. Some "luck," one of them thought. For each had accomplished an invisible feat. Said nothing but each gave thanks in their hearts. Their silence was perfect: harmonious, aerial like the flight of an acrobat.

At that moment a sort of climate lighter than breath prevailed in each. Were careful not to make it heavier with a word. But did feel that each was protecting something precious like a soul's vapor, some essence of cheerfulness, a state so rare to obtain, so crystal clear. Felt they had produced such fine, unrepresentable sensations.

Each had this extremely rare sensation of coolness, which spreads within the soul. It is like a moist blessing. What is the name for this perfect delight, which is to have at the same time a thirst and its drink: it is a question with its answer. It is a desire with its quenching. None knew the name for this sensation, which is at once material and spiritual. But the miracle was: all three were sure that all together they felt "that." Despite not knowing the name, each felt that they felt too. Were inwardly blessed with the same climate that prevails when the soul is unshackled from all anguish, which is so rare, and then feels young, beautiful, and womanly, because—each joyously dared to think that all dared to think that—under the influence of cheerfulness the soul always reveals itself to be able to be a woman. And also all were flooded by the color green. Because hope is green. Nobody knows why, but it is one of the seven obvious wonders.

Thus, at that moment, what allowed itself to be tasted was an intoxicating acid green. And all were thrilled at this flavor.

Yet none said a word. Being equally shy.

Another miracle is that none were afraid.

Being shy without being fearful. A shyness made up of a sublime reserve. Let themselves be filled with joyous wonder like children discovering the sea that they will never understand, do not need to understand.

What they felt could be said was an admiration: had their lips parted because they find this invisible oeuvre they had just accomplished so beautiful. They admired one another: this is what made them laugh a lot a little later.

—So this is when this story began?

—What had just started was perhaps "their" story?

But the one I called the-most-beautiful-story is part of that one. It takes place just afterward.

What began was "their" story: it was then that they understood they would remember, one way or another. Because they had managed to meet in a deep region where the things that happen can barely be grasped with words but imprint themselves in the fabric of time and are ineffaceable. So that, for whoever has the patience to behold the fine weft, they are legible.

Then each remembered it all, in their time and in their own fashion.

Each later, each in their own lateness.

—Were already remembering? None remembered already. No. None wanted to lose their lives remembering it, at that received moment. Precisely because what they knew is that they had given themselves time, or rather had given themselves the place for the time to come. Knew like a profound serenity that they would always have place to remember. Later, each their own, there could therefore be a kind of story that would not be summed up in what is called "story": this would be again a place of a dazzling simplicity like this small, discreet, sacred chamber, like a temple for close friends, where events too infinitely refined to be kept within the mesh of a narrative could happen again.

What happened then was their full, warm, moved, regular silence: the breathing of their triple confidence. All three in one single understanding listened to the gathering of three attentive desires in the middle of this small room, to the agreement of three emanations into one single magical, indescribable constellation, to a friendship being born of a concord lighter than the air of any speech. Being born and beginning to believe—because they were fairly discreet, a certainty that was unspoken, would always be unspoken. The room was soon filled with small iridescent distances, which almost brushed against one another; traces of the thoughts that they were edging slowly toward one another.

So this is not a story? I don't know. What is the name: when three characters go out in search of the most precious thing in the world, knowing it is perhaps merely a thought, which makes them like relatives in seeming to be mad. Take three different paths, knowing only one is the right one. Thus go to the end of their three lives, separately but always together in the same desire. In the meantime meet one another and each time make one another's acquaintance again for the fist time, then leave again, knowing that only one will find the thought to which all three dedicate all their errings? And each time they meet they know this wonderful thing: if they are together it means they are not far from it. For when the three of them are in the same place, truth is among them. This is why none of them are ever really sad. But what is the name for this life in three lives, these three lives for one? This path with three ways?

But-the-most-beautiful-story-of-all-my-knowledge, I have not been able to "tell" it before: it would have been inaudible earlier. From those who got weary of the length of the path and withdrew long ago or recently, I ask for forgiveness. From those who are still here now, I do not need to ask for forgiveness. Since they know.

From this scene, which I will tarnish with words, I ask for forgiveness with all my blood.

I will make the introductions in a deliberately cold and distant voice, out of humility. Out of convenience I shall cover souls with names. The one who looks is called Max. Is also the one who introduces. Spoke of one to the other, from one to the other, spoke in advance. Of F. to O., of O. to F. Thus F. knows that O. is blind. Thus O. knows that F. knows: "O. is blind." Of one to the other, from one to the other there is the word, of one to the other. The blind word. But who knows? And all three thought and thought. Because a sentence came before the encounter and said: "You know that O. is blind." Afterward each had a hundred thoughts in their own fashion. And one thought:

"Who knows?" But who thought: "Whoever sees cannot imagine how a blind person sees."

Then comes the day of introductions.

Now Max will complete his oeuvre. It is an October afternoon.

Now all three together. The first time.

Then there is this Saying-nothing.

Now already there is this hope.

Now according to the order it is the pronunciation of names.

Max pronounces both names. The "blind" word is in the room too but mute.

Now comes the scene:

What takes place then:

"While Max is introducing F. by his name, F. bows in front of O. without saying a word."

—That's all?

—So to speak. From the point of view of the one who sees, that's all.

—Maybe I should have narrated this scene much later?

—Everything is already there?

—It was only on the following day that everything was clear to O.

—Everything is already there?

—Almost everything. The miracle has already happened.

(Maybe the coherence would be to narrate this scene at the end of the last book?

Maybe should not have narrated it. Because now that I have said almost everything, beauty should be staring one in the eye. But maybe I have . . .)

—Maybe I used words which were too big, too visible? And which close like shutters and shut out the radiance. I have said almost everything: the three persons, the one who does not see, one pronounces the name ceremoniously. And without saying a word, F. bows, ceremoniously, in front of O. You see? I wanted to show the beauty of something that would not allow itself to be seen. Would do without a witness. However, there was a witness, but an unforeseen, utterly invisible one: not the one who looks, precisely not. That is the absolutely unexpected element. Because, from the point of view of F.'s secret desire, everything has already happened, as aforesaid.

Maybe, if I repeated, the miracle would become less imperceptible?

But maybe on the contrary the scene would lose some of its radiance? Each word casts more shadow.

And thus: While Max was introducing him to O. (who lost his eyesight when he was a child, a fact which F. had been apprised of), did not F. bow *without saying a word*? Because if he had said a word, nothing miraculous would have happened. This is obviously a wordless scene.

—That's all?

—From the point of view of the sighted, that's all. The ineffaceable of this story is F.'s effacement: in order to make such a delicate gesture, one must have become as transparent as a dragonfly, as light as a grasshopper, as absolutely discreet as a Kafka, one must have reached sublime unrepresentability of one's own free will alive. What makes this scene so fragile, a word could break it, is that it has so to speak almost no place, because it happened in the invisible. The unspeakable delicacy of the gesture: is to make a sign to be seen in front of this blind man: and thus not to deprive him of the most diaphanous respect.

Because if you bow without saying a word, in front of somebody who cannot see—so ceremoniously, so silently, it is inspired by true love: because if F. had not bowed in front of O. as if he were not blind, if he had not bowed, because O. was blind, then he would have doomed O. to the darkest night, if he had forgotten to bow on the pretext that O. could not perceive this gesture anyway, then he would have removed from him again the chance to rise back to light, he would have sent him back to his night, and himself would have remained invisible and cold in his cold day, he would not have delivered him, if he had said a word, O. would have fallen back into darkness crying. What if F. had not bowed without saying a word? The room would suddenly have been traversed by a dazzling flash and would have disappeared, as a city to the bottom of a sea by an evil spell, and F. would have found himself alone in the darkness flowing out from his own soul, on the edge of the world.

But F. was not somebody who has to be reminded that within any person there is light. He does not forget the inner light more than the blood within his own body and he does not forget the other's blood more than his own. And the blood keeps watch. And F. always feels that the other blood also keeps watch within the other person. F. is somebody who also thinks inside the other. Also thinks of respecting what he cannot see from the other. Therefore he forgets neither the invisible light nor the invisible blood, this is why he does not fail to bow with good reason in front of this man who was—totally blind, so that—*he gave him back his eyesight.*

The wonderful thing about this story is how F. manages to give, even if O. is apparently not in a position to receive.

And indeed when one gives in such a way—and it is an invisible gift—, since there is no spectator—, it is the most intimate gift possible,—then something from the rigor of the stoppages of the world seems to allow itself to be swayed, as if the law were slightly moved, yes, then, during a vertiginous moment, the being-sighted is granted to the blind, the being-with-song to the mute, yes—and during a moment of almost unbearable happiness, the gift is well received.

—O. saw?

—To tell the truth, O. stopped being blind in the very instant. And this instant becomes the most precious secret of his spiritual story.

—To tell the truth F. started giving him back light as soon as he entered the room; but perhaps O. would not have received this gift at this very instant. However, O. really stopped being blind in this very instant. Thanks to the uncalculated element of this story:

The miracle has already begun taking place. Remains the additional feature: the unexpected effacement of F.'s effacement. An almost imperceptible detail, which precipitates everything:

Later on O. will tell:

"It is a kind of chance: F. knew he was at a blind man's house. While M. was introducing him to me, he bowed without saying a word. It was, one might believe, a formality devoid of meaning for me who could not see it. Yet a lock of his brushed-down hair lightly touched my forehead; probably because of my leaning excessively. What I feel then is such a painful joy that at that very instant I could not clearly distinguish the cause, I could not contain this passion, all the tears gathered since my childhood wanted to flow at last . . . "

And this instant becomes the most precious secret of his spiritual story and perhaps even the first instant of another life. At the time he does not assess it, and cannot explain it, for all his sensible strengths are not enough for him to bear the crushing joy that hits him.

"For the first time," he began to think the following day, "somebody had regarded my disability as a fact that solely concerned me." Began to understand and from then on the days ceased being like nights to him. Then he understood: F. had just freed him from a spell. And he understood: because F. had known how to enter the presence of somebody who cannot see without shutting him up deep in his blindness. And he had gently removed a night from in front of his soul. What if F. had not bowed without saying a word in front of O., the night would have become darker . . . Every day O. understood this mystery a little more clearly, so that he was allowed also to live from then on in another day hidden beyond his night . . .

—That's all?

—That's all O. and M. told later. But there still remains what O. did not want either to tell or to allow to efface itself forever, that, which he dared confide only to beings who would live long after him, after F.'s life, and M.'s life; a secret detail; which O. out of respect for the purity of F.'s gesture did not want, in his lifetime, either to reveal or conceal. But took care to leave it to the chances of a private paper. Thus it is that someone was able to read this last narrative: "Today, on this the tenth of October 1904: to one of my still unborn descendants, I need to confide this: Yesterday M. brought F. to me. There happened something too violent for me to be able to explain it right now. In a way it was nothing. A sort of chance. At most a light touch. Yes, only the minute sensation of a lock of hair lightly touching my forehead. Yet it was as if thunder had struck me. I felt in contact with this hair a pain too shameful to tell my friends, but it was *a joy* that caused me this pain: I could not hold back my tears. They seemed to spring directly from my heart. Then, as if through the violence of the streaming, a night canvas was wrenched from my pupils, I thought I could see—I am lying: I saw—with certainty—with my eyes as if I could suddenly see the light, I did see, I swear, blue-gray, attentive eyes, I saw as clear as in a dream, under thick, black eyebrows, and I also thought I could see, but I was crying so much, on thin, well-lined lips a fine smile floating, yes, with my own poor eyes, I saw F.'s face: I had the impression of seeing the whole of his being, who was one single look at once light and piercing plunging softly into my eyes, I could feel him at the same time looking at me without touching me and penetrating me, with a sort of piercing, discreet kindness, I do not know how to describe that, because I still feel this shame and this enjoyment that drive me mad. Today, I see nothing. I only have a deep sensation of blue gray. Feel terribly awake, terribly unhappy; but—strong—I was on the verge of calling Max to ask him to describe F. to me, but I hung up straightaway: it seems to me that if I told *that*, if I touched *that* with a word, I would lose my eyesight a second time. Nor can I keep the secret either."

—That's all now.

And why did O. confide nothing to Max? Had no doubt that F.'s eyes were of this blue gray that from then on served as a secret day to him. Said nothing out of respect for the gracefulness of the gift. Because F. had risen, in the reserve of this silence, above calculated kindness up to the incalculable kindness of nature itself. Had risen very far beyond banale sanctity. And as he had given in silence, in silence such a perfect gesture as this had to be received, yes in the perfection of silence, which is effacement. And if O. had said "thank you," F. would have been mortified. For had accomplished the thing in secret, with the fairylike transparency of nobody. Because if he had said a thank you, he would have returned to F. what F. had given absolutely, and the gift would have been annuled. However, it was unbearable for him not to shout thank you, because such a great joy is like a pain: cannot be contained in the cramped human body. This is why O. wrote this narrative, and, while he was typing, his soul full of this blue-gray clarity, a treasure and a proof, it seemed to him he was going to the far end of their lives and to the following generation, to meet his daughter's daughter, it seemed to him, who was twenty years old, that he was crossing his life, and one more till the third life, to which he was going to confide his secret; and thus one miracle triggers off another. And O. knew he would beget this future daughter, because he had a gift to hand down to her. That day, he needed children. And he was thinking all that, sitting in front of his typewriter thinking such great thoughts, greater than any he would ever have, and he had the impression of being mad and he was not afraid of this madness. That day nothing of what was greater than him frightened him. And he also thought about his and F.'s deaths without dread and fear of ridicule, because he had something unforgettable to pass on from life to life. And all this, he dared think that very same day, had been begot by F.'s superhumanity; with one single invisible, inaudible gesture had begot this inner day, had begot this harrowing light, had impregnated O.'s shy, skeptical soul, and had all at once forced it to grow and produce, had taught, under the seal of the most beautiful secrecy, the prudence necessary for generosity, the courage and self-denial of intelligence, which must not speak what it knows, had even begot his descendants, that Saturday, all three were barely over twenty years old, and yet O. was thinking ardently about what his grandchildren would be thinking.

And he said nothing: because he had understood almost everything. . . .

And he said nothing. He did not say that he knew what F. had just done. For he knew that F. had acted in the most simple secrecy. By effacing himself naturally.

Because he had understood: this gesture was nothing. Was not supposed to be perceptible. "It was, one might believe, a formality devoid of meaning for the-one-who-could-not-see-it." It was the supreme sign of respect for that very thing. As he bowed thus, F. remained strictly faithful to the respect owed to any living person. Respect cannot be divided. Cannot be detailed. As he bowed thus, F. respected himself in the respect he was showing toward O. Respected the delicate essence of respect that does not depend on the earthly look but on the spiritual look. Respect does not make itself conspicuous.

This is why O. said nothing. Did not say there had been an unexpected witness of this gesture. He likewise did not touch the thing with words either. But there was a witness, whom F. did not notice. And this witness was himself, O. Because in spite of F., in spite of O., in spite of the carefully respected respect, a certain discretion was interrupted, unexpectedly. For O. in an unhoped-for manner. There was the light touching of a lock of hair.

And all of Saturday and on the following day, O. never stopped thinking it over. But he did not utter a word. Refrained from talking about the lock, out of delicacy. Still felt on his forehead this pain of the light touch, which was not really a pain, but prevented him from thinking and made him suffer as would too subtle a caress; what he called pain was the violence of the revelation. A contact so faint, and involuntary, giving away a vertiginous secret.

And the real pain, on Saturday and Sunday, was the stormy torment not to know what this unique moment would have been without the accidental indiscretion of the lock; otherwise, he would not have known? In two days O. felt all the worst and the best feelings caused by chance, and all his thoughts started by "what if . . . " And he got scared at the idea of what might not have taken place or might have. And at the idea that perhaps a lock of hair had decided his destiny. And perhaps a hairdresser then. And he had vulgar thoughts and others of a religious kind, resentments and gratitudes. He believed in God and turned away from God. He was cross with F. and then was doubly cross with himself. Because, if one gives so delicately, perhaps one deprives of the gift? Because to give while effacing oneself is to give absolutely, but one perhaps effaces the gift? Was tempted to shout "thank you!"

Would he thank the lock? Chance? But was it a chance? What if he had leaned excessively? Just excessively enough? Did not know. Knew nothing. But on Sunday O. no longer felt like complaining he had been touched by this chance. (A reconciliation was beginning: from then on he knew how to love the unexpected.)

. . .

Translated by Laurent Milesi

8
LOVE OF THE WOLF
(1994)

This is a bo(u)nd for a wolf.

On November 11, 1967, Clarice Lispector wrote in favor of fear: "I am certain that in the Stone Age I was exactly mistreated by some man or other's love. A certain fright, which is secret, goes back to that time."[1]

Some paleolithic man or other, a sort of ravishing monkey. Another woman, Marina Tsvetaeva for example, would say a wolf, and another a tiger.

The Stone Age, for Tsvetaeva, is the age of blood and passions, the age of the garden at the Convent of the Flagellants. First blood. Game of blood: the blood rushes up and down, one grows pale, one blushes, the blood rushes away, called back, disobedient.

The landscape of that age is one of anguish and nostalgia. The little girl is running. You can't tell if she's running away. Or if she's lost. If she's running after the tiger. Or if the tiger is running after her.

Following in Tsvetaeva's footsteps, this reading *is a bo(u)nd for a secret wolf*

▦ ▦ ▦

Tsvetaeva is "descended" from Pushkin, according to her own version of her genealogy. She comes running from every direction out of the works of Pushkin.

The initial fright that inspires Tsvetaeva comes from Pushkin's fear. And out of all of Pushkin, her first Pushkin was "The Bohemians."

I had never heard such names: Aleko, Zemfíra or—the Old Man. As for old men, I knew only one: Ossip, in the Chapel of Taroussa, One-armed-Ossip—his arm was like an oxbow because he had killed his brother—with a cucumber. Because my grandfather, A. D. Meyn, was no old man: you don't talk to old men, they live in the street. I had never seen any Bohemians, but I had heard of a Bohemian woman—she nursed me.[2]

Her first Pushkin was on the shelf, it was fat, she would read it in the dark. Her Pushkin, her source, her strange origin. He would always come from outside, that stranger, the one who carries her away. There is a door. The door opens, in comes the Outside, even inside he remains the outside, the Outside in person, that which I do not know, who strikes me very hard and loves me, thinks Tsvetaeva, the woman who loves the devils who carry her away. They are always beings who remain in hiding, who attract and then flee, who flee while attracting, who attract while fleeing, who escape and who call—bizarre beings, cossacks, funny words, clicks of the tongue; they have common, ordinary and yet extraordinary names, terrible names that sound like nothing, *kid, the guide*—they pass, and in their footsteps comes the word that the little girl had read in books, those foreign lands—

Here's a brand new word—love. When it burns in one's breast, there, right in the middle (who doesn't understand me?).[3]

The parenthesis divides the world between those who understand and those who don't. Love always sets up its parentheses in the middle of the sentence, pitches its tents of silence.

. . . when you don't say anything to anybody, it's love. From the beginning it burned in my breast, but I didn't know its name—love. I said to myself: it's the same for everybody, always the same. No: that existed only among the Bohemians.[4]

One day, I don't know when, it was decided to call *love* a set of strange, indescribable physical phenomena, is it pain?—but from the moment that the name is given to that burning in one's breast, the violence of the strangeness is interrupted and the ancient horror, hidden behind the new word, begins to be forgotten. Let's go back to before language, that's what Tsvetaeva does, let's go back to that disturbing age, the age of myths and of folktales, the age of stone, of fire, of knives. Before language there is the fire that bites but doesn't kill, the evil that, like all pain, separates us, the dehiscence that opens in us closed organs, making us seem strange to ourselves—and all that begins with: "when you don't say anything to anybody—that's it—it's love." It begins with the kept secret, with the silent separation from the rest of the world. You love yourself [on s'aime]: you sow [on sème]. You throw the others off track. You go underground. You leave the world in broad daylight. You betray it. You're cheating. It's a crime. It's a kind of glory. Love abjures in order to adore. It burns in your breast and the world is burned.

Don't say anything to anybody—because it's forbidden? That would be the case of Romeo and Juliet. No—it *is* allowed, but you won't say anything to anybody anyway. One says nothing to anybody because one rises to the absolute; one begins speaking the language that no one else speaks—a language spoken only by two. By these two undivided individuals, a language [langue] that makes of two but one, especially when it's your tongue [langue] that I have in my mouth.

(N.B Ah, I shall always regret in French the absence of those words that in other languages name the set of one made by *two* when it fuses two individuals who from then on are no longer two; I shall always regret *both, ambos, beide . . .*)

Joyfully you become incomprehensible—two strangers together. You begin to adore a god that nobody else bows down to. A very powerful and very fragile god, very threatening and very threatened. Nobody else believes in you except me. This very-much-god must be well hidden in order to protect it from incredulity. My god is made of glass, poof! and it's broken. But so long as it's intact it gives the universe. Invisible transparent god made of glass [verre]. I meant to say of verse [vers].

But the amorous break also speaks of the danger of winning. The danger is when you create a world, designed as a whole and for a whole people, made up of two individuals. This world-of-two depends for its survival on a single other person. The world-of-two is immediately surrounded and threatened by death. Death closes in around it tightly. Love immortalizes me. Only that which gives me life can take it away from me. That which gives, gives to enjoy, that which gives to enjoy, gives to fear its loss. Give to lose. The gift and its opposite.

It is on the basis of love that one recalls mortality. We are mortal only in that high region of love. In ordinary life we are immortal, we think about death, but it doesn't gnaw at us, it is down there, for later, it is weak, forgettable. But as soon as I love, death is there, it camps out right in the middle of my body, in daylight, getting mixed up with my food, dispatching from the far-off future its prophetic presence, taking the bread out of my mouth. It's because I love the beloved more than I love myself, you are dearer to me than I am to myself, you are not me, you don't obey me, I was sure that I was myself immortal, otherwise I couldn't live, I live only in that assurance, but what about you? I do not order your immortality. I can no longer live without you. That need overwhelms us. That's why anguish bursts forth: because the need pushes us toward the realization—no matter what, yes, I must die.

In *The Kid* nothing—not need, not infinity—can stop it. That's what the prose of the text says at the opening:

And this is again the story of an old mother who knew too much about future things[5]

Go, go, little girl!
Youth has but one time[6]

Maroussia: Dance, mother,
                        Smashing into everything! . . .
The mother: Your senses are eager
                        Your heart is blind.[7]

Knowledge from experience: the heart goes blind because the need is stronger than anything else. Your ego is blind, your id is eager. It will get to the point of smashing everything. When there is a danger from outside, you bolt, but when the danger comes from inside, how can you bolt? The danger from inside is that complicated thing, the love of the wolf, the complicity that attaches us to that which threatens us.

When the I-ego and the I-id are adversaries and friends, inseparably, like the wolf and the infant, flight becomes unthinkable. When hatred and resentment show their teeth, we flee—but when it's love, tortuous love, who shows us their teeth?

Don't say it to anybody, love is so delicate, it's mortally fragile. A passerby could pulverize that god made of glass. But if you don't say (it) to anybody, this departure, this madness, you're at the mercy of the god. Nobody will come to your rescue the day the god takes on the aura of devil.

"Don't say it to anybody," it's the same refrain that runs through a splendid text by Ingeborg Bachmann, *Der Gute Gott von Manhattan*. Don't say it—

—to anybody. Nor even to yourself? Not even to the other person? But who is the other person? For Tsvetaeva?

The one whom you keep secret even from your mother, the one you don't name, not even to him? The one you keep. The one you kee— Shhh!—

Without being wary of him. The one whom Tsvetaeva, in her poem,[8] is careful not to call anything but *The Kid*. The Kid [*Le Gars*], one word, one syllable—a brief sparkle, a single phoneme, the very one for whom the glory tolls between Genet and Derrida. But in the off-stage commentaries it takes place differently. From afar, from outside, it names:

> I read a story by Afanassiev, "The Vampire," and I couldn't figure out why Maroussia who was afraid of the vampire insisted on denying what she had seen, all the while knowing that naming it meant salvation for her. Why instead of yes, no? Out of fear? ... No, not fear. Maybe fear, but—what else? Fear—and what? [...] Maroussia loved the vampire ... and that's why she lost, one after the other, her mother, her brother, her life.[9]

Why instead of yes, no? Out of fear. But the kid also says clearly to his lover: if you don't tell that I'm a vampire, your brother is going to die, then your mother is going to die, and then you're going to die. What Maroussia wishes to hold onto is love as fear, and fear as love. They are inseparable. This is one of the most obscure experiences that we can ever have. Some of us really like what scares us. Just to be scared. It's appalling. O my love, my terror. "O my son, my terror," says Akhmatova in one of her poems. There is no love except where there is fear. Love run by fear, escorted by fear.

We love the wolf. We love the love of the wolf. We love the fear of the wolf. We're afraid of the wolf: there is love in our fear. Fear is in love with the wolf. Fear loves. Or rather: we are afraid of the person we love. Love terrorizes us. Or else the person we love we call our wolf or our tiger, or our lamb in the manger. We are full of trembling and ready to wolf down.

Love is vertical. First you go up. There is a ladder. Maroussia climbs up. Once you're at the top, you see, you fall. You've seen what you've seen. Seeing the other knocks us over. Seeing the wolf. Fear makes us fail from the top to the bottom, taking us back to the age of blood, in infancy, as we crawl among the odors, the appetites, the food, the earth-worms and the dead.

"I loved a wolf," says the little heroine of a text by Selma Lagerlöf, "Herr Arne's Treasure." And in the end of course, it kills her, or else it's she who kills herself for it.

As soon as one speaks of loving, it is there.

Love begins with a cat. A lost, accidental, fuzzy baby appears. A kitten one might think. A kitten *par excellence*: the found beast, the abandoned creature meowing—as in Aeschylus's *Agamemnon*. It comes into our home one fine morning, a poignant, mysteriously poignant figure of the unplanned child, and without any need of biological mother, or of father for that matter.

This kitten given by nobody, a gracious creature, is loved without being asked its name.

> One day a man reared in his house
> A lion cub still suckling, and he weaned it.
> The beginning of its life was full of charm.
> A friend to children, a joy to the elderly,
> Fed in one's arms, like a baby,
> Its ardent eye kept watch on the hand,
> Its appetite for food making it cuddly.
> But the time came
> When it showed its hereditary character.
> And to recompense the ones who'd nourished it,
> Needing no invitation, it feasts
> On a flock of sheep it massacred.
> The house is flooded with blood,
> Endless sorrow for the people of that house.
> Vast, devastating hecatomb.
> Sent by a god, an acolyte of Misfortune
> Had come into the dwelling

To have a hand in the breeding.[10]

Eternally cruel seduction of the Foundling, whose frequent figure haunts those texts tormented by the riddle. Who is this child born without pain but bearer of a pain that we cannot help but suffer, in whom we cannot help but recognize ourselves, whom our narcissism nurses, who, at first feeding on our need, begins to devour us? And who is named at one time Oedipus, at another Heathcliff, and at another Nicolo alias Colino?

A stiff, black, withdrawn, silent savage, all the more loved in that he turns upon love with an appalling look. How is it that we love him—him of all people? What have we found in this foundling who fascinates us?

As soon as we embrace, we salivate, one of us wants to eat, one of us is going to be swallowed up in little pieces, we all want to be eaten, in the beginning we were all formerly born-to-eat, wolfing it down, eating like a horse; we are starved, full of whetted appetites—but better not say it, or else we'll never dare to love. Or to be loved.

Love is always a little wol-f-ishy [*loup-che*]—a little peckish, it's not nice to say, but . . .

(How) can a wolf be loved? By instinct, says Tsvetaeva. In what way is the wolf lovable? It's not the race of wolves that we love, it's nor the wolf. It's about *a* wolf, a certain wolf, a wolf-but, a wolf-surprise.

> *I said "the wolf"—I name the Guide. I say "the Guide," I name Pouga-tchov: the Wolf which—just this once won't hurt—spared its lamb, carried it off in the deep forest to love it. . .*
>
> *I'd say I loved that Guide more than all my own, more than the strangers, more than my favorite dogs, more than all the balls that rolled down the cellar, more than all the lost penknives, more even than my mysterious red armoire—where he was kept secret, mystery incarnate.*
>
> *More than the Bohemians, because he was blacker—darker than the Bohemians. And if I could say loud and clear that Pushkin lived in the secret armoire, today it's scarcely with a whisper that I can affirm: not Pushkin . . . the Guide.*[11]

"I said 'the wolf,' I name the Guide . . . I loved that Guide more than all my own." I love my ball because it rolls down the cellar, we experience love through the loss it inflicts upon us: whether the ball is in the cellar or in the house, the ball is the possibility of rolling down the cellar. A penknife you have you don't love, but the *lost* penknife, yes.

O ancient pleasures of hide-and-seek, the first game of all, the game inscribed in our flesh (kitten flesh, newborn flesh) for millennia before our being born.

O the mystery of the mystery-game,

that all of us, of all species, children, felines, dogs, celebrate.

Crying "look for me I'm hidden I'm lost find me." How good it feels to be lost, to be looked for, to be found, to tremble with all those fears together: fear of not being discovered, fear of being discovered, fear of not trembling with fear.

I can't find the word to name the essence of these frightful delights. Look for me, says the hidden thing. Let's say I find it: that's *losability.* Not a very pretty word, but this concept is life itself. We feel like we're alive only through the painful excitation of our seventh sense, the sense of loss.

There is a connection between love and *being lost.* In familiar meta-phoric terms, when it's a question of passion, we get lost, we run wild with a panting metonymy, we are lost, all the more so by being helped by the personage posted there to produce objectively being lost: that's the case of Pougatchov, known as the Guide. The guide leads astray. Guide to getting lost. Guide to the secret.

Let's follow the Wolf—that is, The Kid—that is, the Guide—whose name in the end will be Pougatchov. Careful because if we follow him closely, "the Guide" could lead us to the deepest, the most remote place, down to where the roots of good and evil are gripped together in a single root, down to that depth at which we are all mixed together, the guide and I, *Pushkin and Pougatchov,* where Tsvetaeva is Pushkin, where Pougatchov is Tsvetaeva. *The Guide,* therefore, the one whom Tsvetaeva loves, makes appearances and disappearances in these little autobiographical texts in prose, mirrors of Tsvetaeva's unconscious, in the figure—not of a person—but of a scintillating Signifier, magic word, beacon beam, allusion, *promise,* let's say "thing." A strange sudden appearance, comparable to the sudden primitive appearance effected, at first indecipherably, in the mother-text, Pushkin's.

It is in a whole lineage of Pushkin's amorous mysteries that Tsvetaeva inscribes the genealogy of her own imaginary. This always involves duels, dual relations that are so intense, so red-hot, so white-hot, that the dimension of sexual difference, in the dazzle, is actually forgotten.

Such as the Pushkin and Pougatchov couple. *Pushkin and Pougatchov* is a title that sings of the passionate relation that Pushkin—himself the literary mother of Tsvetaeva—had with an ambivalent personage, an impostor, a cossack. One of those messianic figures from Russian history, a popular cavalryman who has come from the steppes to try to take the tsar's place. Now Pushkin wrote two texts inspired by Pougatchov: on the one hand, a historical piece, written for the tsar, and entitled *The History of Pougatchov*; on the other hand, a fiction, the short novel *The Captain's Daughter*. As an occasional historian, Pushkin describes the cossack just as the archives reveal him, a vile, cowardly personage complete with all the vices. But in *The Captain's Daughter* a complex Pougatchov surfaces—cruel, destructive, yet at the same time capable of an unexpected love for the little young man Griniov. This sixteen-year-old hero, Pushkin's creation, arouses in Pougatchov a tenderness such that the wicked creature will remain loyal to the boy till the end of his days. Pougatchov appears first as a "black thing" that draws near during a storm in which everyone is lost, trapped in a *murky whirlpool*, bereft of all landmarks, in which everything comes loose, shapes are seen disconnected from their origins, everything is swallowed up in a huge white whirlpool, nothing is recognizable any longer: it is in the midst of this turmoil that all of a sudden there appears—a *what*—

What is a what? It is not a shaft. It is not a wolf. It might be a kind of peasant who will guide those gone astray, the little young man and his coachman, toward an invisible inn. And that's the beginning of the love story between Pougatchov—because it's him—and the little Griniov. The guide who rescues people from being lost will reappear, later in the tale, in an inversed form. In historical "reality," the guide leads astray all of Russia, and all those who follow him, and does not lead them toward salvation. The one who, in the completely white turmoil, is a tiny black, shiny point, will dissolve, become murky, incomprehensible, yet will remain *the thing,* this obscure, unanalyzable link between the young man and Pougatchov. At the very moment of the encounter, a tremendous thing, Pushkin recounts the dream that little Griniov has in this inn where he has been rescued by the guide—the one that leads up and down, toward death and toward life: in the dream the little Griniov goes home. His mother is anxiously waiting for him because his father is going to die. In the father's bedroom the young man draws near the bed of the person he so dearly loves. Then the father gets up suddenly and pounces on the little Griniov bran-dishing a hatchet. We are overwhelmed by fear. At that point what the little Griniov sees is the look, at once gleaming and incredibly tender, of the paternal assassin, who turns out to be Pougatchov in person, the "guide" who loves him and whom he loves, the crazed, blood thirsty one, the monster of love.

Tsvetaeva takes note of the history of the two narratives and points out that Pushkin wrote *The History of Pougatchov* BEFORE he wrote *The Captain's Daughter.*

In other words, the poet is aware of who Pougatchov was when he writes his fiction. He thus paints *his* Pougatchov in glowing colors—and his is perhaps the true one. We don't know. In any case, it's the one that Russia, the peasants, and the cossacks loved, loved to invent and invented to love, as one should be loved: without telling anyone except in dreams. And for her part, Tsvetaeva—Griniov—Pushkin:

> Oh that guide—I fell in love with him right away, from the moment when, in the dream, the usurping father, the black-bearded peasant found in the bed in place of Griniov's father, looked at me gleefully. And when the peasant brandished his hatchet, when he started wav-ing it around in every direction, I knew in advance that we—Griniov and I—had nothing to fear, and if I was entirely overwhelmed by fear, it was a dream fear, the fortunate fear of being inconsequen-tial through and through—fortunate for me not to have fear to go through inconsequentially. (Thus in dreams we slow down—on purpose to scoff at the assassin, knowing that at the last second we'll grow wings.) And when the peasant—the monster—started to call to me tenderly, saying: "Have no fear! . . . come let me give you my blessing! . . . "—there I was already blessed by his blessing! . . . there I was before him, pushing toward him with all my little girl might—Griniov. —"Now go ahead, now, go ahead! Love him!" I'm ready to burst into bitter tears because Griniov doesn't understand (Griniov is in general the tight-fisted type) that the other loves him, that he'll massacre everybody else, but that him he'll love—as it the wolf suddenly held out his paw, and this paw . . . you refused.[12]

Yes, love of the wolf is indistinguishable from love of fear. When we were little, how we loved to be scared silly! That was an extremely pure fear. The child is capable of two things at once, first to believe absolutely in the danger, and then at the same time not to believe in it. That's the way he gets his pleasure. Later we hold on to no more than half of these beliefs—it's either/or, and farewell dear wolf: either we believe absolutely in the danger, or else we don't believe in it at all.

The secret of the fortunate fear is in the strange scene in which Griniov throws himself on his dying father who is in the grandmother-wolf's bed. Today the reason the children's version of the story of Little Red Riding Hood probably has no pay-off for us is that the split between grandmother and wolf has taken place in advance of the story's narrative. On the one hand, there's the grandmother whom Little Red Riding Hood loves and is bringing food to (but then the grandmother has been eaten by the wolf), and on the other hand, there's the wolf. When we are told this story, when Little Red Riding Hood is in the bedroom with the grandmother in bed, we children who are listening are horrified by the grandmother in that bed, because we know it's the wolf. Now, this is not right in terms of the truth of love. The truth of love is both-at-once: from one perspective, as little red riding hoods, we jump into the wolf's mouth, we think it's our grandmother, but it's no longer grandmother pure, and we love grandmother all the more so because she's the wolf—for loving a candy granny is easy; but from the other perspective, it turns out this grandmother-wolf who eats everybody up makes an exception and doesn't eat us: we are the grandmother-wolf's favorite, the wolf's chosen one. Now that's the escalating value of love. There is no greater love than the love the wolf feels for the lamb-it-doesn't-eat. The other side of the scene is the paradoxical, refined, magnificent love of the wolf.

It's not difficult for the ewe to love the lamb. But for the wolf? The wolf's love for the lamb is such a renunciation, it's a Christ-like love, it's the wolf's sacrifice—it's a love that could never be requited. This wolf that sacrifices its very definition for the lamb, this wolf that doesn't eat the lamb, is it a wolf? Is it still a wolf? Isn't it a delupinized wolf, a non-wolf, an invalidated wolf? If it were a false wolf, there'd be no interest. No, we've made no mistake, this wolf is a real wolf: right up to the last second it could eat us, the axe doesn't stop hissing past us, up to the last second, with the little child's faith, true faith, we believe in the wolf and we're afraid. Then the grandmother holds out a furry paw and we are bowled over by the solemn honor. Thus the wolf, double-wolf, more than-grandmother, sacrifices itself herself to us. And we triumph without ever having gone to battle!

Grown-ups pretend, but children get a thrill. The wolf says to the child: I'm going to eat you up. Nothing tickles the child more. That's the mystery: why does the idea that you're going to eat me up fill me with such pleasure and such terror? It's to get this pleasure that you need the wolf. The wolf is the truth of love, its cruelty, its fangs, its claws, our aptitude for ferocity. Love is when you suddenly wake up as a cannibal, and not just any old cannibal, or else wake up destined for devourment.

But happiness is when a real wolf suddenly refrains from eating us. The lamb's burst of laughter comes when it's about to be devoured, and then, at the last second, is not eaten. Hallelujah comes to mind. To have almost been eaten yet not to have been eaten: that is the triumph of life. But you've got to have the two instants, just before the teeth and just after, you've got to hear the jaws coming down on nothing for there to be jubilation. Even the wolf is surprised.

I've just described the lamb's laughter. What about the wolf? Where is its joy? I'm getting to that.

In Aeschylus's *Eumenides* the Furies pursuing Orestes, their prey, spend years saying to him: I'm going to eat you. The victim believes it, knows that at one time or another it just could happen. The horror of the situation is that it drags on and on; and the person being pursued bolts, knowing he's just a piece of meat. But in that case, it's a question of satisfying anti-love, really shattering the boundary between flesh and meat.

For us, eating and being eaten belong to the terrible secret of love. We love *only* the person we can eat. The person we hate we "can't swallow." That one makes us vomit. Even our friends are inedible. If we were asked to dig into our friend's flesh we would be disgusted. The person we love we dream only of eating. That is, we slide down that razor's edge of ambivalence. The story of torment itself is a very beautiful one. Because loving is wanting and being able to eat up and yet to stop at the boundary. And there, at the tiniest beat between springing and stopping, in rushes fear. The spring is already in mid-air. The heart stops. The heart takes off again. Everything in love is oriented toward this absorption At the same time real love is a don't-touch, yet still an almost-touching. *Tact itself: a phantom touching.* Eat me up, my love, or else I'm going to eat you up. Fear of eating, fear of the edible, fear on the part of the one of them who feels loved, desired, who wants to be loved, desired, who desires to be desired, who knows that there is

no greater proof of love than the other's appetite, who is dying to be
eaten up yet scared to death by the idea of being eaten up, who says or
doesn't say, but who signifies: I beg you, eat me up. Want me down to
the marrow. And yet manage it so as to keep me alive. But I often turn
about or compromise, because I know that you won't eat me up, in the
end, and I urge you: bite me. Sign my death with your teeth.

We love, we fall into the jaws of the fire. We can't escape it.

Open arms
Facing forward—
Red blaze, white birch[13]

This is the portrait of Maroussia hit at point-blank range, a portrait in
green, red and white. It's the fall of Maroussia, struck by a mouth shooting off, by a shirt going off, and hit, pierced by the kid's gunshots.

That's what love is: falling into the jaws of fire. It opens up. There is:

The door opens,
—Hello, everybody!
Cheers, have a good evening!

Neither gleam,
Nor flash—
Kid in red shirt.
Neither ember,
Nor blaze—
Fine-red shirt.

Greetings all around,
Purse on the table,
Shiny money streaming down.
(26–27)

It happens so fast, much faster than lightning, so much fasten than
lightning that I don't know how I can tell about it. The way she does
it: forcing, with gusts of wind, shots, signifiers, axe-blows, with the
tiniest metrical denominator imaginable, tri-syllabically (not even in
threes—in fewer than two beats),

skipping causes, the effect remains, paring away, leaving out, prun-
ing, syncopating, equivocating.

The door opens, in comes—someone? no, in comes the word—in
two words—

Hello, everybody!

The telegraphic utterance, the tonic accent strikes, sets the beat.

Neither gleam,
Nor flash—

In four words, a dazzling scene of bedazzlement.

"Neither gleam nor flash" means also yes-gleam, yes-flash, that's
what Maroussia thought she saw, the dazzle of the dancer and the
complicity of the narration—neither feminine nor masculine, lighting
effect, neither gleam nor flash then it's *kid in red shirt,* kid no article,
neither the nor a,

as soon as she can, she gets rid of the semantic function, which
allows the substantive to pass from the level of discourse to the level
of language.

It's therefore possible to do without the article.

The a is missing. *A* kid? *A* could designate the first appearance.
Once upon a time there was a kid. No. It's: Kid without a. Thus no first
appearance. Kid as though he had always been there, always or forever,
kid like God —Red kid—or were(wolf)kid? There's still the shirt to
cover up the wolf. O the shirt, that's what's so fascinating to the glares
and the gazes—that's all that can be seen in it, just its red. A round in
three times, mine, yours, his, in three persons, mine yours his, the third
figures the space, the third wins, whether I dance or you dance, it's
nothing just a blank. But the kid dances on fire.

The kid fires. Three times.

Mouth, shirt, eyes—
Fire! Fire! Fire!
(28)

All that can be seen—all that can be heard—is fire

Into which falls, open arms, the woman who is now nothing more
than fuel for the blaze.

Fire! It's the order to shoot. Who gave it?
The wolf. Wolf, who are you?
The kid says:
Fire—I am,
Hungry—I am,
Fire—I am,
Ashes—I shall be!

(29)

A disturbing lover who tells not his name but his impulse, his appetite, his choice of object, his food

—Her I shall choose
A fresh-faced one among the fresh

(28)

Time watches
Oven all the graves it digs.
At the edge of the ear:
—It is I, my sleeping one!

(109)

It's the angelic-demonic voice of the Kid. The person who remains
nameless and whose voice one hears—that's the Kid. "*It is I*" proclaims
in terms of absolute intimacy that *the person who does not give his name
is right now inside the person who is listening: it is I.* I read also "It is I, my
sleeping one," as if in apposition: my sleeping one is me.

Hot cry from the womb:
—It is I, my promised one! (110)

—Wolf, who are you?—Kid.
The Kid says one time:

At the edge of the ear:
—It is I, my sleeping one! . . .

Hot cry from the womb:

—It is I, my promised one!

The only one who can say *that* is the kid—and the internalized kid, the voice from the womb. Who cries? Is it the womb that utters the cry, or does the cry come from the womb? It could be the kid transformed into fruit of the womb.

No first name. Just this word, this single syllable, *Kid* (or fire, or soot), just a phoneme, a stifled sigh. One hell of a signifier this kid [*gars*]—who, being just one *l* away, if I let it slip, could sound Derrida's knell [*glas*]. Nameless kid, abrupt, sharp-edged, clear-cut at times by enjambment with hag-/gard-, playing, aggravating, flirtatious, chilling, burning, gnawing the text everywhere, leading the dance that throws you off, drives you crazy. Not counting the double-play that arises from the difference between this kid [*gars*] which literally posts a warning and, when sounded aloud, as *ga,* suppresses it.[14]

He's irresistible—the kid, the wolf, the fire. And for good reason: fire catches *before* you've even had a chance to see it, you can't get away, it bursts into flames and you're already in it, in the wolf, in the circle, in the dance, in the red, or else you're drowned in the devil's gray river. She can no longer extricate herself from him. We are born-eaten.

⸬ ⸬ ⸬

But sometimes it's the wolf that falls into the jaws of the lamb. The wolf, out of love, falls backwards into the circle of fire. It goes around so fast, it just so happens that the lamb catches the wolf, the double. A marvelous occasion for Tsvetaeva to plunge into the wolf's heart and to contemplate herself in there, she along with us as well, as in the mirror of a subtle narcissism: a mixture of heart throbs and nostalgia for our own goodness.

What ties this wolf to this lamb, she figures, is the fact that it hasn't eaten it. Painful mystery of the gift that returns through reflection: what the wolf loves in the lamb is its own goodness. It's thanks to the lamb that the wolf accedes to the plane of love—the love that gives of itself without hope, without calculation, without response, *but* that nevertheless gives *of itself,* seeing itself give of itself. The wolf given to a lamb of the Griniov type who doesn't even notice the enormity of the gift—that's really love. There remains the infinite solitude of the wolf, invisible and unrecognized except by itself. What interest does Pougatchov have in not eating the lamb? The ascetic and dangerous interest of self-love. The lover loves the beloved, which is the occasion for generous love. But thereafter—thereafter there is the aftermath. Now the wolf can no longer break away from the lamb, for the lamb retains, for better or worse, traces of the gift. That which is given in love can never be taken back. It is me my entire self that I give with the gift of love. This is why the wolf can't stop loving the lamb, the chosen one. Repository of the wolf. All of the wolf. That's how love can ruin the lover.

And this is not the end of it. What else? One more riddle: "The black thing that loves the frail whiteness." Me loves non-me. Othello loves Desdemona. But Desdemona loves the black thing as well. The round goes on. The lamb loves its wolf. The wolf turns all white and starts quivering out of love of the lamb. The lamb loves the wolf's fragility, and the wolf loves the frail one's force. The wolf is now the lamb's lamb and the lamb has tamed the wolf. Love blackens the lamb.

Wolf, whom do you love?

It only I knew! . . .

Love—that's: it. That's id. That idself [*ça même*]. And it/id loves me [*Ça m'aime*]. And the fable is called the Wolf is the Lamb.

Translated by Keith Cohen

9

ON FEBRUARY 12, I COMMITTED AN ERROR (2005)

FROM *LOVE ITSELF IN THE LETTER BOX*

I had tried to commit this Error for the last ten years, its catastrophic phantasmagoria had presented itself to my mind at various times, and I had dismissed it too easily, as may happen when one plays at scaring oneself by imagining being led to make a mistake whose harmful consequences can be guessed at, so as to teach oneself a lesson or as it happens with me, and too often but I can't do anything about it, to represent to myself what I fear, that is to say the death of someone dear, with such an energetic scenario such striking images that I bewitch myself into a state of terror-by-probability or verisimilitude that is equal to reality. The fear that this imagined scene might be true overcomes me, a poison of despair spreads throughout my body, I don't move, I don't dare undertake to verify if my fear is real or if it remains confined in the horribly nearby realm of phantoms and nothing can undo the spell I have cast over myself, and which can take an altogether material form, except the apparition of the being whom I am in the process of dying out of fear of losing, in flesh and blood, on the garden path, quite alive and whose miraculous view brings me back to life.

I can do nothing against this mania of threatening myself which is a little crisis illness of my soul. So as to assume responsibility for it I've learned to use these morbid moments like firemen's exercises:

since I can't prevent myself from being played with by fire, well, let these simulations be changed into maneuvers. Suppose there is a fire, and that one is ready to extinguish it. This fire would be perverse: one would have started it oneself. In the same manner each time, in past years, that I imagined myself causing my own ruin with an incurring act that is strangely called an *acte manqué*, I had seen the danger coming in imagination and I had sworn and sworn again never to let myself go near the edge of the cliff, a suicide happens so quickly.

Didn't I see the cliff coming that February 12?

Or else did I want it to come but behind my back, was I able to counter-wish for a feared accident?

Or had I pursued myself with wishes that were just as undesirable as they were desired much as one sees the chase between the Princess of Clèves and Nemours become more and more inexorable, good and evil having the same face?

We were not sitting on our divan, but on another, did this simple alteration in the setting of our intimacy suffice to unbalance my habitual resolution? The non-bedroom of our desert was not ours, it has more than once happened that we are in a borrowed place but with catlike quickness we have always reconstituted when travel-ing the eternal arrangement of our bodies in the habitual sky, me always sitting on your right, our knees slightly apart, the grazing of the knees caressing always furtively even when there is no one in the scene.

The date as well may have had its role. It is an anniversary date and one of great mourning for me. But we have always changed days of mourning into days of joy, our presence being the response *par excel-lence* of resurrection to misfortune. I am looking for neither an excuse nor a cause. I am depicting the circumstances and their incalculable ways of continuously turning upside down downside up.

I was thinking about life—thus about the death of my mother, with and without fear, nothing new because I think about that every day, I live on my mother, as on the earth, I live from my mother and in my mother who serves us as mother, nest, olive tree, because I consider every day as a day with her and without her as earth so I was thinking as I do every day about our death as the maternal chapter of our life, with and without fear knowing full well that what one expects is not accomplished, that our death would not be accomplished, and that it's an unforeseeable death that would be accomplished instead as always

I was thinking about the upside and the downside of life, about the downside of the upside where we were, sitting on the divan, with the word divan opening slightly its Persian lips, we are at the *douane*, the custom-house I was telling you as-always, and I was thinking about the upside of the downside that we have always been.

You had just written your *Belated Answer to Celan*, you had just given me the *Answer*, I had it in my hands.

Celan, I thought, our non-witness.

"One is only through what one possesses" you were saying to me and "so many of our memories leave on journeys far from me, you were saying to me, I have millions of them, thus I lose millions of them I would have to have bodyguards, you are my true bodyguard." I have never forgotten your noncoming to Olivier de Serres and the events that followed, I was thinking. The "gods" who blaze a path for the unforeseeable are not more clairvoyant than the mortals over whose blindness their divine blindness throws a cover of clouds called destiny. No one saw anything. No one knows anything. Celan didn't ever know anything. My mother knows nothing. Those who make the sky and the earth know nothing. You know nothing and you forget everything, I remember and I know nothing more. I had just written this book, I wonder if it is on the side of the upside or on the other side of the downside, I was thinking about the mystery of the book that is neither truly true nor truly false and that had ordered me to go back over our steps to look for the letters that were the authors of this incalculable total that is our being and that tell stories about us that we do not control. I am the guard of the true body, I thought, I keep everything, I write everything. I write the-book. I write the letters in the-book. The book sends me the letters. Am I inside—Am I outside? I have just given you this box of letters to read

And it's at that moment that I perhaps started out on the path toward the cliff.

When you began to recite our memory
what we do or don't do depends on the times as if we were
reciting a *prayer*:
to make the resurrections return:
one time in bushes along the Marne river
one time at St John's College Oxford
one time at the Porte de la Chapelle station Paris
one time at Grand Central Station New York

one time at the Barrio Chino, the plane tree

one time—millions—you were saying, and for all the times that we found ourselves again together at the said place and time except one

—Do you remember at St George's Hospital after the News?

—I was sitting on the divan in 1990.

At that moment the telephone rang, I should have gotten up and answered but you answered: "The Police? It's a mistake." You came back and sat down. You said: "You attract the Police." It was the Police, I'm convinced of it. I should have taken this into account. —I was sitting on the divan. At that moment the telephone rang. The news was good. I fell on my knees.

In the darkness I didn't see the extremity of the cliff.

We did something we had never done, I said.

And there I should have stopped. I pricked up my ears. As if I could hear the edge of the cliff approaching. What were you going to say?

—We went to Kremlin-Bicêtre, you say.

To Kremlin-Bicêtre! Suddenly I bumped against the name of your forgetting. I stumbled. It was the moment to turn the lights back on. To change the subject.

At that moment, I committed the Error. I said: not Kremlin-Bicêtre. Bicêtre! I thought the word pained me. I said: Avenue de Choisy. Even then I should have turned left and run away, it would have been vitally prudent not to say "you said to me something there that you have never said in your whole existence," but I let fly that long, coarse sentence as if to hang myself from it.

—What?

I could no longer turn around to go back the cliff stood there and had a great simplicity. I was seized by panic: each step is a false step, *un faux pas*. I couldn't stop myself anymore. I tried not to go any further and I *saw* myself trying, it was miserable, it was two stories at once, in a noble version, in a vulgar version.

I heard myself saying: "I'm afraid to tell you," meager washed-out miserable words. "I can't" I was saying

—Exactly, so tell me.

Now all of a sudden I didn't want to speak of it anymore, I didn't want to have spoken of it anymore, I didn't want you to come near the delicate and wavering beauty of my scene, I didn't want you to come near the prince of Avenue de Choisy whom I imagined you had perhaps been, the adored one that I had perhaps procured for myself through fraud, through a false memory,

I couldn't say to you: "I'm afraid of you," that would have been to insult the one who you are and perhaps were not, "I'm afraid that you'll kill me, I'm afraid that you will destroy the silk of my story," I couldn't "I'm afraid you'll renounce the secret religion of my text," I couldn't say to you I'm terribly afraid of losing the most precious thing in the world (1) that you have forgotten you gave me (2) that you perhaps never gave me (3) that I possess alone and in secret (4) that I enjoy thanks to your phantom, what if I said it to you and then you say: me, I'm supposed to have said that? or: I've forgotten.

I was so afraid that I didn't know exactly what I was afraid of. My history, my phantom, my sublime scene my unique, what if you chased my thing away! No, I will not tell you, I say to myself.

I was afraid you would confiscate this moment, so brief and frail, thanks to which I have lived a crowned life, my very sweet and very fine improbable glory.

—Tell me

—Another time, I say. I was in despair. At disobeying you. I was gripped by bitter jealousy, but of what, of whom? It seems to me that I was jealous of the one that I had been until now.

I was on the point of surrendering the only witness of the Avenue de Choisy. The disavowal would be resounding. How happy I had been when I lived with the phantom of an event. I could tell myself whatever I liked, I did so, I had just done so. I saw the moment of the abyss coming. The betrayal come from farther away had taken the secret path so as to enter into my interior temple and lay everything to waste.

No, I will not tell you.

And then I tell you.

What I say is very small.

I say: "you said the words . . . " and I murmured those two paltry words as if I were blaspheming, "it burns my tongue and palate without my having ever been able to know if you knew what you were doing." I say this sadly in embarrassment I confess a theft an indecency a very small great crime, I committed an Error and its double.

It's all my fault, I should have been silent but of the two of us you're the one who keeps silent me I keep Speaking and all wrong. I look at the ground, I don't dare look at you, I sense that if at this moment I phoned you out of the anguish of traveling it's someone other than you who would answer me. My gaze escaping from the cage that I myself have made runs to the back of the garden and stops before the piece of sacred ground to the left of the portal where Thessie our witness had elected her secret sojourn behind a spray of thujas when she lived outside my heart. But the hiding place is no longer, the thujas were torn out, the wall remains naked. Nowhere for Thessie to hide her shadow. The image of our witness hidden behind her trellis through which she used to watch us has no refuge anymore. And I myself am the one who in an act of violent inattentiveness ordered the removal of the thujas. I thought I was attacking networks of branches rotted by age. I caused the ruin of the trace. I said these cherished words that I'm not sure I did not dream and there is nothing left of them from now on except a withered breath expiring in the impermanent air. I lower my head, I look between my feet, all is nothing, I am dispossessed.

You get up. Sadly I take pleasure with an unspeakable sadness in feeling the power of nothings in the realm of Love, the need to take in my arms the being that I will never again be able to take in my arms plants its sharp little claws in my breast, tiny blessed bite of vain desire and I suck slowly the bitter powerlessness of love. Marvelous idiocy of my soul that undermines itself. You have gotten up. You say "come I am going to show you some photos." I get up, I go look at the photos. Your Egypt. We look at this Egypt for a long time. As if we were looking at the photos of the Gods. We do not see them. But they make their way in the mire. Were they already there on Avenue de Choisy in the acacias licking their lips saying to themselves: in ten years we'll get her?

Or else is that your Response? I wondered.

Or else you wanted to safeguard the unique mystery of Avenue de Choisy, the barbarian was me. I should therefore be delighted with your non-response that was in truth your response.

You said nothing. You got up. I still had your book to Celan *Belated Answer* in my hands. Time has no age for you I thought. Was I thinking in 2005 after J.C.? Were we not in 2005 before J.C.? Could it be Amon Ra master of the Air and Fertility who arranged our unforeseen affairs?

Perhaps he will answer me in thirty years. This idea makes me laugh. Myself I had just received and non-received some letters dated forty years ago or almost. Some book letters. I saw us in thirty years. I was

watching you as you put away the photos that is to say threw them like
fistfuls of dust into a box. It was very dark. I took advantage of these
very brief instants to note down my state in my pocket notebook. He
is so strong and so fleeting. I note the fleeting. One can't imagine two
more dissimilar beings. At that moment a storm took up the whole
stage of the sky thundering for a long time with surprising uniformity
then letting loose the first waters as if the master of water had opened
wide all the sprinkler pipes up above. My thought followed the movement. One heard nothing anymore except this diluvian Speech, beau-
tifully regular. Our little human words were put back in their place.
You turned toward the window and you said something, but under the
cannon roars it sounded like the murmur of a field mouse.

It seemed to me I heard something like "*Bon, on a ou*, once when
it will be the last time the weather will be like this" or something like
that. Naturally, I didn't say "what?" My voice too would have been
swallowed up by the rain. I am almost certain of having heard more or
less the sentence I quoted. I said thank you silently to the Forces. One
cannot say that you might have ordered the Storm. But if there had
not been the Storm?

The Unhoped-for happens at the end of *Helen* at the last minute.
There is no one left in the play. We have nothing else to do but listen
to the Storm stronger than everything. You sat down beside me.

Now the Thing has been said, I thought. Now never again. There is
nothing to be read on your face—its habitual gentleness.

One cannot listen again to the Unique Word. I will have to remember the Event. Am I going to forget it? Had you forgotten it?

Now all the years that come will be afters and never-agains.

"Did I hear what I heard? Do you think I heard?" If there had not
been the accident of the Storm in which to slide words like a book
into a worldwide letter box nothing would have happened

It's an Accident and all the same it's a wedding, I thought. And so
late and so early.

I don't know what you're thinking. Your thought put your right
hand on my left knee.

I don't want to forget, but I don't want to remember, I thought. But
there is no master for forgetting or for remembering. When I return to
my mother's, after the Storm, it is almost fully night, I am late because
of the bad weather. She had waited for me to have dinner. The essential with the essential according to her. As for me I don't want to eat

I want to think. I see that she has prepared some *Kartoffelpfannkuchen*. That means: "I love you" in the language of potatoes. When I was little I adored these fritters made from raw grated potatoes. She says: I made some *Kartoffelpuffer*. I hope they're still hot. I say: *Pfannkuchen*. She says: no: *Puffer*. No I say: *Pfannkuchen*. She says: *Puffer*. She says: I didn't remember anymore how they're made? It's been at least twenty years. I say: you grate the potatoes, you strain them, you save the starch. I recite the recipe of Omi my grandmother the mother of my mother the mother of the fritters. Did one have to add onion? says my mother. I say no. Paradise: with or without onion? Sad paradise. My rose mother. I don't say a word. Except *Pfannkuchen* and she: *Puffer*. The cats are dancing with joy. The simple life lives. Life lives. I will never forget . . . says my mother.

Translated by Peggy Kamuf

····· 4 ·····
THE
ANIMAL

In Hélène Cixous's world, animals are important characters: we find not only cats—the most popular—but, among many others, we also meet birds, hedgehogs, donkeys, squirrels, cocks, moles, dogs, and wolves (as we have seen in "Love of the Wolf"). Cixous disagrees with most philosophers—with some exceptions such as Montaigne or Derrida—who consider animality on the other side of the border of humanity, excluding beasts from all that is considered "proper to man": thinking, laughing, suffering, mourning, and above all, speech.[1] Poignantly to the contrary, Cixous states that whoever does not hear the "cat's speech" is bound not to hear that "of a woman or a Jew or an Arab or any subject belonging to one of these species which carry the fate of banishment."[2] The author's ideas on animality resonate with what Jacques Derrida called "*la pensée de l'animal*,"[3] a "poetical" and "prophetical" way not only to ponder animality and humanity but also to look at the world differently. An "animal's thinking" may contemplate the world through a wider perspective than one belied through only human parameters. In *The Animal That Therefore I Am* Derrida notes that an animal expresses "the point of view of the absolute other."[4] The other—above all the absolute other the animal is—cannot be "assimilable" nor "digestible."[5] In an apparent paradox, Cixous observes that animals have a "profound humanity," because they are capable of giving themselves without submitting.[6]

This unselfishness of animals can be appreciated in the first piece of part 4, "Dedication to the Ostrich," the first chapter of the book *Manna for the Mandelstams for the Mandelas* (1988). The book is first and foremost an homage to two men, the Russian poet Osip Mandelstam (1891–1938), and the South African leader Nelson Mandela (born in 1918), but it also honors their wives, Nadezhda and Winnie, who supported them and subsequently carried on their fight for freedom. Osip Mandelstam, born in Warsaw to a Jewish family, died in a gulag in the Soviet Union, punished for his so-called anti-revolutionary writings. Among many poems and essays, he had written a famous epigram against Stalin's dictatorship, was first condemned to exile in Voronezh and then to hard labor in a camp. His wife later wrote a testimonial account of these events. For his part, Nelson Mandela was the leader of the African National Congress, an organization that fought apartheid in South Africa, a fight for which he spent almost thirty years in prison. Released in 1990 (after the publication of *Manna*), he became the first democratic president of South Africa and led a politics of reconciliation for which he was awarded the Nobel Peace Prize in 1993. Both men are symbols of the struggle for freedom as well as the human cruelty that condemned them to imprisonment and torture. This fate links them, even though they belong to different generations and lived in very different parts of the world. They also have a signifier in common, a part of their name: *Mandel,* which means "almond" in German. Almonds, like all seeds, in addition to being nourishing, represent a promise of the fruit to come, that is to say, the future. *Manna,* the other signifier associated with these two historic figures, refers to the food miraculously supplied to the Israelites on their journey out of slavery narrated in the biblical Exodus, but it also means "spiritual nourishment."

In a poetic way, both Mandelstam and Mandela are compared to sacrificed animals in this fragment and, more precisely, to ostriches. Ostriches are the most "tragic" beings, says Cixous, because they are birds but cannot fly. The author imagines ostriches as ancient gods who saved the human species by offering their wings in sacrifice. In the same way, Mandelstam and Mandela sacrificed their personal freedom to fight for collective liberation. In this sense, they are "winged avatars of the prophets," profoundly free and "uneatable" (in the sense of irreducible and untamable)—although ostriches' eggs are like manna for African people. These "prophets" share a faith, and a trust in *every* other, that human beings always betray. But "the truth of the ostrich" is that she prefers to die keeping this trust than lose it and survive, the latter being a choice apparently common to humanity. Nevertheless,

Hélène Cixous does not oppose animals (good) to humans (evil). The contemplation of the African landscape (assimilated to the narrator's interior: "I am nothingness flown over by flocks of migrating birds") stirs up an ancestral memory in her, that of "the age when the separation of animals and men had not yet been accomplished, when Creation was complete." Ostriches are complete beings also in the sense that there is equality between males and females in this species: they both take care of their eggs and their "children." They are "noble, powerful, courageous, and peaceful": like a "nonviolent lion" (Cixous is also fascinated by Gandhi, who inspired Mandela). But the best beings always perish under the common cruelty of men: they are betrayed and abandoned to a solitary death. Like Jesus on the cross, they cry "why have you forsaken me"—a cry we find in the two texts selected here—while their death saves the rest of the world.

The second text of part 4 comes from the book *Messie,* published in 1996. Its first part is entitled "Imitations of Thea." Thea is the name of a cat, who in another Cixous story is called a "minuscule . . . messiah [*messie*]," her "daily prophet."[7] In fact, the name Thea is revealing because it is the feminization of the Greek *theos,* which means "god." As for the ostrich, two apparently distinct, and some might think distant, categories, animality and divinity, are united here. Thea embodies the other, as we shall see, and this text deals with the possibilities of communicating with a radically different other. For instance, at the beginning we read that the cat gives "orders . . . but one is free to obey or not obey." This is a good example of how Cixous's writing deconstructs oppositions: if these demands are "orders," the addressee is not free to obey or not. The text continues: "God implores me;" but God does not implore, He is implored: a god who implores is no more a god. It is important to note that the cat only asks for what is beyond her capacities, which is "an honest way not to reduce the other to slavery." The relationship between the cat and the human narrator implies, thus, strong demands, and even a relation of power, but it escapes from the master-slave dialectic. The situation described by Cixous could be banally resumed as one of a cat asking her owner to open the door in order to let her outside. But what Thea wants, says the text, is in fact to trespass "the last veil . . . stretched taut between these continents and the Other." In a very Cixousian way, we have passed from everyday reality to metaphor, as the title of the chapter ("From Menagerie to Philosophy") already suggests.

The cat's principal problem is to make herself understood. Her "struggle for speech, before speech," is also a beautiful image of what the act of writing may be. Her "foreign" tongue not only consists of bodily manifestations of moods and feelings, but it is as capable as human language of producing linguistic signs that express ideas and concepts. Cixous, as in the first text of part 4, makes a strong statement against the difference (of race, sex, species . . .) that is at the basis of inequality. For instance, we usually consider a pet to be owned by someone. But whose is Thea? She is "the cat whose cat I am," a sentence which again deconstructs again the relation between *mine* and *yours* (as in the subtitle "Mineness Thineness") and installs a reciprocity that also has a physical aspect: "The night strokes me. I stroke the night." These caresses are not successive but simultaneous: the relationship between the cat and the narrator is intimate but respectful, made of "a tenderness which knows hunger and feeds on it. Hunger to give and be received. The reflexive form of gratitude." These thoughts on reciprocity echo the Derridean concept of the gift developed in part 3.

The absence of boundaries between the cat and the narrator is depicted by the expression "the human cat"—one who explores the inner self, that space through which passages of alterity move. This recognition of the other within can only happen when one is mature: "It takes maturity to accept and respect the animal in oneself. The animal in itself." Animals are thus equal and different to us; they reveal to us the ancient past when there was no separation between animals and human beings, as we have seen in "Dedication to the Ostrich." However, the acknowledgment of this is impossible for "society persons" who want to materialize "everything in the form of things one can put in boxes one can take in one's hands ," which is what traditional philosophy does when defining concepts so that they, too, can be "put in boxes." Cixous refuses to "materialize" into an academic discourse what she has already said through poetic images about alterity and writing. In the following passage, the narrator compares "the soul of [her] body"—able to face all obstacles of "the physical world"—to her anguish in front of the "intellectual trials" inflicted by "the university the civil the economic police." Through this opposition, the author ironically alludes to the distinction critics have made between her fictional and theoretical writing. She does not imply, however, that she feels more comfortable in fiction, but rather, that such an opposition is artificial, because all of her writings are "physical," that is to say, they come from the body. But "civilian society" does not understand such a hybrid text, both poetic *and* philosophical, and therefore requires the author-narrator to answer questions based on "what-is." Hence, she must give a lecture on "What-is-Poetry," though she would prefer to "have eaten the enigma, so it's become a bit of [her] flesh and [her] blood." This process of acquiring knowledge, which is described in the last section of the text, is rendered through the image of several animals, forming a real "menagerie." The first creature we meet is a hedgehog called Ceres, which is the name the ancient Romans gave to a goddess symbolizing the nourishing land as well as death. This reference suggests that poetry is related to life and death, and, more precisely, like a hedgehog rolled up into itself, it holds the secret of these two mysteries. Thus, poetry, as radically other as animals are, can never be reduced to a concrete concept.

Finally, poetry is defined through the figure of the cat: "It is the way my cat and I have solved the telephone problem. How to telephone one another? The need to telephone has existed forever for it is a matter of life and death to call my mother back. And all mammals bear a trace of the first telephone cord." Poetry "is," thus: first, the need to communicate with the other, who is both radically different and my "mother"—as I am hers. This is not an allusion to a biological mother, but to "the mother person. Who may be a son a husband a lover as well." Moreover, communication with the cherished other is not only intellectual but also physical, as the beautiful and surprising image of the "telephone cord" indicates. This is an aporetic image because it combines the most intimate and primary link (the umbilical cord) with the physical distance of the telephone—the Greek prefix *tele* meaning "at a distance." But we must not forget that one of the subjects who wants to communicate is a cat, thus belonging "to a race which cannot talk long distance." The solution is "to telephone in person," by touch. This light touch reassures both of the subjects implicated, because they are allowed to go through their lives, together and separately at the same time. The final sentences of the text ironically emphasize Cixous's rejection of *academic* discourse: "No lecture! Never!" The author turns down "theory," preferring to it a sort of fable dealing with profound philosophical questions.

"My Three-Legged Dog," the third and final text of part 4, comes from the book *The Day I Wasn't There* (2000). The theme of the chapter—and of the entire book—is, once again, abandonment and betrayal, embodied by "the son other," a "Mongolian child" who died when he was still a baby on *the day his mother was not there.* He is fused with two other characters: a dog called Fips (who suffered from neglect after the death of the narrator's father) and a "three-legged dog." Taking a walk in the park on the first day of May, the narrator runs across an abandoned dog who has only three legs and pleads to be taken in. She cannot adopt the dog because her mother and her cats would reject him. She feels the failure to do so is a betrayal and it reminds her of all the abandonments she has suffered and committed throughout her life. In a broader sense, the dog Fips and the three-legged dog are both figures of "all the forsaken of the earth," the persecuted and sacrificed innocents, such as the Jews deported to concentration camps or the colonized Arabs of the narrator's Algerian childhood. The worst perversity is that these victims are rendered "guilty" of their fate. The absent fourth leg of the abandoned dog is not *his* fault, but symbolizes that "there is a fault, the fault of a leg, the fault of time, the fault of patience, the fault of tolerance, all these faults are not his fault but he is accountable nonetheless, because of his fault of a leg."

Animals in Hélène Cixous's world act as a revelation of the unconscious. For instance, at the beginning of this chapter, the narrator is shocked by the cruelty of animals she sees in the park: a swan who violently attempts to expel two geese from the lake and a drake who tries to drown his duck in it. Animals are thus like actors; the author also qualifies her cats as "the great tragedians (as it was said of Rachel or Sarah Bernhardt) of my passions."[8] Then the appearance of the three-legged dog stirs up the suppressed memories of her childhood in Algeria, during the Second World War, when her family suffered the worst abandonment: the death of the father, also felt as a betrayal because it left them alone and defenseless in a *foreign* culture.

In a poetic passage that recalls a lament or a biblical verse (including Christ's cry: "Why have you forsaken me?" present as well in "Dedication to the Ostrich"), the topic of abandonment takes on a metaphysical dimension, as abandonment touches everybody and everything, becoming a condition of human life. The final reference to Oran alludes to an apparently banal anecdote told by the narrator concerning her myopia: when she was a child she was often lost in her own hometown because she could not clearly see the otherwise familiar streets, houses, and museums that suddenly disappeared from her view; she took these "vanishing museums and churches" as "fatal betrayals" due to her own "fault" and "misdoing." In fact, there is no need of a reason to forsake or to be forsaken; Cixous deconstructs the usual sense of this verb, which seems to follow only one direction: someone abandons something or someone. Here the abandoned abandons too, by dying and thus leaving the survivor alone. Abandonment is therefore circular and often remains hidden to ourselves, until a "prophet" or a martyr, like either of these Christlike dogs, unveils the mystery.

The conclusion of *The Day I Wasn't There* (not included in this excerpt) seems pessimistic, even tragic: "I've saved no one. Save one cat for one million abandoned. You can't not live, says my mother. Live abandon kill not look desert." Nevertheless, the worst of abandonments is not death but oblivion, and the book comes to unearth these buried beings and memories concerning humans and animals. As we now know, animality is not considered inferior to humanity by Cixous. On the contrary, the animal often represents the best among human capacities, like compassion. Thus an innocent being, capable of loving the other without seeking reward, becomes the savior of humanity.

10

DEDICATION TO THE OSTRICH
(1988)

FROM MANNA FOR THE
MANDELSTAMS FOR THE MANDELAS

E come augelli surti di rivera
quasi congratulando a lor pasture,
fanno di sé or tonda or altra schiera,
sì dentro ai lumi sante creature
volitando cantavano, e faciensi
or D, or I, or L in sue figure.
    —Dante, *Paradiso,* Canto XVIII

When the terrestrial earth is lost, the celestial earth remains.

No more plateaus of perfumed skin, no more hills raced up and over by horses and gazelles, no more waves swept and rowed by branches, no more streams, their bellies full of animals,

There remains the earth above, the boundless sea, its belly full of stars The airy earth remains, all traversed by birds.

⠿ ⠿ ⠿

In Voronezh[1] of the four winters, OM was living his last winter, remains of a great poet chased from the earth, chased like the starling by the storm, cast here, there, below, no, no more below, above, beyond, no hope, no rest, no companion no compassion, the world is a bad caving in,

Living on nothing, on the remains of memories, on the remains of fingernails, the remains of terrestrial tissue, on the remains of language once numerous and proud, today laid waste, a man with a worn-out name, with a heart consumed by the cold, the banishing hurricane, raging thoughts,

And into his verse only stars would come this last winter only stars would still come and certain birds.

(Until at the end of this last winter came a day without light, and Osip Mandelstam upon lifting his head saw only a sky swarming with worms of verse.[2] And all the birds and all the stars remained in his verse)

Happily there are birds, without which exile would be infinite, the desert would be uninterrupted, there would be no more dams to the deluges, no more hope at the boundaries of hopelessness,

and hell would not only be infernal but wintry and congealed.

Happily, when there are no more letters, no more bridge, no more mail, all wires are cut, and when man arrives in a place deprived of all space, that roars like the sea in a squabble of contrary winds,

there are the cranes up above who go on singing their lay, and, forming a long line in the air, rend the distance with their riotous wings

there are the swallows that go on losing and finding their nests again, making and undoing the fabric of our lives,

And in a single song of Hell crowd together at least ten species of tender gracious birds, the indispersible remains of warm stolen lives of flight

We need doves to cope with the worst.

:::: :::: ::::

Ultimately it is to the ostrich bird that I would like to dedicate this book,

The ostrich is the most discreetly tragic living being of all prehistoric creation. The ostrich is a bird that is not a bird. It is the greatest bird in the world.

The History of the world began in Africa. At the beginning of Africa was the ostrich. The ostrich has a destiny. This destiny is tragic and tragic: it is comparable in misfortune to well-known tragic destinies, like that of Oedipus, that of Achilles, that of Prometheus, but especially to the destinies of forgotten heroes.

The worst misfortune of the ostrich is that almost everyone is unaware that the ostrich had a destiny. We have forgotten the truth, the myth, the goodness of the ostrich.

The ostrich is an unsung heroine. Without the ostrich, for millennia there would not have been in Africa either human being, or justice, or light.

When man was still but a tiny chilly wildebeest, a clawless animal, a wingless bird, a rootless tree, a motherless suckling, the ostrich was a great bird like a tree, with wings more powerful than the eagle's and a pensive gaze. Her entire being radiated order, strength, and justice. Her immense innumerable feathers were all of the same length. At noon they were light and cool like the morning mist. In the evening they became warm and thick like a fox's fur. Seeing the ostrich flying among the mountains one had to believe the gods existed, and they were good. But seeing the wildebeest stark naked and trembling could cause you doubt.

The whole History of Africa began thanks to the ostrich's sacrifice. It is she who saved the human creature, it is she who revealed the secret of fire: it is the ostrich who gave a gift of life, of intelligence, of light, to the weakest of animals, the human animal.

The ostrich gave us the keys to the world. And in exchange—she paid. We wrenched her own keys from her. Her beautiful feathers of fairness were clipped and paralyzed. She was condemned to prison, she lost the air, the clouds, the happiness of seeing the earth from the celestial viewpoint of birds. She became the bird that does not fly. The bird in vain. The plaything of the gods.

But that's not all. She lost everything, and she gained nothing. She didn't gain men's gratitude. The sacrifice effaced.

Only the Egyptians in the time of the pharaohs were faithful to the ostrich's truth. Their kings always kept flyswatters trimmed with ostrich feathers, to make the air of justice and inner light that the ostrich gave to humanity flow through the heat of their palaces.

The free ostrich is now extinct. Today African ostriches are chickens raised in huge henhouses for their eggs and not for themselves. One ostrich egg makes an omelet for a dozen people. In South Africa one eats scrambled ostrich egg for breakfast.

The ostrich has always trusted. Trust is the cause of all misfortunes and all joys. A life without trust is a night without stars. Whoever accords her trust to human beings must also at the same time accord her forgiveness. For her trust will be betrayed, her eyes will be gouged out, her wings will be clipped, and never grow back.

But whoever accords her trust to no one, whoever gives herself up to trust as one surrenders to incomprehensible and mysterious life, whoever puts her trust in a magic bottle and entrusts it to the sea, whoever yields to trust without expecting any recompense, shall be recompensed.

When Samson forced himself to accord his trust he was betrayed, naturally, and just as the distrust hidden in his trust had anticipated. It is a rather complicated story to tell, but anyone can understand it, for we have all betrayed our own and been betrayed by our own, just as we betray ourselves.

But when Samson was plunged into darkness at Gaza,[3] without eyes, without wings, and his ankles in irons, then his soul soared in the flight of the ancient ostrich and lifted itself beyond human walls up to the moon. And there above reigned a radiant trust. You have never seen a day as dazzling as the one that rose in that night. That is why Samson left the ruins of life smiling with joy.

Another name for Samson: Nelson.

:::: :::: ::::

The ostrich hides her head in her coat so as not to see the furious face of Brutus. This is how she protects her look of trust. Was the ostrich betrayed and assassinated? Or did she give herself up to death out of a love for trust?

The truth of the ostrich is that she preferred to die trusting, rather than to outlive trust. One might think she died of trust, but she died so as never to have to witness the assassination of trust.

I insist on protesting against the calumny the ostrich has been victim to: the ostrich does not hide her head in the sand when there is danger. It is we who close our eyes from fear, and pretend the ostrich no longer exists, since behind our stingy eyelids we can no longer see her.

The ostrich has extremely piercing sight, she can see so far away she always feels very alone, far ahead of our nearsightedness.

The ostrich is noble, powerful, courageous, and peaceful. The roar of the angry ostrich is a magnificent warning. The ostrich is the lion's possibility. But nonviolent. The Mandela family counts among its royal ancestors the first descendants of the ostrich. It is a line of majestic angers, controlled by the will to not destroy.

Moreover, equality of the sexes has existed from time immemorial amongst ostriches. Males and females take turns watching over all the eggs and all the children of the community.

This book would like to be a declaration of love to the forgotten ostrich, to this fire-giver and to all the fire-givers who pay with their wings so that human beings can see a bit more clearly in the dark.

To those who have been punished for having disrupted the uniformity of the night. Punished by a night without stars. To the seers deprived of the light of day, to the prophets of hope, to Nelson Mandela, who is being kept in a cage for having flown so fast ahead of his time.

To the poets who had the strength to not drop their pens in the heart of times without future. All that still remained of tomorrow held alive and sheltered in their frozen hands. To the women, to the mothers and sisters, without whom there would be neither flight nor ascension nor erection nor resurrection. Nor Divine Comedy.

And to all the winged avatars of the prophets, all equally free and uneatable: eagle, lammergeier, griffin, goshawk, vulture, kite, crow, sea gull, sparrow-hawk, swan, pelican, cormorant, stork, heron, hoopoe, ostriches of every genre and every species, signs, letters of augur flying across the voices of space and time.

This book is going to think a lot about Mandelstam, who while I was being born was dying and writing in star-filled snow to tomorrow's address and no one and never

And to think at the same time about Mandelstam and Mandela, two men who do not know each other, but the same sorrow knows them.

From Voronezh depart poems, which, descending the stairs of the universe, blindly divine and seek the one who does not know himself to be sought and divined.

From one continent to the other birds are passing, shouting with glory above our lands. And they are heard, these cries, they are received by unknown ears. All I know is that from one hemisphere to the next, pity takes a deep breath and moves on.

▦ ▦ ▦

Mandelstam, Mandela, almonds in the bosom of the world,
  Tomorrows sheltered in the century's shell,
  Whoever has an ear must hear the future ripening within the walls
of bitter time.

▦ ▦ ▦

If I write in a broken way it is because I am in the process of contemplating in me the South African landscape. It is a landscape that takes my breath away. It is so ancient and so untamed. There is so much sky and so much earth and so little man. Minuscule, stirred by the wind, intimidated by the flocks of mountains suspended above the bush, judged weighed measured by the white bones which the creatures human and animal have abandoned just anywhere upon leaving, in the middle of the immortal continent, I see the world of before and after me. I see my mortality. And I see the time of forever. Whoever sees the African space perceives eternity.

I see her violet and innumerable nipples that nourish no one. I see her oceans of golden earth. I see my own little bones, invisible from the hilltops, no bigger than milk teeth. I see the beautiful, powerful carcass of a buffalo, reposing without anguish beneath this too much eternity. Ah, I nestle my tiny remains near the tranquil skeleton. And it is with the intoxicating sensation of the infinitely small within the infinitely great that the calcareous fragment that I am sets herself to thinking. Thoughts born in Africa are grandiose and sloped like those that come to us in a cathedral. They go from the lowest to the highest. They start at nothingness and cast themselves into the sky, hoping to find a port. I am nothingness flown over by flocks of migrating birds.

The wind blows very hard. Thoughts change forms and color like huge clouds. Sometimes they are clear and close to me, and I see them distinctly like stains of paint on the body of a young Xhosa[4] initiate, and I seem to be able to decipher the most ancient secrets. Sometimes they retreat suddenly to infinity, all the way back to where one cannot tell anymore where the sky begins where the earth ends, if it is the earth that mounts in the light or the mountain chain that kneels to sleep. Into my sky cloud silently palaces, giant barges, battles, temples, whales. All is vision. The air reveals. One believes one is seeing the unthinkable. To believe in seeing is such a joy.

The ostrich's feathers are black. They are of a brilliant whiteness. A white ostrich feather was standing on the goddess Maat's[5] head while she watched over the weighing of souls in Egypt.

The feather is white but I see it as a brilliant black. At the back of my eye the goddess Maat weighs the colors of day and night.

⦂⦂⦂ ⦂⦂⦂ ⦂⦂⦂

On May 1, 1986, Winnie Mandela was wearing a black hat, of black straw, a milliner's hat, and the hat bore long black feathers thrown backward by the wind. Beneath this hat, a great black woman who looked larger than nature. The hat attracted everyone's gaze. It was an extraordinary hat. She spoke before one hundred thousand African strikers.

The crowd was extraordinary. And what was most extraordinary was that in this crowd all you saw was her. I had never in my life seen such a hat. Such a glory. Such a pride. Such a woman. Such a victory. Those feathers were the future. This was clear to everyone. Winnie Mandela began to speak. She said: Nelson Mandela says: I am in prison. My people are not free. But how could I lose faith, when I know that the future is ours. In prison I am free. Everyone looked up. At that moment a flight of birds went by very very high in the sky just above the crowd, but so high that at first no one saw a thing, all one heard was their cry rending the air, and suddenly there they were, and everyone saw the immense black majestic V descending slowly toward the plain, then climbing again, climbing again, and blending finally with the light of that day, yes it was the future and the one hundred thousand strikers saw it, just as I saw Winnie Mandela's hat.

⦂⦂⦂ ⦂⦂⦂ ⦂⦂⦂

Winnie's hat is her standard, her crown, her sword, her black horse, her panache, and her shield. At home, Winnie wears a brightly colored scarf. And she is called Zami.[6] At home she is even bigger, because the house is so small, but once the hat of glory is taken off, it is quite clear that Winnie is in reality an enlargement of the little girl Zami, from Bizana.[7] These are the same eyes that can see over walls and mountains. And she does not watch where her feet will land.

∷ ∷ ∷

Her feet pace a soil at the bottom of my breast. If it sees the light of day, this book will be the fruit of a haunting. I want so much to tell the story of Winnie Mandela. Because for several seasons, thanks to her, what is stretching out in me is Africa. Not the non-African Africa out of which I came, the Africa of the North, but the other one, the ancient one, the first, the one I felt beginning behind my back when I was little. And now, without my being able to defend myself, she has won me over, invaded and overwhelmed me. I am resting peacefully. I want to lie down burning and astounded and dry and heavy and of a golden color. How this came to pass I do not know. It happens in the depths of my body behind thought, there where me stops governing and gives way into world. Me is the door to Africa. Past the door, everything mysteriously immense. I carry the traces of animals on my soil, along my roads over which for days all that passes is the sun, the rare shadow, and with a leap the antelope. And it's as though a memory I haven't had since birth is given back to me. Thus am I returned to the age when the separation of animals and men had not yet been accomplished, when Creation was complete, when we ate each other without hatred, when we weren't ashamed to be naked, and when each was in the elegance of her own skin. So much so that had I been in the bath with Zami, I would not have started to wonder if she saw me naked white or if she were wondering if I saw her naked black, nor if I should see her black, nor if I were able not to think of the color white and the color black, nor if skin had a memory of eyes and teeth, nor if I should think of the past, of the present of the future, nor if she were thinking that I was thinking all this, and so wondering weighing till the water that washes all cleanses my spirit. I would have been in the bath, without thought, with pleasure, without the shame that is the shame of human beings, without the shame that is the skin's malediction, and I would have bathed myself with my sister, a magnificent gracious corpulent woman, in the blackwhite water of golden whiteblack gleams.

And to think that so much misfortune and fatality have existed for so many centuries just because so many men are afraid of the night and of their mother's womb.

Happily there are, all the same, some people who love their mother's womb! And who know: white comes out of black and black comes out of white. All teeth are white and the pupils of all eyes are black.

Now I've said enough on this subject.

▦ ▦ ▦

How will Zami have one day entered my cold core, my inner north? And I find her giant and much bigger than me, in me.

By a stroke

By a stroke of words, of voice, of face,

By a sentence that pushes my heart head over heels,

By the song of three lines that fling the soul into the sea

By a look that doesn't look at me, that passes before me and continues on, pensively, interminably, flowing toward the back of the world, by a gaze that travels far away, toward what I cannot see and would like to see, by the stroke of a wand, of feathers, of magic teeth, you strike and enter me, rending Unknown, opus or woman, poem or poet, like a blade that cleaves my forehead and does not hurt me

Zami entered me by the stroke of a hat. Then she went away like a bird in winter. But when I heard her tell the story of the wedding cake, it was then that I ceded her all the space in my soul and she entered forever without harm and as though she were at home, and as though her story were my own grand mother returning to sing to me the most familiar lieder, in the kitchen returning as usual back from among the dead, as soon as I ask her sing again and tell, one more time. It is an imperishable, grandiose, and familiar story, like a quote from Dante, cruel and musical and painfully familiar.

Sweet and nourishing on the tongue is the bitter plaint molded by Dante, my grandmother.

> *E come li stornei ne portan l'ali*
> *nel freddo tempo, a schiera larga e piena,*
> * così quel fiato li spiriti mai,*
> *di qua, di là, di giù, di su li mena;*
> * nulla speranza li conforta mai,*
> *non che di posa, ma di minor pena.*[8]

Presently I am going to tell the story of an extraordinary cake. The story of its life. This book then will not be without sugar, without eggs, without spices, without succulence. Nor without famine, nor without desert. It is the cake's story that is sweet and nourishing. The cake itself might be rancid, but its essence is inalterable, I believe.

Thanks to the existence of the cake, the courage to write this book came to me: that there be pastry in hell, not merely torment, is what allowed me to advance sentence by sentence but not without shyness in this sweetened hell. I entered it then through the kitchen, with one soul, shy, and the other soul, audacious. And there in the middle of the kitchen, the great black Egg was smiling, the Lady of the divine panache and on her head the sun for tomorrow.

In the kitchen amid the white chickabiddies Zami broods Africa, and on her head is tied the white scarf imprinted with gold and silver suns. She turns on herself and shines. He, meanwhile, turns on himself in the vault of stone. Around him the wall is dead bone. In his midst, his own house, his continent.

In their midst, the hard joy causes distance to boil in its cauldron. Distance expires.

Without a telephone He calls: "Be my bird of the sea, and come to me in a flap of black wing, come, Zami, blade of Love, cleave the sky's sands, cleave the veils of time, come through the hundred fissures in the world's concrete come, cross over, come my army of the sea, my dove of war, and set yourself on the suffering egg of my chest, brood my heart Zami, where tomorrow sprouts."

Whoever has a sublime ear hears plainly these voiceless words.

▦ ▦ ▦

How shall I dare to speak of all these events, which apparently haven't happened to me? And which are superiorly cruel and superiorly gentle, superiorly to my experience. How shall I dare to speak of a black destiny, me, whose destiny is apparently white?

Once upon a time there was a man who had been told in childhood the marvelous story of Abraham put to the test by God, losing his beloved son and finding his beloved son again, in the midst of life losing life, and once dead finding life again, and all this, death, life, death, passing by like the hard heels of God on a single heart, and all this all alone beneath the heartless feet of God, for God has no heart, has no need to have a fragile human organ, and all this, this crushing, this extirpation of joy, this transplantation of the heart, without trembling, but not without hiding all his tears from the father of the world.

This story was so terribly beautiful that the child became crazy about Abraham. Grown up, he had only one desire: to see Abraham. His entire life became a taut bow, an immense tension of his soul attempting to see with his eyes, however they might be, of air or of flesh, the one no eyes had ever seen—since God alone saw Abraham put to the test, God who has no eyes.

So you see, this man, ancient and sometime child, wanted upon aging to be the child seeing and understanding the incomprehensible, which only the new child, whom thought has not yet woven into its web and inspected, can see.

And he spent his life growing old in reverse and trying each one of the millions of paths that Abraham laid out with his slow and solitary step upon our docile earth.

· I am then neither the first nor the only one to die of the desire to approach the sublime stratum that stretches above my height. I hear their feet walking wistfully on the sky's floor.

And I too I am dying and living of the desire to see the absurd unimaginable face of the person who hopes in hope, after the setting of hope, who believes without the aid of reason, whose soul flies in reality just as I know how to fly in dreams, who gives birth every day to a new hope, then night kills the child and swallows it up, but in the morning each day's hope sees the light of day.

And I too I try each morning to make my way, climbing in the direction of those I have no hope of ever overtaking; but I don't despair of climbing and imagining in their direction.

The ancient and sometime child had only one desire, the impossible: to have witnessed these events without witness. He had the desire but not the hope.

And I too with the absurd eyes of she who wishes to behold the hidden, I want to be present at that to which I'm not a witness. And above all, I want to bring my heart up close to the fire where the Devil didn't throw it, and give it an inkling of the martyrdom it will never know. Why? Because a life without the intuition of absolute grief is a life without light without water without salt without miracle and without bliss. And because "why was I born this color and not another?" is a question I do not want to forget to ask myself from time to time, and that I often forget.

▦ ▦ ▦

At Voronezh perished, without crucified mother, without mute father, without olive trees without stone without tree, all was under a sheet of snow, no one knew who,

> Mandelstam, unknown to the passersby.
> And no one to cry out to why have you forsaken me
> Without last word without last breath without last anger
> No one knew when
> Perished lost and unknown, and become
> No one
> A foreign snow cradled him
> Only a snow knows

⠿ ⠿ ⠿

Unhappy the dead from whom we have stolen not only their life but also their death; they die forever without reprieve.

. . .

Translated by Catherine A. F. MacGillivray

11

MESSIAH (1996)

It's urgent. Orders are what she gives, but one is free to obey or not obey. The imperative of hope. Right away she forgives. God implores me. Her trust, how beautiful it is. She only speaks to me gravely intensely and reasonably. Only asks help for that which is truly beyond her own strength. It's an honest way not to reduce the other to slavery. Her sublime manner of dealing with frustration: without resentment. A spiritual balance. Divine versatility.

She asks me to make her dreams come true: to be a butterfly, to stop that rain, may I have some squirrel legs, fly without wings. Alas I cannot grant such just and concrete desires. My magic is abstract. Never mind she says without sadness. I take stock of my impotence. So finite am I that I don't even contain the idea of having wings. She has her body for soul. Me I am separated.

All the same what a struggle for speech, before speech. She addresses me in her foreign tongue and, aware of this, patiently she speaks mute to me, as to someone who doesn't understand her language she sends me innumerable messages, attempting to reach the ear not yet born in my brain, to rend this membrane, this swaddling that straitjackets its language and I'm all eyes listening to this mutinous pythia toss me clues. She tenses her body to make it the arrow toward what's not there, and I am struck on the temple. It's my turn to purr I hum I meow some litters of damp words to charm the ear she lends to me.

Turned toward the world that stretches beyond the world nose tipped toward God, dumb she cries:

—See see see see see see see see see see see.

—Oh! me too! me too!

We are born to see, to want to see and not be able to see to cut through at whatever cost to the other side of the last veil but where is it, is it over there, canvas stretched taut between these continents and the Other? or is it in my eyes? Nose to nose with you dumbly I cry out: I want to see you! see see see see!

She wants to go there. Outside the black toms flex cheetah soles, paws flash bare knives. The older brother's dangerous look, the father that old reprobate. The kid brother a big burly knucklehead hides out in the bushes he'll pounce from behind. I'll take my little knife and stick it in the big guy she tells me, and she will I know, but I'm not up to it. I look at the slender little knife for sure it'd go in but have I the force to skewer mister macho? While I torture myself resisting from the mortal doorway she cries come come I grip the knob, I'm about to give in, I haven't the courage to resist when suddenly she gives in and comes and curls up across my chest. The joy that submerges me: in an instant suffering forgotten, all is forgiven me.

MINENESS THINENESS

It is with emotion and nostalgia that I touch the sweet, ferocious touch of Thea the cat whose cat I am. The night strokes me. I stroke the night. I stroke her the way she wants. This is perfection, I am caressed caressed from my hand right to the tip of my soul the stroking spreads out warm soft small gathered seamlessly into the yoke of an impersonal goodness. It has its effect. My heart opens into a flower. Why isn't there any warm and soft adjective formed from the word well-being?

I am in well-beingness. It is not in the least sexual. We are representatives of love's gifts, a tenderness which knows hunger and feeds on it. Hunger to give and be received. The reflexive form of gratitude. The well-being that hides in the doing good. It's like licking your body while you sleep you wake marvelously regenerated. I feel a kind of goodness that nourishes the body's starving soul and from the touching emanates an intoxicating gratitude, sublime beverages. Sorts of magic.

The act of grace is without acknowledgment.

Each day the cat crosses a new limit. She conquers garden after garden, space unrolls at her will. The will is not hers: to see her bound away in a silver gallop her silent hooves shooting off sparks at daylight's first gleams is to feel that she obeys. How far will obedience take her? Who is calling her? Her own mystery: is some changeling angel the ideal-of-the-cat?

The same for all of us inhabitants of this book: we obey, we go, with one insuperable leap we clear wall after wall, and this is the entire plot of this tale. Things might well go on this way right to death, this is what I try to forget, writing. As for my characters, on they go, escaping me, as is always the case in a book that doesn't pretend to know that which it never knows. Like the cat they do as they wish, and the author goes after them. They only listen to their horse paws, their stubborn and vertiginous heads. I stay close behind them. I love them, I talk to them like friends, I am dazzled by their willpower. And when two days ago the woman told me: stop talking about her and let me talk about myself, by the next page it was done. She said I. Not that she is any the wiser for it. But is there anyone who has the physical force to keep a human cat from going in search of herself? One believes she is exploring the universe, but she's using the universe to explore herself. She goes in pursuit of herself.

She says:

At a very young age I had sons, daughters, I fed them, now we are six. As a grown woman I had my cat, before I was ready, it takes maturity to accept and respect the animal in oneself. The animal in itself. And after having learned not to believe in having what one believes one has had, and all the same we six are in a single superior kind of belonging. The limit to the great freedom that unites us is that we don't engage in sexual incest. Only when a person has passed from the age of having to the age of being can she venture into the zones where life is very ancestral. In those regions one feels one is really not far from the future. The not-far is almost behind the door.

When the door opens, we'll set off to discover it, the future, like cats.

We absolutely don't know the future, but it's much closer to us and more favorable than society. This is a question of age and maturity. Society persons live forever in the age of having. That's why their greatest effort goes to materializing everything in the form of things one can put in boxes one can take in one's hands.

Me and my life meet up with extraordinary difficulties and extraordinary facilities.

First of all in the matter of space and the innumerable obstacles the physical world throws up along the way I can absolutely count on the soul of my body. In the end I've always come up with solutions for all of fate's blows geographical, topological, problems of relief heights peaks abysses sheer walls opercula intestines skimped corridors citadels without doors . . . Anything to do with bodily genius, my mental will never lets me down, I have invented, I have known the steps the pains and every sort of dare and I have come out safe and sound out from every attack, and in every discipline and on every occasion things which began in the worst possible way, each time taking me by surprise and impressing upon me that I am a finite mortal nonextensible human creature subject to the laws of my bodily matter and nature's, programmed to walk run go up come down move around according to the possibilities of my species, these harsh and adversarial things that loom up against us on earth under the earth in the air and in the water and in thousands of ways, I have not hesitated to face up to them, I have set in action all of my powers of response to extreme situations and I have never yielded to any inner dejected speech. A fatality of victory has always helped me without in any way lessening the real and redoubtable excesses of the trial. I simply accepted I forged ahead I passed and I have no doubt I'll escape blows to the day of my death. Thanks to my efforts and my capacity to go where I have to go by the most direct route and necessarily the most original. In every case I find something else, and always at the cost of a total contraction of my soul.

However, dealing with the countless intellectual trials the university the civil the economic police inflict upon me: a disaster. I can be several days walking away from the obstacle already I am lost going in circles gasping. I am a beast and without intelligence, everywhere I see invisible barbed wire, I find neither light nor knowledge nor hallways nor lines of flight, I am a sack of nothingness I am battered by insults my throat's a plug of dried-up words my soul inside me weighs a ton and I haven't the strength to lift it, no one can conceive the sluggishness of the tank of my thoughts we crawl along, a few centimeters a month and maybe a year, this is not absolute immobility but all the monstrous pain of paralyzed movement. Doubts? No. It's my deep truth, it's my fate, it's the doughy what's-to-become-of-my-brain the moment some member of civilian society has the involuntary misfortune to ask me to answer a question beginning with "what is"—or to invite me to speak in a circular theater, yet another way of expecting I'll respond to some What-is or other. Now, any What-is presents itself to my conscious as a very powerful ghost which begins by confiscating all the messages of the senses, I don't see it I don't hear it I don't smell it, my mind is nothing but a fly strung up in the night of a spider web, and living in total despair of itself, totally incapable of catching the least word, moreover there is none. Ask me to cross the veins of the earth on an airbus ask me to make my inner camel traverse the eye of a sergeant major, I'll do it; but ask me, as is your right, to give a lecture under whose title skulks the What-is question, on the spot I am a blind sheep on the edge of the cliff and I don't even know whether an abyss really yawns at my feet or not.

It's not that I hate this question. On the contrary I acknowledge its force its grandeur its legitimacy. I myself wish passionately *to know* "What-is-Poetry." What I mean by knowing personally to have eaten the enigma, so it's become a bit of my flesh and my blood, and that henceforth it lives and dwells in its precisely archived splendor on the head of a pin of the book of my head like a talking illumination forever irrevocable.

But I did not come into the world to be paired up with an enigma. Nothing in my constitution is capable of perceiving the sounds the senses the outlines the directions of this vague monster. I can listen to my night as long as I like, examine my entrails, nothing takes shape nothing comes.

But one day I heard a very fine scholar respond to the enigma What-is-Poetry: Poetry is a hedgehog;[1] and then I had a marvelous vision, I saw the hedgehog big as life with a soft skin like tiger silks and the hedgehog brought forth a high meadow that made for the earth red- and yellow-spotted corollas, and the meadow brought forth an admirable dead woman whose stories and tales are the cities and lights of my inner existence, and the hedgehog was in the center of the springtime like the spirit of resistance at the heart of great leaps of growth. As if on an elevator, the dead woman had gone straight up to that which lives again and she spoke to the hedgehog in the voice of a beloved. She spoke to it as "Ceres," in a voice whose gentleness was stronger than any authority. Seeing that, I understood for myself the mystery; but that a hedgehog which puffs up in case of danger be called Ceres doesn't make a lecture for an exacting public.

And to say: "Poetry is a hedgehog" is a bit short. One phrase does not a lecture make.

But hold out your hands, and into them I'll put the word hedgehog and the word Ceres. Keep them safe, each of them will bring forth harvests.

Last Saturday I was supposed to chair the department meeting. The room was a madhouse, literally. I myself was one of the deranged I was no longer really me. Except for my anxiety about being unprepared, which I recognized. The room was buzzing. People coming in, a general hubbub. A colleague warned me that they were going to ask us to provide sculptures on pedestals for the university gardens. Oh! no, I said, I want my sculptures free as birds. The crowd was getting thicker and thicker. Someone announced the arrival of some big shots. Sitting down I felt like a tortoise in a forest. I stood up to assume my hostess duties. I greeted the important people in a friendly manner. Their ladyships glanced at me and turned their backs. My throat became so dry I was sure I'd choke. I needed water. There were enormous carafes on the table and all the glasses were dirty. What had started smoothly was turning sour. I reacted violently. "Make no mistake," I said. "If I am a civil servant, it is by choice. "Stop," said my inner angel. But it was too late to stop. "With my gifts and my strengths," I said, "I could have been Prime Minister and head of the government," I said despite myself, slamming on the brakes just before I got to king. "And if I am not, it's because the only thing that matters to me is poetry," I cried. One way or another this impressed them.

But I hadn't wanted to say that! In the intoxication of the affront my head spun, I ate the cock's comb, I arched my spine like a Spanish dancer, in one bound I leapt onto the back of the ridiculous. Here I am rigged out in the world's passions. I no longer knew how to get rid of my anger, it'd clamped its little claws so deeply into my belly, it's as if I'd swallowed an eagle, live.

In truth love is the only thing I care about. Had I lied? But maybe poetry is the Latin name of love?

Would I, they asked, agree to give a lecture Monday on the following topic: "But what-is-poetry?" After what I'd said, how I could refuse? But I am not a scholar. A lecture! Chastisement—count on it. And to say I'd meant to spend Sunday with my beloved. Already I could see him glowing like a soft deep red sun. Whereupon Monday was upon me so fast I didn't even see Sunday. What-is-poetry was still the question, and I still didn't have so much as the beginning of a response in words, and after my rooster act how could I talk about hedgehogs? Yet. It was time. The students filed in, sat down, notebooks out, pens poised. I backed off. To begin with, I say, fill out these forms. A docile young man asked: should we write our personal details? —Yes, I say grateful, whatever might interest me. I want to get to know you. The time to fill them out gave me one more chance. Quickly I went out. I knocked at this one, that one, I knocked at all the doors, at each I asked what-is-poetry—had they heard it speak, was there a book, a dictionary, a list, a collection, cave to cave I went, right to the very last, it was the first, to go there I clambered over a huge trunk that had fallen into the rubble. The thing looked impassable but I found a way between the rocks and the trunk tangled with branches. I crawled on all fours ruminating, my movements impeded by brambles and tangles I couldn't jump. In short I didn't stop. Somebody opened the door. It was where the two Marias lived. Who are they, you ask? But they are the first two sisters. Maria opened to me thinking it was Maria. I saw where they lived. Hard to conceive of anything simpler and more ancient. It's nice, here, I say, it has charm, two Marias like a pair of quill-less hedgehogs they didn't have the answer either, you need to grow quills I said, as I left the mud cave just behind their molehill I saw an infinite chaos of naked rocks, best not to look that way, it was sinister in winter with the snow one must be buried, one could go no further without loss of life. Retracing my footsteps for a moment I thought I couldn't get back over the hump of the trunk and the rocks, but I found the way again and I overcame the obstacle so as to return to my place where the students were waiting for me.

So what-is-poetry? The question dogged me. During my trip I hadn't forgotten they were waiting for me without suspicion and without hate.

I sat down inside the circle *and I went on:* "It is the way my cat and I have solved the telephone problem. How to telephone one another? The need to telephone has existed forever for it is a matter of life and death to call my mother back. And all mammals bear a trace of the first telephone cord. It's about our need to be sure she is there, that's all: that she's alive. The mother person. Who may be a son a husband a lover as well. Between people who give life to each other this is what telephoning is: Are you there? I'm here. Good, then I can get on with my work. —How's life? I can run around the world without worrying about my line being cut? —My life is in good condition. You may go.

But how to do this when one belongs to a race which cannot talk long distance whenever the forever urgent need to check on the life comes to me? Here's what my cat and I have come up with: we telephone in person. So several times a day she comes to give me a little telephone call on the leg, using her own body briefly as apparatus, for the number she rubs: everything fine? —Everything is fine. And she hangs up reassured. As for me, able to call long distance, several times a day to do her number I whistle three notes like this: : : and from the end of the world up she pops everything is fine. Two different kinds of life which exist for one another by means of touch. In conclusion, I say, I asked myself what-is-poetry, and this is all I came up with. For me it all begins with some small-in-size sentence like: Is everything OK? One hardly notices it. But if one pays attention then this is life humbly appealing on the phone for life. But it can't be a question without an answer, that would be terrible. One is asking for permission to go on living. And the permission is an order: live."

But the strongest love is that which is poorest in words. It's hands touching.

And is the poetry of the poetry the dumb emotion arising from phrases that graze the legs with the chastity of an absolute passion?

So now if someone were to ask me "what-is-poetry" I'd say: my cat's expression of chastity—but to know? I'll never know. No no! No lecture! Never!

Translated by Beverley Bie Brahic

12

MY THREE-LEGGED DOG (2000)

FROM *THE DAY I WASN'T THERE*

ARCHIVES OF 1 MAY 1999

It was the first blue day of the year.

Blue as an angel I said. It slipped out. But my mother wasn't listening.

We set off very early for the Bois. I always want to arrive before everybody else. —Where? —Where. Where it begins. Just before the sound and the fury, perhaps. It happens every year: I go the Bois to add to my book of never-to-be-forgotten days. —Never forget what? —Never to forget: come back to oneself. It's a matter of taking the same walks, every year there's the miraculous non-miracle of re-beginning and re-budding. It's the law. And yet: I can't get over it. We take note that we are still here. No forgetting along the walks. Then there was a rip in the murmured silence. The traumas began. The rape of the lake: plastic bags simulations of lumpy carcasses, banged-up cans. Two gray geese screamed alarm like sirens on the bank: it was a swan cruising, stiff-necked: No geese allowed! No geese allowed! The two geese didn't dare and screamed haunted by forebodings of massacre. Water off bounds! patrolled the brandished swan. I went down toward the bank armed with the pussy willows of before all memory, armed with the too-light catkins of chestnuts that I pitched violently, fistfuls of them, at the swan crying angrily mean, cruel swan, cruel mean! Go away! Go away! Note that I didn't insult it, the enemy being a swan, I didn't shout bastard! or brute! or dirty rat. I cried swan, I summoned it go away go away. Slowly the swan veered off obedient. Immediately the two geese set sail.

I thought about meanness. I thought about powerlessness. I thought about the will to power and about the powerlessness of the will and about the force of power. I thought about the mainspring of the soul: how to think the unthinkable while it is happening.

And to which god were the two geese screeching their prayers and their imprecations?

About the drake which yesterday was trying to drown its duck and there was nothing I could do about it or at least I did nothing. He mounts it he grips the little beige head in his beak and he holds it under the water to annihilate it. I screamed. Yesterday too. Deaf as a post. I could scream till I was blue in the face. The power of assassination was absolute. My cries were drying in the air. I did not wade completely dressed into the polluted pond. I am telling the truth. I went away, disgusted. I thought no more about the drake with his duck. But the inaudible cries of the duck under the water of the back of my mind added themselves to everything else that would keep us from living if we thought about it.

We were on the island nestled in the middle of the lake. What is a lake isle? For a while any persecuted person can find shelter there, it's the cradle, and it's the trap. Once the period of respite has passed you are caught and besieged. We were embarked on the island and it was the sweet luxury of metaphor, ship house shelter ark desert that's when: when my temporary deafness ceased. For a quarter of an hour I had not been letting myself hear the distant cry, my hearing busy with the buzzing of young, hardly-formed flies. It was a yelping which, once heard, became inextinguishable, inevitable. The creature was insisting, superhumanly. We were all under a dreadful spell: my mother, my daughter, me, a stout little lady and two pooches humanized with ribbons and hair-slides, all six of us bound in a single spell by the distant barking. —Who is it? I say. —For half an hour. Says the lady held for half an hour in the note of uninterrupted hope. As long as the cry lasts we are unable to move. It was a young voice and which was crying crying crying don't breath cry not breathing cry crying. You really can't go away. The voice is speaking *to you*.

At last I saw it. I glimpsed it, not very well. Because of the freshness, the youth, I asked who is that crying, what creature, with what angel's voice? —It's a Tintin dog, said the lady with the beribbonned daughters. And she had that look: struggling not to let it become the awful pity. At that moment finally I set eyes on the dog, and I will never be able to act as if I hadn't seen it. In the middle of the spring meadow with its tender cloak, on the other side of the lake, cries cries cries a neatly-drawn white fox terrier with a black spot on its left side, it was calling like a spirit that has never known discouragement. It was so long, I began to have doubts. At the end it bounced, it spurted from the fabric of the meadow and I saw that it was jumping on three legs, it has three legs I say, it only has three legs my daughter says, it's missing a leg says the lady, it is missing its right hind leg says my mother, this leg suddenly we were all missing it, or rather it hit us, it was running fast, running with all its strength right and left meanwhile a lady arrived on a bike. She stopped and gave us the explanation, saying: it doesn't belong to anybody, and there's nobody. And she said: they abandoned it, it's the first of May. It was the first of May the day they abandon the little dog, three legs is all it takes, one does not kill, on abandoning day it is always very blue, the meadow is a human allusion, there is no one on earth, the moment they let it go in the meadow the dog gives a little drunken leap, the grass is so fragrant that doesn't keep him from feeling ashamed because he smells all the perfumes of all the thoughts, and although he is not guilty there is a fault, the fault of a leg, the fault of time, the fault of patience, the fault of tolerance, all these faults are not his fault but he is accountable nonetheless, because of his fault of a leg, you need one to bear the weight of the family sins, so it's him, it's him who has failed to be pardoned.

The bike lady was saying: no caretaker the first of May. The day of abandonment and no witness. The dog lady said: sooner or later he'll find a restaurant. And off they went.

Left to chance again, the stray frisked about calling: nice! nice! nice! I am nice! Besides with three legs you are still good for running jump-ing eating playing, it's only slightly fewer legs, it doesn't keep you existing, I am nice! nice! nice!

Me I say nothing. —Every year they abandon the first of May the bike lady said.

The first of May, feast of the abandon. Instead of killing. The dog acquitted. Pardon! Pardon! Pardon. Pardoned.

And me too? And me too. And you too.

What to do

I abandoned

I have been abandoned
And that's what has always abandoned us,
—The Answer—
Already when I was three and so many abandons and things abandoned, myself included,
I didn't know, already I did not know what to do with such and so
many abandons
Already I felt I so forsaken on the one hand and so forsaking on
the other
and all eaten up with knowing how to ask already at the age of
three and not-ever-knowing what how to answer, with all the forsaken
of the earth what to do,
with all these dogs in whose image we have been created in order
to be forsaken, punished for having lost a leg which however doesn't
prevent anyone from running and crying very loud and pleading saying "I-still-am."
Already when I was three, in Oran,
what should could would I have been done seen
when I was already an atheist on the earth
crying for a quarter of an hour without stopping
the cry why have you forsaken me.
Already I had the look of a three-legged fox terrier
The worst is not to have less it is this less that doesn't keep you from
existing in order to be abandoned on the first of May
each year all those who are driven into the meadow
having only three of four legs is this a crime
round and round, rounding up your thoughts
—should I go and get the dog—
my heart swung back—forth—back
—back—for one whole minute

My mother at my side was thinking: if you go get that dog, I'm going
to slam the door, I'm going to go away.
At her side I thought: ah! if only you hadn't been with me! Then
anguish. Sadly anguished: would I have adopted it? the question in me
asked itself—and I didn't know how to say loud and clear: yes.
Because at that moment the cat in me thought: if you bring an animal back to the house the way you did to me last year, coming through
the door with another creature in your arms that I thought belonged

to me, I will burst into terrible cat sobs and I will rake every face with my claws until I die.

My daughter beside me thought: I am going to break into a heart-rending cry I shall burst, I am bursting. Let's go, let's go, I am bloodied.

In conclusion—

In conclusion I thought: dear dog cherished on three legs, everything keeps us apart including myself.

He with his terrible doggy freedom which was pleading: take me, pleaded and pleading believed. Believed.

My mother tugged on my leash. I followed. The dog followed me with his eyes, I had his eyes in the back of my neck. Head down I walked off along the path with my mother.

—A three-legged dog needs to be sssschot, and that's all, said my mother, adding four s's to the word shot, and shooting it at me with all the strength of her conviction. For, to strike, she never uses a knife or a blunt or sharp instrument: her operative mode is to increase the number of consonants.

She sslipped her arm into mine

and I let the stray race back and forth in the meadow. Far away. Far away, its dwindling voice. Kinship increased. Its voice crossed the world. Will someone else respond to it?

One more dog I didn't save. I strolled amongst the roses, my heart bleeding, petals clenched. Once upon a time my cat was saved and in being saved saved me and since then I have not saved any other crea ture nor other creatures or perhaps I have but not on purpose since I have not been saved, but everything kept me from it, I'm not going to accuse anyone, my cat doesn't want to share me and I don't do battle with it, I have already chased two cats away for love of my cat in weakness and in strength, perforce, forced, but I am not going to accuse anyone, no one wants to share and me too neither I don't want to divide myself into hostile cats and I don't do battle with myself.

I would like to find the argument that pardons.

I am a woman who always has courthouses in her head, all because I was not deported, that can neither be regretted nor not regretted nor be said, it can only try to blunt the thorns on the roses, a never-ending trial, my mother neither was not deported, and she never deports herself from the straight and narrow, without regret and without regret for regret. Whereas I, separated from deportation by a verdant meadow and a deep blue sea, I have always in my skull a bench of judges who abandon me to a searing absence of punishment.

Later in the morning, with all these animals in my head, some female, the others threatening, the trusting, and the birds which I always think my cat is thinking of, I forgot the fox terrier.

When I got home I told my cat all about it. She curled up in the May light in my image, offering her white belly to my lips which she does not have to fear sharing. I smiled at her, there is nothing she likes as much as my smile, I smiled at her with a little abandon stuck in my guts. Stretched out on the bed, I leafed through the big book of archive photos from Algeria. All the photos, Jews, Arabs, brave settlers, leading citizens, the Kabyle woman, the rich European and his wife, from 1882 to 1945 and nobody smiling agas, horsemen, kaids, the black servant, the dignified old man, players in a game of chess, douar chief, candy seller, ouled-naïl, free-woman-capable-of-inspiring-Delacroix, French family settled in Miliana, colonists about to make their fortune, travelers on the Setif-Constantine bus line and nobody from 1882 to 1945 to smile.

I lived in this country. I knew.

Already when I was three years old, Boulevard Seguin, in Oran, I saw the photos this country would leave. I ran up the steaming streets as fast as I could so my cut leg wouldn't trip me up. But I could never get past the square with the cathedral without being stopped, petrified by the enormity of that face hardened into the gold.

All the time I lived in Algeria my native land not stopping going to school then to secondary school as if in exile, I was dreaming of arriving one day in Algeria though it was my own native land, to find the door at last while I was going every day to school along a corridor of to my eyes irascible streets, and yet so fragrant, skirting the invisible walls reserved for immigrants who keep step with them whenever they go from one part of town to another, I was dreaming of one day entering my native land as I used to wade into the welcoming sea, to melt in, to be part of it, no longer prowl around the outside of the body of my city in the heart of town, which is what was happening to me daily, even on the Post Office square, even on the Government square, even on the City Hall square, even on the Cathedral square, I wanted so badly to be one day invited to a wedding or a birth, and then go my heart pounding, finally penetrate to the heart of my kind and be born of them like a human being or another, like all the other human beings save us, I saw myself at last with henna on the palms of my hands and feet, I saw myself at last stuffing my mouth with couscous with beans and whey, my hands full of the sugary grain, the difference with the couscous at my grandmother's being the henna and the hands, but I never found anything but closed doors in my way, I see myself knocking at an olive green door or an almond green door banging my little fists on them and squealing: Come in! or Come in! for a long time for nothing in my ignorance of the password, if there was one. Another difference or another misunderstanding it's that I was smiling. On all the photos I can see myself smile, I was always smiling, there was nothing I could do about it, though the others were not smiling and perhaps I offended their no-smiling and without any reason, no inhabitant of the Two Worlds having any reason to smile without mistrust while I was living in Algeria. With my mouth open and all my teeth gleaming on display I was like a wound that I kept reopening even when I wanted so badly for the scar to heal. My smilingness was beyond my control, I was ajar, I signified come in, I was miming what I wanted and not really what I had to offer, I was longing for visits, I was expecting travelers, I had the soul of an innkeeper set up in the desert, come, come, I said and my eyes followed with devotion the pointy swallows cutting out the high blue metal with their scissors. Nobody came. We were too widowed a family, too woman, too girlish, we were bad, we were repulsive and not veiled. And me trusting, in the stubborn expectancy of no one. Without fear but not without anguish every morning, schoolbag in hand, off I went again to try and gain admittance to the heart of hearts of this native city Oran followed by Algiers which in no time at all slipped out of sight in a flutter of mists and veils, I was running blinded guided by my sense of smell between columns of spicy perfumes, while ahead of me, to my immense dismay, vanished, snatched away by some incomprehensible sleight of hand, now the cathedral leaving only the proof of the equestrian statue already half swallowed up, now the Municipal Theater, now the harbor entry and drowned quays where gigantic barrels of wine were bobbing, each time everything had been but was curtly denied me, and these denials felt like fatal betrayals, it wasn't fair, I couldn't get used to it, this whole city which I loved nonetheless was leagued against me in an attempt to throw me off balance by means of my vision, a powerful argument for someone as near-sighted as me for these brutal mists, these vanishing museums and churches, these sudden doglegs in the avenues, perhaps they were my fault, my misdoing, perhaps it was I who missaw what was right under my nose all along. So I was always ready to accuse myself of the wrongs that I suffered.

One evening when I am coming out of the Theater after dancing class suddenly I am struck with limping. This time the spell takes me by the feet, I advance as if I were walking backwards, my sandals attack me, I have two dogs at my ankles, one crushes my toes, the other wags at heel, I stumble and trip, obstructed, trapped, it's already dark when I finally manage to get cast up at the house, I drop at last I have the right to drop since I no longer have to hold my head up in public, I collapse, crumple up on my knees head dangling. Then I notice two strange shoes on my feet, one brown and the other gray that I'd never seen before, causes of my misery and consequences of my unreflecting short-sightedness and my credulity. For I always head straight for the supernatural in Algeria. Meanwhile my own sandals abandoned in the changing room where nobody will have wanted to inflict them on themselves. You get the wrong shoes and it's exile wandering and solitude. You walk with your feet twisted up, mocking, foreign, and all time is out of joint, shelter recedes infinitely, the road climbs sheer as a wall in front of this uninhabitable, footloose body. And all the magic of my city out of sight. A city that I knew by foot in every sense. Losing time, losing blood, but not the earth.

Translated by Beverley Bie Brahic

5

DERRIDA

Hélène Cixous's and Jacques Derrida's works, however singular each of them may be, have always maintained a bond; though quite invisible at the beginning, it has grown increasingly conspicuous over the years. Some critics have inferred that Cixous's thought is indebted to Derrida's, implying that fiction is subordinated to philosophy and even indulging in a sexist prejudice, but this influence is not a one-way process: the thinker himself even admitted[1] that sometimes he did not know which one of them had first coined this or that word—such as the case of *animot*.[2] In her earliest texts, Cixous already mentions Derrida's work, which she discovered at its start and found illuminating. Both of them have described their first meeting, in the Parisian café Balzar (at her request, because she wanted to show him some of her writing). This meeting took place around 1963–64, before Cixous had published anything; Derrida, whose international reputation was not yet established, had already begun to develop his ideas in lectures and articles. The young and rising intellectual was astounded by Cixous's manuscripts—they became her first book, *Le Prénom de Dieu* (1967)—because they did not resemble anything and he thus qualified them as "unidentifiable literary objects" (a wordplay related to UFO, and therefore implicitly containing the verb *voler*, "to fly" and "to steal" in French). This meeting ushered in a lifelong intellectual and personal friendship and with it a mutual impregnation of ideas and images. Derrida said in *H.C. for Life, That Is to Say . . .* (2000): "I-met-her-some-thirty-five-years-ago-maybe. . . . It is *as if* we had *almost* never been apart." The publication of *Veils* in 1998—a book that interweaves a text by Cixous ("Savoir") and one by Derrida ("A Silkworm of One's Own")—brought this dialogue between two of the most influential intellectuals of our time to the public. (In fact, their intellectual exchange had already been opened to a larger audience as early as 1990, at a conference held in Paris on "Lectures de la différence sexuelle.")[3] The reading process that takes place in *Veils* was totally new: while Derrida's text is written in response to Cixous's, it maintains a total autonomy. Both texts are, in a certain sense, confessional, but their autobiographical component acts mainly as the foundation of a philosophical questioning about identity.

Though they had never encountered each other before their meeting in the Parisian café, Jacques Derrida shared similar origins and experiences with Hélène Cixous. He was born in Algeria seven years before her (1930) to a Sephardic Jewish family of Spanish ancestors. He also suffered exclusion because of antisemitic laws: as he explained more than once in his work, he was expelled from school in 1942 because of quotas limiting the presence of Jews in public institutions. Soon after, he moved to Paris (1949–50) where he studied philosophy and began his career as intellectual and writer. Many of the topics developed in his essays are also relevant in Hélène Cixous's work, such as hospitality, friendship and love, Judaism, animality, personal and collective identity . . . One might consider the main difference between them to be that Cixous composes mostly fiction, whereas Derrida writes philosophical essays. However, if it is impossible to establish a firm distinction between fictional and theoretical writing in Cixous's oeuvre, in Derrida's it is also difficult and even an oversimplification to separate his autobiographical writing from the philosophical. For instance, "Circumfession"—included in the book on Derrida by Geoffrey Bennington, published in 1991[4]—is perhaps his most personal text (a sort of journal kept while his mother was dying, where he speaks of her and his family, his childhood, and his first memories), and yet it is also a reflection on such themes as death, circumcision, Jewishness, and identity. Cixous commented on "Circumfession," in a deeply personal way, in *Portrait of Jacques Derrida as a Young Jewish Saint* (2001). She had also previously devoted a text to Derrida's work—"Quelle heure est-il ou La porte (celle qu'on ne passe pas)"—a paper given in 1992 that inaugurated an exchange of homages they paid to one another.[5] The most recent book by Hélène Cixous on Derrida's work is *Insister of Jacques Derrida* (2006), published after his death in 2004. As for Jacques

Derrida, he devoted two book-length studies to Hélène Cixous: *H.C. for Life, That Is to Say . . .* (first published in 2000) and *Geneses, Genealogies, Genres, and Genius* (2003).[6]

The first text of part 5, "Second Skin," comes from *Portrait of Jacques Derrida as a Young Jewish Saint* (2001). Quoting Derrida's "A Silkworm of One's Own," Cixous evokes the *tallith*[7] as an image related to the veil—and to truth as unveiling (corresponding to the Greek concept *aletheia*)—a topic on which he has written extensively. She remarks that the philosopher "circumvent[s] the masculine law" of the tallith and the veil, causing them to become, instead, images of the "perfect love," the one "you feel with the tip of your fingers," that is to say, by touch. As we have seen in part 4, "Love (and) the Other," Cixous associates this "other-love" with femininity. Without distorting Derrida's thought—on the contrary, she keeps herself at a close distance to it—Hélène Cixous points out the concepts and images in Derrida's texts that are also present in hers. In this excerpt, two themes stand out: the relationship between the philosopher and the French language and—through another language, Hebrew—the acculturation suffered but also encouraged by the Algerian Jewish community. As for the first theme, Cixous describes the tormented relationship that Jacques Derrida maintained—as if it were a passionate liaison—with the French language. Cixous personifies this language (language being a feminine noun in French) saying that *she* reciprocates this passion and is also "wild about him [Derrida]." But French is also "his eternal adversary friend interlocutor," adds Cixous, meaning that Derrida loved the language and wanted ardently to possess it, all the time acknowledging that it was perhaps because the French language was not *his*. In his book *Monolingualism of the Other, or, The Prosthesis of Origin* (1996),[8] the thinker himself developed the idea that, due to the particular situation of the North African Jewish community, he felt in some way excluded and/or in an illegitimate position within it—this statement resonates with those expressed in Cixous's first texts, discussed in part 1. For her, this tormented relationship with the French language is what makes Derrida write in a "French that surpasses French"; he places himself, therefore, "beyond the French language," yet, at the same time, what he writes can only be said in French. His writing is, therefore, untranslatable—translation in its literal and figurative meanings is a main topic in Derrida's work—as only that of poets. Cixous, indeed, regards Jacques Derrida as a poet—she even compares him to Rimbaud—which is not usual, as philosophical discourse, since the Enlightenment, is supposed to be based on reason, whereas poetic discourse allegedly emanates from the irrational and the unconscious.

On the other hand, Hebrew—unknown in both Derrida's and Cixous's family circles—symbolizes the "comfortable acculturation" of which they were, as members of the Algerian Jewish community, "victims" as well as "accomplices." Cixous calls Algeria this "disease of autocolonialized communities," this "autoimmune craze" for French language and culture that made residents like her, and Derrida, move to France as soon as they could. This uneasy feeling about the colonizer's culture—a culture that had rejected them as Jews—was the reason for Derrida's "troubled identity," with which Cixous also identifies. The lack of a clear social and cultural assignment provokes a constant questioning about personal and collective identity: "what does it mean to be a Franco–North African Jew is that something you add on or subtract or maybe you take it away from any attempt at collective action?" Both Cixous and Derrida resist the social need of defining oneself; they react against "this verb to be, the great persecutor." However, from what can be judged a "malediction"—"a belonging constituted of exclusion and non-belonging"—comes, finally, a "benediction," as, according to Cixous, "the greatest works of art" are always the outcome of "certain wounds." In this sense Jacques Derrida's origins (and the same could be said of Cixous's) are in part responsible for his caution toward any form of belief or certitude—but this caution cannot be assimilated to the nihilism he has been accused of. As Hélène Cixous says, Derrida is "the one who knows that one cannot say I believe without doubting, without crossing out *I* and *believe* and *doubt*."

The second excerpt comes from a seminar given by Hélène Cixous and Jacques Derrida at the University of Barcelona (Spain) in February 2002, published in a bilingual version (French and Spanish) under the title *Lengua por venir/Langue à venir. Seminario de Barcelona* (2004). They responded to questions addressed to them both in turn. The selected part deals with a highly debated point in relation to Cixous's and Derrida's writing: that of each one's *style*. Both writers have been accused by some critics of using a precious and unnecessarily obscure style. This criticism is addressed to "deconstruction" in general, but it is harsher when aimed at Derrida's writing because, as earlier stated, philosophical discourse is supposed to be rational and clear. Some theorists have talked about a "linguistic turn" in twentieth century thought, meaning that modern and, above all, postmodern thinkers have focused on the relation between language and philosophy. Derrida not only developed all sorts of topics related to language, he also, as Cixous stresses, carried out these reflections in his own writing, elaborating his thought in a performative way. In *Lengua por venir* he speaks out against the concept of style—as he had done in earlier works such as *Spurs: Nietzsche's Styles* (1978)[9]—considering it a "phallocentric" category. "Style" is associated with incision, penetration, violence; in a text, it is the signature of the author, expressing thus his "mastery" of what he has written. If the author has the last word, "nothing else happens," says Derrida, who believes, on the contrary, in the capacity of language to provoke "events." But, for events to arrive, "one must give up on performative authority;" going beyond the opposition between activity and passivity, Derrida suggests the concept of docility (the writer must be willing to follow the language, while keeping himself alert). Instead of style, he speaks of idiom, which is "what is proper," but also "what can't be reappropriated": its own author cannot recognize it, then. Moreover, Derrida feels that his manner changes in each book: for him, every new work means signing a new "charter" or establishing a new "constitution," even though he admits obvious differences between his philosophical essays and his autobiographical or "circumfessional" texts.

On the other hand, Hélène Cixous thinks that Derrida "writes in Derridean": throughout his writing "there is a creation of language"—and that is what interests her when she studies Derrida's work. In her answer to the same question on style, we can see the similarities and differences between their conception of writing. First, as she points out, Cixous does not separate literature from philosophy as an "act of creation." She believes, as Derrida, that the author must renounce being the "pilot" of the book: it is language itself that commands writing, but instead of using the word *docility,* she suggests *submission* to this *mystery.* However—and Cixous herself notes this possible difference between her and Derrida—she is more concerned than he is about the fact that an oeuvre is a link in the chain of literature: she sees how one "inherits resources" from all these "parents, friends, ancestors" who—in her case, whether writing in French, English, or German—also contributed to this "transmission." This is called intertextuality in academia, but Cixous prefers to speak of a conscious and unconscious *memory* of language, as if it were a living being. Nevertheless, the role of the author is also important: she must let this memory spring freely, and even encourage the flow, at the same time acting as a *witness*—in other texts Cixous has used the image of the midwife who assists in childbirth to illustrate this point. One must be trained to do such work, and this apprenticeship can only be accomplished by reading and acquiring a thorough knowledge of tradition (this is why Cixous does not separate reading from writing). Moreover, what interests her in this process is the capacity of language to "disturb" certitudes. Contrary to the most common belief, she states that language makes one "think" precisely because of its "unreason"—bordering on "madness"—whereas thought is usually related to reason, as seen previously.

In the third and last excerpt, which comes from the book *Insister of Jacques Derrida* (2006), Hélène Cixous returns to some of the topics already developed here, such as Derrida's passion for the French language, his capacity for creating words that convey new ways of thinking, and the relationship she and he maintained together. From a factual point of view, one might consider the main difference between this book and the ones Cixous wrote previously on Jacques Derrida to be that *Insister* was written after the philosopher's death (October 2004). This information enables the reader to more fully understand the first section of the chapter, titled "Today," where Cixous reflects on the multiple meanings of this apparently simple word, which can refer to the date when she wrote this text ("Today 10 March 2005, I write the word today") to the time we are reading it, as well as to the year (2000) when Derrida wrote his own text that includes the word she is quoting, *today*. She states that Derrida makes frequent use of it ("It is today a little bit everywhere with you"), so much so that it becomes a sort of "signature." One might believe that the thinker's death would put an end to his capacity of "todaying," as Cixous phrases it. However, even though "everything has changed" (with his death)—which is the first sentence of the text—"Nothing has changed": Derrida's work outlives him, rendering this "today" eternally present.

Moreover, Cixous's writing is interwoven with long quotations from Derrida's, continuing the dialogue between them. Their lifelong conversation has not been stopped by the philosopher's physical disappearance from this world: Cixous pursues it with Derrida's texts, which carry not only his voice but his multiple ("ghost-") voices, spectrally. Her intention is not only to pay homage to the great contribution Derrida has made to contemporary thought but also to demonstrate that he continues to live: his voice keeps resonating with the most important concerns of the present. His thinking will never be outdated because it "ventures into the regions of the not yet and the perhaps," according to Cixous. In order to glide in these "groundless, bottomless regions," he must "invent fragile and supple sur-words" because those already existing are often not precise enough. While loving French with "a mad irresistible desire," he treats it as a foreign language, defamiliarizing it in order to exploit all its richness. This is the same reason Derrida pays so much attention to translation: it shows us the uniqueness of every tongue, revealing that language is not an instrument that renders or *translates* the world in a transparent way—for everything, then, would be translatable—but, rather, that language has the power to create the world. Cixous chooses, for instance, the French expression used by Derrida "tu ne l'as pas volé," which primarily means "you asked for it," but also contains the aforementioned meanings, "to fly" and "to steal." She signals the ambiguity of the pronoun *tu* (you)—the second person contributing to the impression that their dialogue is still alive and will be forever—when using it to address Derrida; she is aware that *tu* is the past participle of the verb *taire* (to silence, to fall silent). The untranslatability of these French expressions has its counterpart in the closing paragraph of "Today." In it Cixous explains how Derrida gave her a word "as a present," saying, "You are *my insister.*" The significance of *insister* (which literally means "to insist" in French, but may be read as "in-sister" in English) can only be fully understood in an in-between or "foreign land" that is neither English nor French, neither feminine nor masculine—it is all of these. This is the land where Jacques Derrida and Hélène Cixous come from, and it is from there that they invite us to come and partake in their journey.

13

SECOND SKIN (2001)

FROM *PORTRAIT OF JACQUES DERRIDA AS A YOUNG JEWISH SAINT*

In the armoire, here it is in Hebrew in its transfigure, *the tallith*, "it waits for me tucked away in its hiding place at home, it never travels." In place of the stolen skin, this other, the hidden skin, not from just any animal but from the sheep the ewe or ram (*Voiles*, p. 67) the commemorative skin, the death-commemorating skin of a ewe that was alive and died for the tallith, the skin that *remembers* the *Korban*, the offering that brings close, the proximate skin, the hypothesis under whose protection he murmurs, no, he keeps murmuring, the prayer shawl, the *shawl* he insists and not the veil, the word shawl introducing an Indian note, the skin, of a ewe perhaps, but for the body and soul of *man*.

Yet another male thing? Reserved? Exclusive? Perhaps but it won't take him long to circumvent masculine law.

Here, under the tent of the tallith, an extraordinary hymn mounts to *she* who waits for him "hidden" in her hiding place at home him forever traveling *she* never voyages. I said *she* yes, not a slip of the tongue, I follow the signs of his.

He says and writes of the tallith that it is unique as you've heard. By means of tallith and tongue he delicately introduces the theme of the liaison. He has a liaison with the tallith which is unique, *qui est unique. Tunic by liaison,* probably his only liaison, one that is weightless, that waits, a skin for his skin, that doesn't capture but protects him, keeps watch over him without keeping him. He loves his tunic and he sings of it in moving accents, caresses himself with it, against her, like a cat, as the cat just barely caresses him, a light touch grazing the skin, he is fonder of it than anything else this masculine feminine thing he calls, this is unique in his language, *my very own tallith.*

All his life he has fought against the veil in the veil's counterdance, dreaming of a lifting of the veil that, so as not to be a mere an unreveiling should, might, come from the other, it's the silkworm's dream to be born of the voice of the other, to be called. Without illusion, without the least figment of a veil over or in back of his eyes. But under no condition, he swears, would he dream of getting rid of the soft pelt of his shawl. Without illusion nonetheless. One doesn't forget there's a dead ram in the Jewish tallith.

But calling it *my-own-tallith* is also a way of setting it apart, of differentiating it from other talliths at least trying to draw it away from the memory of the sacrificial offerings, he has no illusions about what in the Jewish religion is sacrificial, not at all incongruous with the idea of the veil that's how it is there is blood on it, except on mine he would like to believe, the tunic unlike others. And who knows perhaps, *white* as it is, his is the tallith of before all talliths, the pre-original shawl. It suffices to believe, weeping

[no] "theory-of-fetishism" can ever measure up to the infinite compassion that comes from brushing up against, from the caress of a tallith, of my tallith, "my very own tallith. . . . I would like to sing the very solitary softness of my tallith, a softness softer than softness,

Do you remember? My child, my sister, imagine the softness of going to live there together

utterly unique, both sensitive and insensitive, calm, acquiescent, a stranger to sensibility, to effusion or pathos, to all "Passion" in short. Boundless compassion, however, a compassion without idolatry, proximity and infinite distance. I love the tranquil passion, the absent-minded love my tallith inspires in me, I feel it allows me this absent-mindedness because it is sure, so sure of me, so little concerned about my infidelities. It doesn't believe in my inconstancies, they don't affect it. I love it and bless it with a strange indifference, my tallith, with a nameless, ageless familiarity. . . . My white tallith belongs to the night, to absolute night. You will never know anything about it, nor I without doubt. (*Voiles*, p. 79)

Love with the seeing-eye fingers of the blind, love you feel with the tips of your fingers, with your lips, it's the dream of love, perfect love.

"I touch it without knowing what I do nor what I ask at that moment, and especially without knowing in whose hands I put myself, without knowing to whom I give thanks" (*Voiles*, p. 46). There is no knowing, only grace and thanksgiving there where there is neither knowing nor seeing.

There he is with his Jewish touch, a Jew groping for his tallith, a Jew with an undecided tallith: not knowing, at the end of the wordless grace, of the life so short but so long, with the tunic he loves that loves him, whether he will be ashes or buried in his tallith, letting his loved ones decide.

Yes but I thought he would never give it up no matter what? Doesn't he say:

Right to the very end, never, no matter what: under no circumstances, whatever the verdict at the end of such a redoubtable "*journey*," does one give up a tallith. One must never, at any moment, throw it out or reject it. (*Voiles*, pp. 68–69).

Yes but after the end?

If there are fire and ashes, then what? I can go no further than the life without violence. I stop without knowing and without seeing. I shall stay with the vision of his astounding union with the white tallith, *this white wedding that belongs to the night*.

We shall never know.

This was the marvelous tale of the Jew of the night. One can only tell it in French, with a French that surpasses French. Just as he goes beyond the French language, so his Jewish being his Jewish not-being [*son n'être juif*] his Jewish birth [*son naître juif*] surpasses (being not being) Judaity Judaism Judaicity Judaica and everything else that might come along with a *j*, *u* and *d*, for *if* as a *Marrano* he is Jewish at least it is *in passing*, between the French language*, in the turns* of French, a passer-by.

THE MAIN CHARACTER OF HIS WORK IS FRENCH

From the very beginning, from the playground at school, that's where he met up with his eternal adversary friend interlocutor, *French*. The French language he will have had his whole life to do battle with. In school he likes it when he *has* French. Then explications, arguments, quarrels, hugs, the figures of his impossible homotextuality.

And then, up from under the floorboards—the theatrical ground of this tirade, this *algarade* (from the Spanish *algarada*, from the Arab *al-ghara*)—making themselves heard by the insistent and welcome—caressed even—hosts, elves and gnomes, come Latin and Greek or perhaps Greek and Latin. A magic nostalgia keeps calling up the two of them his best friends. They (masculine or feminine) are always there, chanted, like a chorus with French as coryphaeus.

French and haunted, French is always speaking to him.

Le Français I say. But she whom he adores is *la langue française*. He is wild about her and makes her wild about him. He sits her down on his lap. She tells him her names. His names. Only to him.

As only poets, perhaps only as Rimbaud.

I said of the tallith earlier that it was Hebrew, but immediately afterward as unique tunic, we could hear it was *Hebrew in French*.

Hebrew, he makes no secret of it, for him it's Hebrew or Chinese if you prefer. For him as for me as for my brother, as for so many victims or accomplices of a comfortable acculturation upon which the aforementioned Algerian Jewish community edified its desire for France in the deformation years of the twenties and thirties. Strange autoimmune craze, hence those whose soul was already formed and who had a keen ear for the things of the spirit had a good laugh over it and a great deal of suffering.

We were gripped by a circus feeling. We would see so many of those let's call them "Algerian Jews"—for the sake of brevity—performing their highwire act in the void. Spangled in French but sporting kippas we called skullcaps, out they swung, having let go of the bar of their old culture, left it far behind them, in Morocco, swimming across the abyss arms reaching out for the other trapeze, the much-desired French, but there's France, hostile, snatching it back. The Jewish trapezists cling to the void. A community out of step with the times. One often spoke a rather elegant French, the language of the denied and oft-flattered enemy. Hebrew? So suppressed. At best one was at the Marrano stage but unaware of it. Humbly my Oran uncles made believe at the dinner table, under the true false skullcap they gabbled away. I admired them: to me they were the last of the faithful or was it just the opposite? Imagine the enormous weight of the word *Jew*, the swelling, the erection of the word, sole survivor of an extinct verbal population.

To think that in the Derrida family they'd naturalized the bar mitzvah, converted it to French. In our house, Cixous–half Klein, Omi kept watch, my German grandmother, French did not do quite the same damage. We said bar mitzvah. But all the same we caught Algeria that disease of autocolonialized communities.

—My bar mitzvah! hoots my brother, what a joke! You had to recite the Shema Israel which is your basic prayer. I was under the arcades on Bab Azoun Street with the rabbi in front of a shitty little synagogue maybe pretty he says. Do you know the Shema? asks the rabbi. The Shema I thought, a shema in the ass! my brother says. Yes, I replied unfazed. So recite it for me. Of course, I exclaimed. I start off. I say Shema Israel Blablablah nice and loud. Fine says the rabbi. He stops me. You can say Shema. Afterward in the tram—after the bar mitzvah—I tell Granny our Oran grandmother with my ritual subtlety risen from the depths of my rage: I hope we're having ham for lunch.

That was 1951. For him it was in 1943 at an Isly Street rabbi's he had to sham.

They would ask these boys my brothers: do you know the Shibboleth, at least a bit of it, hey? It starts with a Shi says the brother. Good says the rabbi. Who will recount the circoncessions of the Isly or Lyre Street rabbis? The main thing is to barmitzvah the boy eyes shut. But don't tell anybody says my mother. She fears the worst sin is not the sin, it's the telling strangers. Some "goy."

The troubled identity, the trouble whereby the tremor passes between us, has also to do with this difficulty of saying, this preaching of not telling, the shame-faced culture unashamed of its lack of culture. But keep it to yourself. Don't tell a soul.

The crime is making believe in bad faith. In those days he hadn't found out about his *marranity*, therefore he was innocent.

How to escape unscathed from a scene in which I take *communion* instead of having my bar mitzvah, what a circummunion! "It's my feast day" he tells himself in French, they feast him, yet another circumcision.

His genius gets the best of these cruel comedies—gives it wings—like Elie

> I did my "communion" by fleeing the prison of all languages, the sacred one they tried to lock me up in without opening me to it, the secular they made clear would never be mine, but this ignorance remained the chance of my faith as of my hope, of my taste even for the "word." (Period 54)

We were always imposters doubled up in an excruciating laugh. Offended offenders. My brother and I at Hanukkah bursting out laughing singing *ma au sau ne chou aussi*, making a mishmash of cabbage and currants and the hermetic hymn.

Not kosher: conjurers. Jugglers with language, swallowers of the ashes of words. What remained of Hebrew.

(Here I owe a mark of respect to my father the circumcised atheist: when I was ten he gave me two teachers one of Arab one of Hebrew. Then he died and I had my two paternal languages cut off.)

At last *Le Monolinguisme de l'autre* came along to say everything one was not supposed to say, a splendor of an apocalyptic testimony in a language that is merciless that owes nothing to anyone, about the plots against the soul, outrages, interlingual persecutions, the whole war beneath the surface of the Algerian wars, our daily lot, a history rich in tormentdreams, in battles between regiments of identificatory phantasms, my grandfather Samuel Cixous as a Zouave, we always were a strange bunch of Zouaves, the great book of our terrors tells it all, interrogations, torture, drawn and quartered by hyphens what does it mean to be a Franco-North-African Jew is that something you add on or subtract or maybe you take it away from any attempt at collective action? Still we ask it and to have to answer, in a language that is Hebrew in French for us, for a belonging constituted of exclusion and nonbelonging, what does it mean to be from Algeria not Algerian, Jew by the other, French by decree, disenFrenched by decree, to be constantly decreeicized, furthermore forever not-like, not like the other not like me, subdivided, circumceded, circumdecided, improbable, what is this verb to be, the great persecutor.

Who can say what it is, this Franco-North-African creature Jew-nonetheless or in-spite-of-everything or Jew-who-doesn't-know-that-he-is, how to know who is better placed to know anything, when are Jews Jews in what way I wondered are my mother and her German sister Jewish more Jewish than Russians Jews perforce, "no Jew has ever nor will ever know anything for certain" it seems to me I read that on the ceiling of Montaigne's library but I am not certain of it, the more my mother and her sister seem sure of knowing what is or what is not to be or not to be the more unsettled I am, perhaps it is enough to be *certain* but in what order are they Germans or Jews English or French Jewish or French sometimes German Jews sometimes German French or on the other hand English Jewish with a German passport also Israeli (infinitely Jewisher in their opinion than the forced-to-be synagogue Russians who know nevertheless and know only that they were Jews but one must say that they are not Jews all they know is that they once were).

Le Monolinguisme de l'autre tells us everything there is to know about the mental anguish to which we owe our books of memoirs— . . .

For sometimes, as in his case, from malediction comes benediction. We are indebted to certain wounds for the greatest works of art.

Such is this chopped up Jewish "community" which thrice cuts itself off from its language

1. cut from the Arab and Berber languages

2. cut from French or even European language and culture

3. cut for—from Jewish memory,

such is this Jewish memory cut off from its memory,

such is the dialogue with his mother 1. that cannot take place 2. that never took place

such is the voyage with his father so as not to work but to be together in a foreign country that never happened

such is the cemetery he visits each year to think in front of the stone

It is to be forever swimming as best he can between two hands of liar poker. If he responds? Lies. Not respond: kill the truth. The lie, wherein lies the truth. It is the obligation to make believe. It is unavoidable. He submits. Such is the betrayal in order not to betray.

It is the language he speaks, the only one, the one he must speak and that does not belong to him.

It is the untranslatable that remains his dwelling place, uninhabitable, it is the word dwelling [*demeure*] that prophesies in his mouth the minute he says it two always die [*deux . . . meure*]. And yet one must go on living. It is France that has no place except as figure a ghostly country, a spectrality but that he imagines so he can get some rest there between one voyage and the next. A ghostly repose. It is fatigue, it is the dream of one day touching something like land with the tips of his fingers, feet, lips, not only a tallith, flesh, duration and, yes, the peace of a belief.

And yet one must continue to get lost and dream of believing what one does not believe, a waking dream of what could be, here, if—

I feel lost without French he says, that's something, at least he feels something, which doesn't mean he finds himself in French except in all these figures of cases in point, but at least he renews and increases its powers. He loses his head over French.

. . .

Translated by Beverley Bie Brahic

14

ON *STYLE* (A QUESTION TO H. CIXOUS AND J. DERRIDA) (2004)

FROM *LENGUA POR VENIR/LANGUE À VENIR: SEMINARIO DE BARCELONA*

The term *style* can lead to misunderstandings but I can't find another term to express this singular appropriation of language in the act of writing-speaking.

Your written work is not easy to understand-read-translate. I believe there's nothing new in this statement, nor do I intend to elude that proper activity of thought this work with concepts is ... However, your *style* points to work with form, with signifiers, in order to disarticulate or dismember the signifieds that lie hidden or are evoked like prefixed suppositions that do not allow for the mobility of thought, of thinking otherwise.

Your thought in relation to literary or philosophical tradition, in relation to the present, operates through a disarticulation of the language that traditionally shapes the discourses of knowledge and literature ... Could you define, explain or justify ... your style? How does it relate to speech [*parole*], to language, and to its potential ability to account for what happens, for "truth" ... ?

Mercedes Coll

JACQUES DERRIDA:

This is a very difficult question, much more difficult for me than the previous one—even if I believe it to be necessary—because of this word *style* . . . We shall give different answers first because, whatever one thinks of the word *style*—and I'll very quickly say something about it—this question surely can't be addressed to both of us jointly, because if there is something we don't have in common, it is style; if something like style exists! We don't have the same style. You say that you can't find another term to express this "singular appropriation of language in the act of writing and of speaking." In general, when one uses the word *style*—which is a classical word—one no doubt designates a singular way of signing what one writes, in a broad sense what one says, in a yet broader sense what one does, one's behavior, because one sometimes speaks of the style of a gesture . . . But when one speaks of people who write, style is the way of writing rather than the way of speaking, thus a singular way of writing, but one that, no matter how singular and inimitable it may remain, is made up of rules, that is to say, recurrences. The style remains the same, one claims one can recognize somebody's style, it is an inimitable style. Nobody writes like Hélène Cixous, but one recognizes a text by Hélène Cixous (in principle) because in what she writes there are things that look similar, ways of doing things that look similar, thus regularities, returns, recurrences, implicit norms; I don't know if this is true—and Hélène will answer.

As far as I am concerned I know that I don't have a style in that sense, that each time I write there occurs an almost constitutional change—in the sense of a political constitution—each time it is a new contract, a new constitution. For each text, whether small, short or long, there's a new charter and this charter orders me to write differently each time. And when I say differently I mean even in the grammar, the length of sentences, a different style. Of course I don't deny that there may be recognizable things, that it's possible for people to say, "after all, between a text about philosophy, a study on Husserl and a text supposed to be more fictional, autobiographical, or circumfessional, one recognizes a few differences," but this recurrence, this resemblance, what one thinks one recognizes, is by definition accessible only to the other. What returns as the same or as what looks similar in a very different text of mine, which I sign, can be legible, visible, sensible only for the other and not for me. I naturally could recognize my texts. If I'm asked who wrote this, I would most often be able to tell, not because I wrote it, but with another's point of view and because I remember things. It's like a photograph, what I'm saying here is like a photograph, I can't see myself . . . The idiom, idiomaticity— if there's any—is what can't be reappropriated; *idiom* means in Greek what is proper: *idiotès*. I would set down as an aporia and logical necessity that what is proper can't be appropriated, what is proper to me is what I can't reappropriate. In other words, I would be the last one to be able to see my style, in a way.

If one now wants to use the word *style* with a slightly sharper edge to it—style supposes sharpness, in your text—there is something pointed at stake; style is pointed. I wrote a little book on Nietzsche called *Nietzsche's Styles*,[1] in which I insist a lot on the sharp, phallic nature of the point. Style is the pointed tip with which one writes. Therefore the insistence on determining the idiom as style, in the figure of style, is what I would call a phallocentric insistence, which consists in thinking that writing is a gesture of inscription with a decisive, incisive point and that where this decisive, incisive, cutting, sharp point is lacking there's no style. But this is also an academic interpretation, since this concept was used in the old-style university; one no longer talks about style nowadays, or very little, it was when I was a child that people were asking, what is Chateaubriand's style? Style now is thus an old academic or phallocentric category in which the style is the man [*le style, c'est l'homme*]—and then I must understand man in the sense of man, not woman. It is the inscription at its most incisive, penetrating, violent . . . but there can be great forms of writing [*écritures*] without style in that sense. Basically I am not sure whether I'd like to make a claim for style; if I was told "now would you rather be considered as somebody who has style or as somebody who has no style?" I would find it very hard to answer. And I think that if I was obliged to, in the end, I'd say, with some precautions, "I'd rather not have style."

But I'd like to do justice to the end of your question, when you ask, "How does it relate to speech [*parole*], to language, and to its potential ability to account for what happens, for truth?" Precisely, if I replied, "I don't want to have style," or "After all I'd rather not have style," it is because if one really writes with style, if style is the last word, nothing else happens. If I write with the incisive, decisive authority of someone who makes things happen, who does what he says, nothing happens. For something to happen, that is to say, happen to me or happen/arrive

[*arrive*] out of language, one must give up on performative authority, which decides what happens. If I want to make something happen, nothing happens. For something to happen, it must happen to me; even if I am very active, I am passive there where it happens. Therefore, for something to happen to language, through language, one must in a way be docile regarding language. One can multiply many activities, but precisely in order to be docile. And my own experience, if I may be allowed to speak about it, regarding language, is an experience of an extreme yet docile activity. When something happens, or happens to me, thanks to language, I receive it from language, and, each time I experience something good in writing, it is in an experience of quasi irresponsibility in which naturally I deployed a lot of responsibility, cunning, work, and activity, but, at the end of the day, for the thing to have come to me from language and to have happened, affected my own docility regarding language: a stroke of luck [*chance*], and each time a clever word [*bon mot*] comes or happens to me, it happened to me, all at once I say to myself, "Ah, there it is! . . ." The silkworm, for example: I deployed a lot of work but the chance of this phrase was within language, and all that happened to me happened to me from language without my intervention, at the end of the day, and thus without style. Therefore something happens only there where style is somehow undone, routed, what happens puts style to rout. There are always several ways of living this rout. One is in a rout in front of language, therefore one suffers, one is affected, sometimes one runs away and each has his or her way of losing, and this is where readers recognize: that's how he records his rout, that's how, after all, he lives his passivity, his docility . . . that's his style, if you like, his signature. But this is not calculated, decisive, authoritarian, and pointed style.

HÉLÈNE CIXOUS:

I am thinking, because I am looking for something to add to what Jacques has just said that expresses my own experience.

First I shall return to Mercedes's question and stumble over the theme of the disarticulation of language. I am grateful to Jacques for taking care of the whole question of style, which indeed is irrelevant both for him and for me, but this does not exclude the theme of the idiom nor of language. I think that Jacques writes in Derridean, which is extremely difficult to define, just as one could say that Rimbaud speaks Rimbaldian ... These are still languages, there is a creation of language, but, as he puts it very accurately, it is not Derrida who can account for what Derridean is but we who read it. In fact I try hard from time to time to portray it, and it's not easy, but I notice possible ways of drawing its originality, its absolute singularity. I would keep away from this word *disarticulation;* it doesn't correspond to the way in which, for example, I let myself be carried away, led and enchanted by language, for that's still what it's all about. Admittedly what Jacques was saying a moment ago is absolutely true. One is not in front in the driving seat, as a pilot, one is carried away by a flow. It's quite mysterious, besides it is an overwhelming experience, but this is so. I retrospectively recognize, as I turn back or because someone points it out to me, the way in which I am the bearer of this language that then yields a text [*fait texte*] in front of me, receives or inherits resources—and then this is perhaps a great difference between us—that I recognize in texts other than mine and that have to do with the way in which language—not only the French language, of course, in this case the French language, but it is the same thing in all languages, therefore with singularities specific to each of them—is disturbing and allows one to disturb. For example, I know that I find in the flow traversing me that which charms me, pleases me, and fascinates me in others whom I regard as parents, friends, ancestors through the wonderful world of literature in French, and not only in French since I often feel a relationship of alliance or recognition with authors who write in German, in English ... All that destabilizes is what I cherish. Indeed it's not disarticulation, on the contrary, it is a weave ... I will allow myself to use terms from rhetoric, from poetics, for example, the amphibological ability and competence of language is something I can't do without and therefore favor, not that I program it ... Ultimately we're arguably almost all amphibologists when we speak, but in general we tend to correct and eliminate ambiguity.

To turn now to the world that Jacques threw some light on, in general one seeks to do, to sort out, to classify, to decide, whereas on the contrary the resources of language are on the side of the undecidable. I myself am very sensitive to this resource and when I feel it sweeping in front of me—since the phenomenon of writing is first one of sweeping, then the author follows, and I am more and more convinced that the one who writes, if I may say so, is the book itself; when I see it manifest itself, that is to say, at the moment when I am the scribe (anyway, I always say I am the scribe, my job is that of a scribe who jots down what the book is producing), I do not, quite the contrary, oppose the disturbance, therefore all that causes a slippage [*fait déraper*] and causes the act of creation in literature—I am not separating literature from philosophy in saying this—well, let's say writing, to produce uncertainties. All that is anacoluthon, all that is a shift in tenses, enallage . . . all that, with me, is, if I may say so and I want to, at once spontaneous, that is to say, it comes, I don't go looking for it, but this spontaneity, which is mine, comes with a simultaneity of perception: at the moment when I am writing there is a tiny lag, which is perhaps only the time of composition [*rédaction*], the time my hand takes to rest on the sheet of paper, and in this time lag I hear, I am not saying I understand what is taking place, and in fact I encourage it, it is granted to me, these are gifts. Jacques was talking of chance a moment ago: something that appears suddenly, that has not been solicited but comes; from time to time a certain system of signifiers is granted to me, and one second or the other, that is to say, the witness [*la témoin ou le témoin*] who follows this race, jotting it down, encourages it. What does "encourage" mean? First it means not to hold it back, then to be in a state of vigilance, which makes it possible for an effect of seeding [*effet d'ensemencement*], in the text, to be kept alive and multiplied; it's as if in me a kind of auxiliary of the multiplication of effects was always at work.

It must also be said that I believe a lot in learning [*apprentissage*], I am a learner in writing, a bit like somebody who plays a musical instrument, I think that somebody who writes just can't do without an exercise like the pianist or the violinist, that is to say, if one stops learning, one also loses an expertise, a subtlety, which doesn't have to do with the speed of execution but with the practice of the ear and of the mind's ear. Then, I've been practicing that kind of learning for decades out of pleasure and necessity, as I would eat, drink, sleep, or dream, and also out of discipline. I don't exercise in the abstract but I am at the paper . . . as if by a need to go deeper and explore farther the resources of language. Then, for example, French idiomaticity, since this is where I exercise, offers something like the practice of anteposition in French; I don't grammaticalize it, if you like, while I practice it, but I realize that effects of accentuation, insistence, which signify, of course, are produced and engendered by forms. Besides, as I do this, I concur with a tradition, I become aware while reading—for my writing practice is indissociable from my reading practice—that this piano or violin exercise is something that has been practiced by all my predecessors. If you read some Proust, some Rousseau, or some Stendhal you'll find exactly the same experimentation, the same research, the same opening, the same availability, the same receptivity to what constitutes the wealth and the singularities of the idiom. This does not mean—and what Jacques was saying a moment ago is obviously essential—that for example Proust writes like Rousseau, or that Stendhal writes like Rousseau, even though, if one is experienced, one can recognize the transmission very well in those texts. There is in literary language a transmission that can be conscious—this is what is called intertextuality when one is in academe—but in fact, it is memory. Language is at once brand-new, each time I write I speak French for the first time, and at the same time it has a fabulous memory, which is either conscious—I have the bookshelves in front of me and I know the texts by heart—but I'd say rather that it is unconscious. There are sayings, there are repetitions [*redites*], but in general it is rather the transmission of a treasure, of a wonder that is handed down from generation to generation, from text to text, and that remakes each text differently, that moves, reinscribes, grafts, and transposes . . .

Often it works not through a disarticulation but through an articulation, a syntactical form, a phrase, a sentence that rebounds from one great text to another in an absolutely admirable way. Then what is most interesting, most fascinating, most necessary is a form of boldness; in journalistic practice it will be corrected by the copyeditor, whereas in literary art, in writing, one will refrain from trying to bring back to reason a text whose vitality lies precisely in the fact that it eludes reason, that it ceaselessly unreasons [*déraisonne*], which does not mean that it is mad, even if it borders on madness. I'll give an example: in Stendhal's *La Vie de Henry Brulard* there is a chapter that begins with little Henry's first memory, which I am unable to narrate to you, but it goes something like this: My first memory is to have bitten my cousin madame du Galland on the cheek, I was sitting beside her, she was so fat and red that I bit her . . . What is wonderful, of course, is that in the marvelous, condensed course of this childhood memory there's the three- to four-year-old little boy who is sitting on a meadow beside Madame Pison du Galland, but in the following sentence and thanks to the possible flow granted by the French language—moreover you will recognize the film technique applied in language at that moment: suddenly, close-up! in fact he's sitting beside the cheek, that is to say that Madame Pison du Galland has become an enormous cheek, and the little boy bites into the cheek . . . It is a wonder of literature because, in one small sentence, a whole scene at once real and phantasmatic appears through a trope [*tour*] of language.

Therefore, what this art, which we exercise, tells us is that language makes one see; it makes one see and think. It is that language, that efficiency of language I love and I attempt to free as much as possible. This is also what Jacques does in his texts, and it is interesting to realize this, especially for somebody one calls a philosopher, because one no doubt tends to think—much more for a philosopher than for a writer—that in action-oriented speech there is 90 percent mastery. And what he was saying a moment ago is true; what is admirable is that, after all, his thought is carried by language, something that may well be disturbing if one really wants to believe that the philosopher is the master onboard. Then, on what style would be, I completely agree with him. I was interested in what you were saying a moment ago, Jacques, about the different books and the different ways of crafting them [*factures*]. This is something that, in the history of my own writing, if I may say so, used to bother me, I felt kind of ashamed because I was saying to myself, each time I change books—no! it's not true, each time I change directions, because for me a book is a direction, it's something that goes, something that goes away and that I pursue—I was saying to myself, it's terrible, I have no style. In the naïveté of my beginnings I was looking and saying to myself, but each book is written totally otherwise; it absolutely obeys the necessity of this quest, since each time there is a quest, a questioning, and the means to go on with this quest, at that moment, must needs be suited to this quest. I cannot cross the desert in a boat, so my text will have to turn into a camel. You were using the theme of docility a moment ago, so I will take up that of submission: one is submitted to the demand of this mystery, which leads and claims the means. And one improvises these means, one improvises them continuously. Then one is a better improviser if one practises at the piano, I know it from experience, not because one has more mastery but because one has greater suppleness, because at that moment the call coming from what goes in front of me receives a much quicker verbal, linguistic response, and this is indispensable.

Translated by Laurent Milesi

15

"TODAY" (2006)

FROM *INSISTER OF JACQUES DERRIDA*

"Everything has changed"   "Nothing has changed"

I write these two sentences on the same line but separeunifying them with a "blank," a voiceless, bottomless, depthless spacing. Today 10 March 2005, I write the word today. Today, a word that you give us with great frequency. I just stumbled on a today, one of your numerous todays, the one on to which I have just stumbled, tripped, staggered, and thus begun to think, is situated page 17 *États d'âme* . . .

> By attempting to take another step, I will be asking whether, today, here and now, the word and the concept of resistance still remain appropriate. Do they represent the most strategic, most economical lever for thinking what is going wrong, what is not going well in the world on the subject and in the vicinity of psychoanalysis, between it and it, if I can say that? What is going wrong? What is not going well? What is suffering and complaining? Who is suffering from what? What is the grievance of psychoanalysis? What registers of mourners has it opened? To be signed by whom?[1]

—but I open *Resistances*, it is there from the first page. It is today a little bit everywhere with you. It's what the weather's like, it's the time of day. How many todays, a herd, an army, the word of cunning and naïvety, the impossible today that's yours, *le vierge, le vivace, le bel* the rebel today.

A signature, a word that you privilege, uproot replant, make pivot, surplus-value, overvalue, from one day to the other text, that you persecute, that expects your perjury, that you make into a perjury, that makes you a perjurer, perjurcuter, that turns you into a ram drives you up a wall, you will never have stopped todaying one has only to read you I say to myself and instantly you today with your eternal mischievousness, you have always been ready for everything, ready and prepared, for absence like presence, absence like the other presence, presence like the other absence, I have only to read you, and you are here. Here and now, it's enough to make you laugh. —Laugh or weep? you say. —Laugh, weep, laughweep, we say, it's the same. —Do you hear what you have just written what I have just read?

A word that has not changed at all will never change his way of working a text, of pricking it, spurring it, making it stagger, or to add another recurrent, insisting word, "*marcher,*" walk, work, run, etc., "making it work, run," putting a text in motion, turning it on and on time—

the same word, totally changed in my eyes, in my soul, sent, sent away, before me, by the wounded heart of my soul,—of my 2005 thinking so changed since last year and yet the same, this today, a later today, loaded with messages and lurking thoughts. It is here now, you say, this today, you say, which one I say, the one of the year 2000 you say, listen, I am talking to you you say, here now, I read you today I say, the one of the year 2005, the same, and so what do you say? Here, page 45 of *États d'âme* . . . you say, I take perhaps a few steps (you always take a few steps, a few *pas*, don't you?) (perhaps):

> I would perhaps have taken a few steps in the direction of the self-analysis that I was evoking a moment ago. My own, perhaps, which does not interest many people, barely myself, for example around the questions that made me choose to speak to you today about the death drive, as I have done too often, but especially about cruel suffering, and that cruelty that is found at the center of a seminar, the last one, that I thought I had to devote elsewhere, and this is not fortuitous, to the death penalty. But well beyond my own, which is not worthy of your attention, it is the direction of the self-analysis of the Estates General of Psychoanalysis that I will take my chances more surely.[2]

And now you worry about the translators, the man or woman translator, how is he is she going to read you, is he is she going to be able to, you worry, with that emotion of tenderness, always on the alert here—you say, you confess, that once again you've made them a present. Thus a poisoned present. You believe—

You are quite embarrassed about it, you are delighted about it

you disculpate yourself of what you accuse yourself of, you know (that) you don't know what you have done yet

psychoanalysis would be, I said at the outset, the only possible approach, and without alibi, to all the virtual translations between the cruelties of a suffering "for the pleasure of it," of the making-suffer or the letting-suffer in this way, of the making-oneself or letting-oneself suffer, oneself, one another, the ones and the others, and so forth, according to all the grammatical persons and the implicit verbal modes—active, passive, middle voice, transitive, intransitive, and so on. Wrongly, in contradiction with these premises, the conclusion one has just read might then seem to accredit at least one difference between two crimes, between two transgressions of the "Thou shalt not kill": between, on the one hand, the murder that consists in killing the other, in him- or herself or in oneself, and, on the other hand, what is commonly called suicide, or the crime against oneself.

. . .

if a forgiveness can be asked, according to good common sense, for the evil inflicted, for the wrong, the crime, the offense of which the other is, by my doing, the victim, can I not also have to be forgiven the evil I am suffering from? "Forgive me for the hurt I feel, my heart, there where no one wants to hurt me, for hence comes the hurt I do to you without wanting to, without faith or law, *sans foi ni loi* . . ."

Avoir mal, faire mal, vouloir du mal, en vouloir à quelqu'un (to feel hurt, to cause hurt, to wish evil, to begrudge someone): I already imagine the sufferings of the translator who would like to respect each of these three words: *d'avoir à faire mal à quelqu'un* (to have to hurt someone), not to mention *vouloir du mal à quelqu'un* (to wish hurt or evil on someone). An apparently impossible translation. The French language seems to me the only one that deals out such a fate or such a welcome to the unheard-of and absolutely singular configuration of these words, these very large words: *avoir, faire, vouloir,* and *mal.*

—Am I somehow to blame for this impossibility of translation? For the impossibility of translating word for word?

—No, of course not, it's in the language. You inherit it.

—Yes I am, on the contrary; look what I'm doing with this inheritance. I'm betraying its truth.

—Is the alibi still avoidable? Is it not already too late?[3]

You accuse yourself of that which you are innocent—

It is endless, the ring of guilt, you slip it on yourself—

You worry that you have once again written some *pasje*—apparently impossible to translate (to the ear: *pages*; to the eye: *notI* or *stepsI*). And you congratulate yourself. It is what you desire and what you wish for yourself, to be always the last of the last, the very first and the last. Your followers-pursuers, whom you are careful to shake off, are between you and yourself, you in advance and you in *après*-sence

"I already imagine," you say; the "apparently impossible translation"

—"Am I somehow to blame for this impossibility of translation?" says one of your ghost voices. Ghost-voice-ghost-writer.

—No of course not says one of your voices

—Yes of course—you say to yourself

You think all the time *à la* translation—(yet another idiomatic French form) with the help of, in the direction of, by force of, you think across yourself, all crossed up with translation, you write with several voices and each one of your ghosts thinks of the other, with the other . . .

You think all the time of defying it, calling to it. Your thinking ventures into the regions of the not yet and the perhaps, zones of trembling approaches, surprises, surceases. Of all those *sur*'s that launch thought beyond its limits.

To go there, into these groundless, bottomless regions, you invent fragile and supple sur-words.

I read you. Chance would have it that I was already of your language, chance of destiny, chance of two destinies which we knew nothing about at the beginning when we arrived each one from his or her side by the same route and the same path from an outer-edge of France to the other edge, called, pushed and called each of us, by his or her desire, a mad irresistible desire, to move toward the heights, toward the north, and the head, toward the capital of the language, dashing straight, each one for himself, for herself toward the lips and the tongue—of French,

each one of us, transported before knowing by the vital need to go gather up as close as possible to the source the flow of the language.

You think *à la* translation I say—

Which does not mean that you write thinking of translation into foreign languages. It is the foreignness, the strangeness of French that strikes you, that you cause to spurt, to spring up again, that you make resonate, the strangeness yours, the one you feel as soon as you rub against this language that you have and that is not yours. It is in the narrow margin of the "monolingualism of the other" that you find yourself and that I am going to look for you.

Among all other languages, the language that speaks French or that the French speak or that are spoken in French, an exacerbated language, galloping until it's carried away, bit between the teeth, over-excited, overidiomed, capable of every kind of mobility in the world, that of the bird, that of the feline, that of the ant, that of the poem, that of Time, that of the unconscious, you initiated by Gide (J.D.) me at Joyce (James?) that of the Swan, which is to say of the *Cygne*, which is to say of the Sign

up to the drunken beating of the wing, the *coup d'aile ivre*

up to the blow of the books, the *coup des livres*

To read in order to deliver with a beating of the wings, with a drunken blow by her, *d'un coup d'aile, d'un coup d'elle ivre*, the transparent glacier of the flights that have not flown

Un cygne d'autrefois se souvient que c'est lui

Tearing, torn, this lecture, but also delivering, *magnifique mais qui sans espoir se délivre*

Beneath the ice, beneath the ice

I'm alarmed by you I say

Tu ne l'as pas volé, you asked for it. *Pour n'avoir pas chanté la région où vivre*

—*Je ne l'ai pas volé* you say. How to translate that? "I asked for it," yes, but no: "I didn't steal it," "I didn't fly it."

Library, archive of stolen flights in flight but always ready should the ice be broken to take again to the air

I do not stop reading you, you do not stop speaking to me "today," of today.

What am I saying there? How do I say this saying?

I listen to myself. I repeat myself. I hear:

1) First, right away, I say *you*, that is, *tu*.

Where did I si*tu*ate myself? Where if you are I, *si tu es je*—I am you, I follow you—

In the interior forum you speak of in *Rams*—

In the forum of uninterruption.

2) I read you: you read yourself to me. You speak to me. This *tu* speaks to me. You play on the *tu*.[4] You tease me this sentence. Certain times you say to me: *tu parles!* [You're telling me, you must be joking, you bet, but also simply, you speak!] This *tu speaks (to) us*. As you would say that the animal looks at us.

Most often, speaking of him in writing, I say *you*, that is, *tu*. This *you* is not in my control, it is stronger than me. As for him, you say rather "she" of me. He says Hélène, or Hélène Cixous, or H.C.

When, in my seminar, I share him with my friends or listeners, it's "Derrida" that I offer to a reading, that I extend. It's because he is, since forever, this *tu* in me that speaks, who speaks of living, my complication, my accomplice, my interior force stronger than me. But everyone knows that there is more than one *tu*, he himself made the innumerable and complex inventory in *Geneses* . . .

To whom is she speaking, with these months and me's, you [*tu*] and you [*vous*] so as to recount my death, yours, your death, and your faces; your death can be hers, that of the me who is speaking and who speaks to herself, the one spoken of from the other place of the dream or the death of the you [*tu*] who, further on, in the same paragraph will be dissected, we shall see, with all the resources of its untranslatable homonymy, that is, of these irreducible French homonymies, whose language all dreams recall (*tu* meaning *toi, t, u, tu*, that which is struck dumb with the silence of the verb *taire* and *se taire* [to hush, hush up], *le tu* [the you, the silenced] of the secret, *le tu* as the genius of the secret: genius *qui est tu* [who is you, who is silenced], etc. Just as months of tears have gone by, like a period of time and the multiplicity of I's or me's who are others, four weeks and just so many *egos*, so there is the *tu* who is you and knows to fall silent or impose silence concerning itself).[5]

There is one for him, one for you, one for the National Library.

Yet this *tu* is indeed him, the one who speaks to me in the tube of the so-very-interior ear that right away I say *tu* to him, I echo internally—Io!—it is the young and green and perpetual *tu*, which I clearly hear, it's true, rise up from among the *tu*'s that have fallen silent or been killed, *tus* or *tués*, or don't know who you are who silences, *qui tu es qui tait*.

Yet, she is since forever for him the cause come from without of an astounding explosion:

> I already wondered what was happening here, the landing in full flight or the take-off lights ablaze of an unheard-of speech, the appearance of an unidentifiable letter and literary object. What *is* this? I asked myself more or less. What is happening here? What is happening to me? What genre? Who could ever read this? Me?[6]

Naturally, there is no opposition between outside and inside, everything that happens happens only at the line of nondemarcation, at the edging, at the self's exinterior, in the outside of the inside, that doubly locked heart that he calls the secret. The event does not happen, does not arrive, it arrives only as not identifiable, it arrives a long time before itself, it arrives for the eternity that has (not) begun (un)beknownst and (nowhere) in plain sight to the designated parties, it comes to be recognized only after itself, a long time after many years after its *landing in flight*, later. To be sure right away there will be promise. And date. But what will later make of the moment an event is the endurance of the promise. It takes time, all of time. Until once again we find ourselves there. When one day this day comes back to us, it's because, having made the rounds of time, it comes back as event.

It is beyond oblivion that an unforgettable makes appearance. Something that had no name, except a borrowed one.

▦ ▦ ▦

—You are *my insister*, he says to me.

This can be heard and understood only in a foreign land where we find ourselves beneath the same *Passat*, Celan would say, with the trade wind for canopy.

What pleases me no end in this word, which you give me as a present, your found object, your genius discovery, this feminine or masculine untranslatable, is that I can likewise turn it round on you. You too you are *my insister. My insisting.*

Translated by Peggy Kamuf

6

THE THEATER OF
HÉLÈNE CIXOUS

REMEMBERING
REFASHIONINGS,
AND REVENANTS

JUDITH G. MILLER

Hélène Cixous writes to re-member and to bear witness. Through words, she offers to the reader's body expressive rhythms that keep memory alive, delivering from silence past events or engrained attitudes, a writerly operation capable of illuminating the present.[1] Her accidental encounter with the theater has made her apprehend words as flesh,[2] for in theater re-membering happens in "real" time, "real" space, and through the sinews of those entrancing and entranced beings she calls actoresses.[3] This materiality creates simultaneously and paradoxically, as theater is wont to do, a world of the imaginary in which all senses contribute to the spectators' knowledge, stretching and often surpassing words. Cixous's theater work thus strains toward realizing the "eye that listens" and "the eye that touches" evoked throughout her writing.

Generous and sensitive to the theatrical process, Cixous recognizes the indispensable place of actors and directors in making theater happen. Consequently, and most particularly since 1984 in her role as company writer for Le Théâtre du Soleil, writing for the theater has evolved as the most collective of the many communal ways in which she deploys her gifts. Her work with director Ariane Mnouchkine and the some-seventy-member Soleil troupe has multiplied the opportunity to reflect on and experience the practice of "othering"—generating through character portrayal multiple and more enabling forms of subjectivity. Embraced by the Soleil and its organic creative methods, she has allowed her theater texts to be cut and edited during rehearsals.[4] On the other hand, she has clearly oriented the Soleil's interest in placing women characters at the heart of its dramatic endeavors. The four plays written to date for Le Théâtre du Soleil—epic in scope, historical and/or mythic in nature—speak convincingly to the shared vision and delicate complicity of artists for whom theater must be both nonvoyeuristic and nurturing.[5]

Cixous, however, also privileges another kind of theater writing, originating plays she calls chamber theater or what we might call tone poems.[6] These works, eight in all, explore, among other things, the construction of women's subjectivity, poetic identity, and the kind of resistance to totalitarianism possible through writing.[7] Freely structured, more lyrical on the whole than her epic pieces, these works often spatialize the radical thinking underlying her essays and prose fiction.[8] They also foreground the slipperiness of meaning, double entendres, wordplay, mood switches, comedic parody, and register changes found to a lesser degree in all her theater work and in her writing in general.[9] Since 1990, director Daniel Mesguich has given voice and dramatic form to many of these pieces.

Despite the differences in the two types of theater work she composes, striking central features permit us to speak of a Cixousian theatrical universe, re-membering being key. For all Cixous's plays not only body forth but also unearth characters and/or situations from the realm of forgetfulness or deceit. They refashion or inflect already existing myths, mythic figures, or mythic departures for understanding social practices and human behaviors.[10] They deal in revenants, stirring up the ghosts of our cultural habits, steaming up the mirrors in which we see ourselves and each other. In this they resonate with the Derridean project of undoing the precisely knitted veil of the natural and the normal, a veil that hides and disguises power. Having both "ethical and spiritual usefulness,"[11] Hélène Cixous's theater mobilizes consciousness.

Four of her plays, excerpted in part 6, *The Name of Oedipus: Song of the Forbidden Body* (1978), *The Indiad or India of Their Dreams* (1987), *Rouen, the Thirtieth Night of May '31* (2001), and *The Blindfolded Fiancée or Amelait* (2004), illustrate particularly well—although quite dissimilarly[12]—the work of re-membering, of bringing back and birthing anew, of plunging into myth to debunk myth. Each of these plays invokes a myth in order to challenge the system that the myth supports and propagates. Each, in its own efforts at "remything," decenters the male figures or idea of masculinity propping up the patriarchal structure—

a structure that is perhaps the hardest myth of all to dislodge. Each thus recasts central characters in such a way that the binaries male/female and masculine/feminine are undone, or at the least troubled, and that the limitations of gender roles and gendered thinking are exposed. All denounce more or less prominently the pressure of political and social expectations upon the individual; the collusion between a certain education and power; political bodies' apparent need to assert themselves by killing and controlling; and the tendency to scapegoat and marginalize.

Oedipus, a libretto for a score by André Boucourechliev, revisits the oedipal myth scripted by Sophocles and remapped by Freud and later Lacan. Through linguistic manipulation and a plurality of voices, Cixous shakes up the incest taboo as understood by Freud to determine gender and by Lacan to determine subjecthood.[13] Whizzing, spinning, dancing a web of words, Cixous's mother and son lovers multiply their relationships with one another. They abolish time, attempting to exist in a perpetual present where invention is always possible and where one can outstrip the limits imposed on the mind.

Cixous paints in the end, nonetheless, an Oedipus who cannot say "no" (*non*) to his name (*nom*). Determined by the myth of "Oedipus" as leader and pariah, he heeds the call of "The City," rather than cleaving to the woman he loves, a love of such intensity that he feels himself awash in the sea (*la mer*) she (*la mère*) represents. Jocasta, on the contrary, the dominant presence throughout the work, exults in her passion and desire. She is neither Freud's "unknowable," nor Lacan's "necessary absence," but rather a celebrant of the forbidden body. She fights against the pull of the "law" that would separate her from her love and holds her couple together by demanding a unitary we: "We," Oedipus sings, "continues." Like Molly Bloom, Jocasta says "yes," urging Oedipus to invent a liberated language, freed from closed linguistic systems.

The Indiad, a six-hour production when first performed by the Théâtre du Soleil, engages with an historical figure whose impact was such that he has become mythic. In Cixous's dramatic examination of the 1947 partition of India, Mahatma Gandhi is at once huge and small, awesome and awed, sweet and determined. He is present but also disseminated, doubled by feminine others (the Baul pilgrim Haridasi, the performing she-bear Moona Balou) and seconded by the most virile of men, Ghaffar Abdul Khan, the leader of the Pathans. Cixous presents a multiplied, maternal, and timeless Gandhi who holds up as hope against civil war and genocide the utopia of a loving nonviolence.

Degendered, Gandhi opposes the many vengeance machines made up of unthinking "men" who refuse to listen: the members of the Muslim League led by Mohammed Ali Jinnah and those of the Congress Party headed by Jawaharlal Nehru. Cixous's *Indiad*, unlike its model, *The Iliad*, exalts the peacemaker rather than the warrior hero and rehearses the pathos in nationalist-fueled killings and blood feuds. It gestures, through association, at the hideousness of all fratricidal wars, particularly those currently decimating many parts of the globe (Israel and Palestine, the former Yugoslavia, Central Africa). Haridasi, the connector between all the various groups as well as between the actors and the audience, reminds us continuously how categories, castes, and marginalization limit the possibilities of healthy being. An inhabitant of several realms, she finds in lyrical verse the reason to continue.

Cixous's *Rouen,* like *Oedipus* a polyphonic dramatic poem, splendidly alliterative and onomatopoeic, shows a Joan of Arc who neither matches the traditional mythic image of the virginal warrior nor reenacts saintly martyrdom to French nationalism. This is not a play about the grandeur of an all-powerful God who speaks to the simple at heart or about the greatness of a France beholden to a miraculous girl child. Cixous's frightened and vulnerable Joan hears no voices. No one even calls her on the telephone. Like the ostracized Jews of mid-twentieth-century Europe to whom she is compared through allusion and anachronism, Joan of Arc is scapegoated, reduced to ashes by a petty bureaucrat. She waits and she longs, but her fate will be to disappear in flames, while the wind (words, music, song) scatter her being over the face of the earth.

Some twenty-five characters, ranging from "the usual suspects" in histories of Joan of Arc—La Hire, La Trimouille, Charles VII, Bishop Cauchon—to medieval devil figures, Napoleon Bonaparte, a moralizing chorus, and a chorus of contemporary sports journalists question her trajectory throughout French history: Is she female or male; a con artist or simply naive? A twinned Joan bandies between her two selves—myths of her sorcery and monstrousness. Joan also understands that indeterminate gender is unacceptable to kingly men. Her most relentless persecutor, Cauchon, a true pig (*cochon*) and thus anathema to the "people of the book," a racist, a clod, and an Eichman-like technocrat, concocts an absurd story to condemn her alleged devil worship, when all she had asked for, again in a nod to the Shoah, was "authorization to continue to live and work." He takes credit for constructing the myth of a Joan sacrificed for France, while his behavior shows him capable of setting up countless holocausts that, in fact, could never be justified. Another Joan emerges in the last lines of the play, one symbolized by the roses that bloom irrepressibly in her mother's garden. A revenant summoning all revenants, this Joan escapes from the combined murderous powers of Church, State, and University. She, contrary to Cauchon, perfumes the air.

Hamlet haunts Cixous's theater.[14] *The Blindfolded Fiancée* takes this mythic theater piece and inscribes it onstage in a loopy and pun-riddled spoof of a text-in-the-making. All the characters are already "characters," their story known. But, thanks to the structure of mise en abyme, their story ripens and changes. Cixous pits the scholar/writer Hamlet—"Amelait" in the play, or a milky (*lait* or "feminine" in Cixousian terms) chaotic soul (*âme*) and by homophony an ugly one (*laid*)—against the author/filmmaker William Shakespeare and the passionate, feisty reader/writer, Reguine (a reworked Ophelia). Not one of these writers, not even the neurotic raconteur Amelait, controls the story, one that finds him dead, as expected, at play's close. Even Shakespeare finds his characters escaping him, usurping plot and dialogue. Against prototype, Reguine manages nonetheless to survive, sidestepping the devastation wrought on her by man-of-letters Amelait, who sends her a tricky, poisonous, and personified Letter (*lettre*) and who toys unconscionably with her being (*l'être*).

Focused on "to write and to be" (*lettre et l'être*) rather than on "to be or not to be" (*être ou ne pas être*), Cixous asks: "In which fiction should we believe?" Of the many themes *Hamlet* proposes, she has not chosen to query vengeance, nor political renewal, nor incestuous longings (although she hints at all of these), but rather to wonder about who creates the stories that create us. Reguine finally perceives that Amelait (truly and maddeningly "a melee" in bilingual punning) tells them both false stories, while Amelait fathoms that he has believed in the silliest fiction of all: longing for the glory of his warmongering father who proves to be a blowhard superego and a self-involved specter trying to clone himself through his son. The additional character of The Mole, a polyvalent figure conjuring up, among other possibilities, Amelait's desire, his unconscious, the tunneling underbelly of the searching mind—a being who sees through touch, who prompts the truth—decamps at the dying Amelait's request. She—for the mole is female—migrates from Amelait to Reguine. The Mole will thus help Reguine carry on more lucidly the work of living. Contrary to Ophelia in *Hamlet*, Reguine's worth shines forth in a feminized Elsinore, where all the servants are female and where father figures have either been replaced by mothers (Polonius by Reguine's mother) or demoted: Claudius/Fredegond is a mere dent in Gertrude/Gerutha's bed.

All four of these plays also summon the liminal or the space of myth—a space free of borders, full of promise and possibilities, in-between and connecting at least two realms, confusing the inside and the outside at once. Singing and talking their "song of the forbidden body," Jocasta and Oedipus breach borders, blending into and incorporating each other, no longer knowing where one stops and the other begins, realizing, as the polyphonic structure of the libretto makes clear, a form of intersubjectivity, a bisexual whole. In *The Indiad* the dreams of separation of the Muslim League clash with the dreams of unity of the Congress Party, but Gandhi and his doubles, Haridasi and Moona Balou, hold everything together, magically transporting themselves from one end of India to the next—from Bombay to the Himalayan highlands on the border of Afghanistan, from New Delhi to Bihar. These border crossers know no boundaries in their quest to blanket, permeate, and disarm with love a warrior mentality. In *Rouen* Joan of Arc's mind encloses all the scenic action, a mindscape that expands by analogy to include the five hundred years between 1431 and 1931 (an analogy suggested by the imprecision of the play's subtitle: *The Thirtieth Night of May '31*). Although imprisoned in a matchbox cell, Joan can both visualize the king who has abandoned her and call forth by allusion a future world where forsaking the sociohistorical "other" marks one of the most abhorrent crimes of the twentieth century. By their secret password, "Outside or inside?" "writers" and "characters" Amelait and Horatio in the Pirandello-like *The Blindfolded Fiancée* reveal the difficulty of peeling away all the layers of fiction that determine their actions. Like the other characters in the play, they float in an unhinged space of reading and interpreting.

Cixous's "remything project" always carries within it the seeds of its own destruction—and by that we mean the destruction of her reworked myth. Denouncing how myths take hold (Cauchon's construction of Joan of Arc, Lacan's Oedipus), Cixous's plays undercut the unquestioned authority of all myths, including her own. Gandhi's universal love in *The Indiad*, for example, does not successfully counter the Hitlerian rage mowing down European Jewry. Perhaps force is necessary after all? Moreover, her reanimated myths, contrary to the narratives with which they play, lack definitive conclusions. Open to interpretation, as are all vital myths, they fade to finish rather than build to a resounding resolution. Still asking questions (Will Reguine write herself? Is a dual-gendered or ungendered dual-sexual Oedipus obtainable? Can humans stop repeating the wars and genocides fueled by extreme nationalism?), Cixous's theater offers myths in process.

"Theater," says Cixous, "gathers and locates and makes communion possible. The pact is to agree upon a secure world within the world of representation. Thus anything can be staged safely."[15] Invoking a theatrical world out of the bounds of realism's constraints, Cixous—like her theatrical family: Aeschylus, Shakespeare, Genet, and Zeami—opens herself and her theater to anything that can happen or be dreamed to happen. In her mythic theater, she layers experience with reverie and poetic meditation and initiates deep psychological change through extreme stimulation of the mind and the senses.

16

THE NAME OF OEDIPUS: SONG OF THE FORBIDDEN BODY(1979)

TWELFTH MOVEMENT

(*Tiresias, Oedipus, Jocasta, Chorus*)

Tiresias:

I hear. I hear them look for each other. I hear the names they
gave each other. T hat was in the first bedchamber.

Oedipus:

Promise me never a lover but me
Me alone: your strength, your child, me
Your father if you will, myself
Your spouse, mother, your lover
Promise me never another king.

Jocasta:

You: my life, my day, my light, I promise you.
No, I will not promise you! I want you to ask me
Again and again. And every time tell me who you are for me.

Oedipus:

If you wish I shall be your impulse, you my grace, I your
new strength, your dance. If you wish, I shall be your
mother, and then I shall be your child.
You—my child first, if you wish . . .

Tiresias:

I hear their voices find each other, their breaths caressing each
other, fleeing, heeding each other.

Jocasta:

Tell me the time, tell me where,
Tell me when, tell me "us" in time, give me our time.

Oedipus:

I see the future. I call it to me. The future is you.
The future is happening to us. It is the present.
There is no time.

Jocasta:

And now?

Oedipus:

Now is the same as ever.
We are beginning. We are beginning.

Jocasta:

You will tell me everything?

Oedipus:

I shall tell you everything. And everything will have no end.

Jocasta:

Everything that you think? That you know.
That you do not know. You will say everything?

Oedipus:

I think so. I know it. Though I also do not know
It will be everything.

Jocasta:

Tell me where you are just now, at this moment in our story.

Oedipus:

I am everywhere your voice calls me. Wherever I am,
I see us.
I close my eyes, I see you before having met you,
from the beginning. I do not sleep. Even in dreams, I sleep

without sleeping to dive into time into your body,
To swim in your flesh that is the sea
Your waves rock me. Say "the sea."

Jocasta:

I say: the sea, the sea, the sea.

Oedipus:

As soon as you pronounce the word, I am on top of you, against
     you, in you, I am awash
in you, the whole of me
But it is in me that you, the entire sea, is rocked.

Jocasta:
    Uncurl my waves,
    One after the other, the whole
    Of me in you. I, the sea,
    My naked billows, my
    Tongue, my fingers, my breezes,
    my hands on you.

Chorus:
    Look to your body for the words
    That set fire to the soul.

Jocasta:
    Are you here?

Oedipus:
    Yes. I am here.

Jocasta:
    Here forever?

Oedipus:
    As long as I live
    I am here.

Jocasta:
    Here? Where? Tell me your
    name.
    Say "I" again.
    Tell me: "I am here."
    Come here again and again.
    Swear to me.
    Swear to me for every single day.

Chorus:
    So very close!
    Between them
    nothing can slip in.
    —Death?
    —Not between them. Impossible.
    But perhaps in her?
    —No.
    —In him?
    —Possibly.
    Death could not separate them,—
    Not happen to them,—
    It might come
    afterward, after their life,
    one day after their death.

Oedipus:

Every day I shall swear it. I swear it to you, today.
I am here. Yes. I am here. I am in Thebes for you.

Jocasta:

No, not in Thebes! Closer, closer. Do not be here. Be the city. Be
the air. Be the sky. Surround me.

Oedipus:

I am the air. I fill the room. It is I you breathe.

Jocasta:

So far away! The room has disappeared! Everything contains
me!
Who are you in this bed? Who are you in my arms? You
are never enough me? I cannot go on! I am torn apart with love.
I do not know you! I
do not envelop you! I fail to touch you! I fail to approach you! I
touch you; my hand
burns on your shoulder. Tell me that I touched you!

Oedipus:

Yes. You are touching me. You have reached me.
It is I, yes, it is my body made flesh by your flesh.
Do you hear me?

Jocasta:

Ah! I have become a stranger to myself. Tormented by such joy!
If you should feel the presence of such love within you, you
would not be frightened.

Oedipus:

Frighten me, then, share your joy!

Jocasta:

How can I stop this suffering? Stop feeling the grief of not
being you, of not being inside you.
When my lips touch yours?

Oedipus:

    We must find a way. I want to go where your heart beats. I will
        enter your chambers and
    take your heart in my hands and caress it.

Jocasta:

    I will be your blood. For it is only there,
    In the flesh, in the folds of the chambers
    That pain can cease. That love can rest.

Oedipus:

    I will go where I am no longer myself. I no longer want to
        have
    a name.
    No other name than you, for you.

Jocasta:

    No longer to know, no longer to think. But to live, to be life, to
        be the fire and the light.

Oedipus:

    There is no word for this. Only gestures . . .

Jocasta:

    This gesture: You are standing, I am in your arms, you turn
        slowly
    and we see the entire Earth together. Say "we."

Oedipus:

    "We" is one. "We" continues.

Jocasta:

    This moment was born of yesterdays before time.

Oedipus:

    Where is the shoulder that reaches further than the edge of the
        world?
    Now I am walking on the grass of your shoulder. I am going
        further than the Earth.

Jocasta:

> Life opens up, it is within me, it is before me, it expands. And it is
> us. A breeze ruffles my hair. It is the breath of life.

Oedipus:

> Why? Why? Why are you woman? How are you woman?
> You must give me the whole of her, everything.

Jocasta:

> Take Jocasta, tear her off, undo her, tear her off from me!

Jocasta:
I remember being
Life.
And now, who?
I remember loving
Love, you, life in person. And now—
Still loving you, but I do not know who you are. No
Other lover but you, but who is
"You," now?
I see the one who was my life,
Looking without seeing me, as if he were
My death.

Chorus:
Now who is loved in the place of the beloved?

Jocasta:

> Tear me apart, empty me out, shred me, weave a new space with
> the fibers of my body!

Oedipus:

> How many hours, how many years were my lips on your belly to
> have embraced you once?

Jocasta:

> I expand to love you further and further still.
> Larger, wider, more vast.
> At night I think I cannot love you more. I have reached the limits
> of myself, of love.
> But this morning infinity explodes, and I love you still further.

Oedipus:

> I will not sleep anymore. I do
>> not want to wake up
> Next to your body.
> I want to live the night that is
>> your flesh,
> Turn the sky and Earth upside
>> down.
> This sky is not motionless; it
>> is the sea.
> I want to climb back up each
>> vein, to follow your blood
> Across all times, up until
> The first drop.

Chorus:

> *Who could believe that there was*
>> *an end to infinity?*

Jocasta:

> *I see my life before me*
> *But my life no longer sees me*
> *And I feel myself dying outside*
>> *myself.*

Jocasta:

> Yesterday, we are beginning; I entered us without delay, carried
> to the center of us—here my blood is your blood.

Chorus:

> *Because it was written,*
> *Expected, promised,*
> *Incredible, so very*
> *Incredible.*
> *Not desired, not hoped for—*
> *A killing blow.*

Oedipus:

> Before your voice called me
> Who was "me"?
> Where was I when I had not seen you?

Jocasta:

Yesterday, you were coming.

Jocasta:

Yesterday, silence is not silence. Yesterday in the room in your arms where we had withdrawn this silence was singing. Do you hear it? It was a peace song. We had given it birth. It lives outside us from now on. It continues.

Jocasta:

That was yesterday. I do not even remember it. Absence has become absence. This silence does not sing. This silence clutches my throat.

Oedipus:

I hear everything, but I cannot turn my eyes.
I hear everything with my dead eyes.

Jocasta:

Yesterday, you must go to Thebes. I know it.
Go. You must go. But love holds you back.
Love prevents you from leaving. You say: I am leaving.

Oedipus:

I am about to leave. Right now. In a moment. Minute.

Jocasta:

Words drift like feathers
On our lips, I laugh. You stay.

Oedipus:

Love is stronger
Than I. I say: I am leaving.
Love decided that I stay.
It wants me to carry you away.
Quickly we live several lives in one minute.

Jocasta:

That was yesterday.
Today: the desert.

The dance is dead.
My arms too heavy, my hands—too weak.
My blood—dried up. A metal hand rips
My heart out. I was us. Now I am no one. I am this desert.

Tonight no longer alive, I see myself dead. I see myself dead. I see
my body lying. I am alone as never before, my body laid in
a coffin, not wept over, not hidden, not remembered. I want
to die.

No one is free to die in such loneliness.
Tell me the word that gives death or life.
Tell me,
Say it. Give me a sign.
How to die, how not to die.
How to end it? When? Where? Why?
I do not know what you want.

> *Jocasta:*
> The worst is to have seen him leave
> Without knowing if he would ever again
> Return the same.

I want, but I dare not. I cannot manage to end my life.
Your silence kills me. Your silence forbids me to die.

> *Without ever knowing what it is you wanted me*
> *To be—for you—,*
> *Without ever having understood*
> *What I might have been.*

Yesterday, I told him:
"If I should die, a breath from you would give me back
My life. If I stopped hearing, if I were lying
In the dark, if I expired, if you lean over me, call me by your name,
I will hear it. Tell me your name,
Oedipus! I shall cease dying."
It was the truth, I remember it was true.

I believed everything. Everything was true.
I believe even now.

Oedipus:
Every word hurts me; every question wounds me,
I am not deaf.
I hear too much.

I feel the past rejecting me
If he does not remember even if he does come back, I cannot come
  back, not yesterday, today, or tomorrow. Nor forget. Nor stay.

Jocasta:	*Chorus:*
Yesterday, I live, I believe, I hear your voice.	*Because he does not turn around.*
I enter, I leave, I have a body, I have a face.	*Because he does not glance* *At her.*
My eyes dive into your eyes.	*He does not utter her name.*
My blood surges; my blood exults.	*Not a word for a month.*
Your voice fondles my heart.	*Thirty days, thirty nights,*
Joy lifts me up, transports me	*Thirty years without life.*
Over foreign lands, around the world.	*He is not here. I saw him this morning.*
I arrive at a wall.	*And his face was hard.*
A laugh of fire springs from my mouth.	*He was gone, he was dead.*
The wall opens wide. I go through	*He was lost.*
between times.	*His body turned into a desert,*
I move on, I roam through bottomless Space.	*His heart rotted.*
The abyss is there, I do not fall in.	
I accept everything, I dance,	
I run on the air, pleasure carries me along.	
I believed, I believed . . .	

Chorus:
This morning. I think he still wants to love.
Love held firm.
Then love broke down. Suddenly
No strength left.
He wants to leave.
He cannot find the door.
No door left. No window.
No opening. His teeth—clenched. His voice—
strangled.

Jocasta:
I was absolutely sure. This morning a burning wind wakes me,
my bed goes up in flames.
Time! Time has caught fire.
Leaping toward you my blood is ablaze.
I dash—
The ground gives way; love does not protect us.
The air does not support me. I collapse.
Infinity deserts and absence
Engulfs me.
. . .

Translated by Christiane Makward and Judith G. Miller

17

THE INDIAD OR INDIA OF THEIR DREAMS (1987)

ACT 1, SCENE 2

(*In the Himalayas. On the Indo-Afghan frontier. 1939. Enter the Mahatma Gandhi and Abdul Ghaffar Khan.*)

Haridasi:

The Mahatma Gandhi! *Jai Guru!*

Gandhi:

Blest is this region of yours, my dear Abdul Ghaffar Khan. Everything here is big, the mountains, the men, your Pathans who from their great height look down on my bald pate.

Khan:

These mountains gave birth to us Pathans. The Himalayas are our mothers. This is the highest point of the High Zone and from here you can see half the world. There lies our Afghanistan ... I can see Kabul and beyond it. That way is Russia and China over there.

Gandhi:

And up there the sky. Which is bigger here too than anywhere else. And this is where India starts! Enthusiasm grips me!

Impossible here to think small. Take me down again. Come, to work! Our Pathan sons are waiting for us. Go and look for them! For five minutes I shall remain alone with God.

(*Abdul Ghaffar Khan leaves.*)

Haridasi:

But where are all the women? Have they hidden them?

Gandhi:

O God, Thou knowest how important this region is for me. These last years I have retreated so far that my back is now against the Himalayas. And it is here at the foot of this rampart that my fate—Thine too—will be decided. Of all Indians the Pathans are the most Islamic. The most virile, violent, and warlike of brigands. So if Abdul Ghaffar Khan and I convert *them*, of all people, to our nonviolence, it will be a great triumph! What an example for the Hindus, the Sikhs, and all those political parties! The whole of India will be enlightened.

(*Enter Hermann Kallenbach.*)

My dear Hermann, I've finished. You can come.

You see how sad he is, my dear Kallenbach, my old companion. Because the West has forgotten about God. His ears are deaf with cannon fire. The shadow cast by Germany has fallen over the minds of men, who cut each other's throats in the dark. Yes, Hermann, we'll resist this universal folly. The clouds at our feet are floating vessels. And I entrust my most far-ranging thoughts to them, so they can carry them on to Europe and America. You see, it's here I shall raise the first citadel of Peace.

(*Enter Abdul Ghaffar Khan, Ghani, Goulam, Tughlak, and Masud Khan the Schoolmaster.*)

Khan:

Mahatma, these two men, Goulam and Tughlak, arrived at dawn from Bannu to enroll in our army. They walked all night.

Gandhi:

That's good, I am delighted to see you.

Khan:

But I'm afraid they are angry.

Goulam:

What are we to do, Mahatmaji? It was at Kohar we became angry. I am wanting to enroll in the army of Badshah Khan's Servants of God. But at Kohar my brother is telling me that a Pathan without a rifle is no man, but a man without. A billy goat without balls! How do I answer him?

Khan:

Am I not a man?

Haridasi:

None but *men* here!

Khan:

Not one of the Servants of God has a rifle. And they're more goatish than the goats, stronger than the strongest, and more human than most men.

Tughlak:

The proof, my king, please. The proof?

Khan:

Listen. Do you love the thought of death?

Tughlak:

No.

Khan:

Yet all your life you are obsessed with it. Your son was born with a sword in his hand, a rifle in his cradle. Before he knew how to walk, over his head you poured all the vendettas of your clan. That was your blessing. He was born to avenge you and shed Pathan blood. Our life is a headlong race for death. Down we go, from bloodshed to bloodshed, from one bereavement to the next. And as we descend the ladder of life toward death, we weep.

Tughlak:

Me weep? Never!

Goulam:

Liar! For your brother Ali . . .

Tughlak:

Say that again . . .
(*They confront each other.*)

Ghani:

Respect! Have respect for my father!

Khan:

Men! Not in my presence! No, we are not happy people. We are
stiff with pride. But our hearts are no more than little pebbles
seeping pain.
We must stop this! Let us cast away the sword. Who is stronger
than a Pathan? A Pathan able to leave his home in the morning
with no weapon. And if he can't, he's a coward.

Goulam:

Do that, go out without a weapon, and this Tughlak shoots me
down!

Khan:

That is what *I* do. No weapon.

Goulam:

One day a neighbor shoots you down. What does your Ghani do
then? The day after?

Ghani:

The day after, I go out without a rifle.

Goulam:

But your father, what would he be saying if you don't take
revenge?!

Khan:

I *am* his father. And he obeys me. I have trained my son and all the Servants of God to rise above revenge. And I have guided them to far greater heights than you have ever reached, burdened as you are with all that metal, all those weapons. Where we are bound, you must be stronger than a man and lighter than a wild goose. We shall gather together way above men, higher up than the Khyber Pass, beyond fear and cowardly dishonor, as high as the feet of all-powerful Allah, up there in the antechamber of the clouds where the angels congregate.

Goulam:

Badshah Khan, that's where I'm wanting to go. But if Tughlak isn't coming, I'll be dead before I'm having the time to get there. Between us there is vendetta.

Khan:

Is that true, Tughlak? Yet you wanted to enrol?

Tughlak:

If Goulam's going, I go too. Because it may be a trick, Badshah Khan. He says: I'm going. Right. I'm getting up, laying down my rifle. Then he is shooting me down!

Gandhi:

My children, perhaps you haven't understood about our Paradise. It is reserved for the strong and the pure. All that hard metal you hang round you doesn't give you more strength, it's a sign that you haven't enough.

Schoolmaster:

How right! Oh, that's good. You peasants!

Gandhi:

I am glad you agree with me, Mr. . . . ?

Schoolmaster:

Mr. Masud Khan, headmaster of the school!

Gandhi:

Let us be clear. I belong to the caste of the Banyas. I know about figures, about weights and measures. Don't think I'd take counterfeit coins for gold. What we want, Badshah Khan and I, is nonviolence, twenty-four carat. You understand?

Goulam:

Oh yes! twenty-four carat! Yes, yes!

Gandhi:

Do you think it's enough to change your shirt when our aim is to change the Universe? You need a change of heart.

Goulam:

Change the Universe, Mahatmaji?

Haridasi:

Exactly.

Gandhi:

The Universe. It's not just on this Frontier that your swords will fall, like so many dead leaves from a tree, but in the whole wide world. That is our ultimate hope this year, this is our magnificent mission.

Schoolmaster:

So you intend our example to be followed by the Christians, Mahatmaji?

Gandhi:

Throughout the Western world, yes. And to start with, of course, in warlike Europe.

Schoolmaster:

That's right, I agree with that.

Gandhi:

There, today, destruction reigns and their Christ is no more than a despised and tarnished memory. Over there, deathly oblivion.

Here the source of life springs up again. And it's our Pathans who will bear the purifying water, first through all India, then as they follow the faltering sun from Asia, ancient mother of countless religions and their absolving rites, to where it sets at the world's end. We shall wipe away the blood, shed our tears, and restore to the face of the earth the smile its horrors have banished.

Kallenbach:

This wonderful explosion of energy may well succeed in stirring the hearts of Indians. As for the West, you're wasting your time. What is happening in Europe is past help and beyond belief.

Gandhi:

If I were a Jew, my dear Kallenbach, and born in Germany, I assure you I'd find some means of transforming Mr. Hitler.

Kallenbach:

Let's change the subject, Gandhiji, please!

Gandhi:

No! I stick to my idea. All we need is one Jew, full of imagination, as brave as your David or my Abdul Ghaffar Khan. And what would he do? He'd gather all his trembling people around him. Mr. Hitler being exceptionally wicked, a carbuncle on the heart of the world, an exceptional exploit is needed, as unique in History as is Mr. Hitler himself. The Jews can do it. So they should all set off together behind their German Moses, young men, old men, women and children, till they come to the top of a cliff.

Kallenbach:

You think they'd ever reach it? They wouldn't. They'd be stopped, arrested, at once in the street.

Gandhi:

But don't you stop *me*! Once on the edge of the cliff, all the people would cry upon Jehovah, and all together, with God's name on their lips, they would leap into the sea.

Tughlak and Goulam:

Allah u Akbar! . . . a whole army?

Kallenbach:

Gandhiji! I grieve for you. You say whatever takes your fancy.

Khan:

Mr. Kallenbach! You don't understand?

Gandhi:

You are wrong Hermann, and I'm right. For I promise you if the Jewish people made this sacrifice, it would set the whole world quaking with emotion. And you'd see the winter of your discontent transformed all at once into a springtime of hope.

Kallenbach:

But who would see the spring? A child that had drowned? The Messiah will come. One day after the world has ended.

Gandhi:

If the Jews take no action, what do you achieve? Death with no hope of spring! They should act and make of their end a beginning.

Kallenbach:

They jump to their death. Hitler says thank you to the sea, and carries on as before. He'll swallow up Belgium and France and soon he'll be facing England . . .

Gandhi:

So the English climb up on their cliffs . . .

Kallenbach:

You are mad, Mahatma. If we listened to you we'd turn the garden of the Universe into a plantation of corpses. Don't you realize that no heart beats in the breast of that monster?

Goulam:

No heart?

Tughlak:

In Assam there are men with no hearts, no insides at all.

Gandhi:

Don't listen to him! Mr. Hitler is a man. Every man can be saved. You should pray for Mr. Hitler, Hermann.

Kallenbach:

Pray for Hitler! Oh God! A man who murders me! No! I'm not staying here! What you're saying is sheer madness.

Gandhi:

Hermann! Don't go! Come back! Mr. Kallenbach!

Kallenbach:

No! I've had enough! I won't hear another word from you!

Gandhi:

Come back!

Kallenbach:

Er ist ganz meschugge!
(*He exits.*)

Khan:

Let him go, Gandhiji . . . Leave him alone.

Gandhi:

How violent he gets.

Schoolmaster:

I was about to say so too. Your friend is a violent man.

Gandhi:

Poor Kallenbach . . . The sufferings of his fellow Jews are driving him out of his mind.

Schoolmaster:

Oh, he's a Jew! I thought as much.

Haridasi:

And you, sir, what are you? Which caste are you?

Schoolmaster:

Me, you nincompoop? I'm a Muslim, aren't I?

Haridasi:

You a Muslim? So am I. Are you a nincompoop too?

Ghani:

Mr. Kallenbach! He's coming back! Followed by the Sardar Patel and the Pandit Nehru!

Schoolmaster:

The Sardar Patel and the Pandit Nehru? The leaders of the Congress Party? Here? In these mountains?! In my school! Impossible!

(*Enter Nehru, Azad, Patel and Kallenbach.*)

Gandhi:

Panditji! What brings you to these mountains?

Kallenbach:

The war, Gandhiji, it's war. Yesterday, England declared war on Germany.

Gandhi:

He Ram! Regrettably, she has a right to do so. But India . . .

Patel:

India! India learned she was at war from the newspapers! With no warning, no consultation, the Viceroy has declared us at war. They spit us out into the dust of battle. Rage and humiliation have added years to my life. What of India's honor now?

Gandhi:

It's the war that should concern us, my friends, not our pride. My God, what are we to do?

Patel:

We are uncertain, divided, Bapuji. I must tell you that more than one of our leaders is getting swept away by great visions of arms and cannons and heroic confrontation.

Gandhi:

It must be Panditji, dreaming about guns.

Azad:

He's not alone.

Nehru:

The moment has come, Bapu, for us to change our viewpoint. England needs India. A trader knows how to balance out profit and loss. The account books are on the table. If India should be lost, it will rock the throne. That's why we've been sent an emissary.

Azad:

And what an emissary! Sir Stafford Cripps! A Labor man! That in itself is a sign. They're holding out a hand.

Patel:

And what can you hope from this noble envoy? What conditions will you lay down? That's what I'd like to know!

Nehru:

Immediate independence. That is what we demand. England must break our chains this very day. Then as we greet the air, the sky, the clouds again, we will at once forget our cage. And the world will witness a young India, suddenly unshackled, emerging fully armed, glowing with pride, to succor old nations in distress: forward with all our strength against what is most vile. For let no one here doubt that Britain's cause is just.

Gandhi:

So everyone leaps into the first war they see like so many frogs into a pond?! Hop, hop! Indians? No! Frogs! And just as we were recruiting all India into nonviolence. Abdul Ghaffar Khan is dis-arming the whole frontier. A hundred thousand first-class warriors. Is he to tell them tomorrow that the people of the plains have changed their minds? "We're to take up our arms again!" Shame, confusion, and folly! I tell you, if you try to mobilize the impressionable hearts of Congress in order to have the freedom to make war, don't count on me! I shall oppose you, I shall disown you, I shall . . . without getting angry of course. There. I have spoken. Whether you listen to me or not.

Nehru:

India is my mother, Bapuji. But my father is the Universe. Today India can't remain crouching under her Asiatic tent while the Nazis go on devouring one nation after the other. No war is a good war, but some wars are necessary. And just.

Patel:

And if Churchill rejects your advances?

Nehru:

If he refuses? We resign! Congress withdraws from all our administrative posts in the provincial governments. We're simply not there. We deny the British government all our help and support. *If* they were so unthinkably stupid as to refuse us.

Azad:

They won't refuse.

Patel:

I agree with you.

Khan:

Sardarji! You're abandoning us?

Patel:

Bapu, I ask your pardon, but today I side with Nehru. I believe in you, but . . .

Gandhi:

But only up to a point! Following that other goat, you believe in Nehru.

Patel:

Gandhiji, above all I love freedom. Isn't that the only thing we've been striving for?

Gandhi:

Not entirely. Go on, forget about Gandhi.

Nehru:

Bapu, it is true that today, without a backward glance, I must distance myself from you. But I go sadly and with love in my heart. Let us go down to Delhi and greet the man who holds our fate in his hands! Follow me into the twentieth century.

Khan:

No, my friends! Please, stop! You are committing parricide. You renounce the Mahatma!

Azad:

I do not. I love and admire him. But nonviolence for me is not a religion. Merely a political weapon. It's just that the time for it is over now. Let us go, Badshah Khan.

Khan:

Then I resign. I can't stay with men who insult the father of every one of my thoughts.

Azad:

I understand you.

Nehru:

Go forward, India! March on for the sake of the world!
(*Nehru, Patel, and Azad leave.*)

Gandhi:

The parting of the ways. For the first time. But it's an unhappy day for me. This is a great defeat for Gandhi. Yet, you know, if I was twenty years younger, I'd have beaten them.

Khan:

Mahatmaji, at ninety you'll beat them all still.

Gandhi:

And now they've crossed over to the other bank, what am I to do? *Kya Karega?*

Haridasi (singing):

If they answer not the call,
Walk alone, walk alone.
Some hope lies in the quarrel,
Walk alone, walk alone.

Gandhi:

"If they don't hear thee on this earth
Talk alone, talk alone.
Go on up, thou lonely climber
Talk to the angels above."
I know that, it's the song of our great Tagore.

Haridasi:

No, it isn't, it's mine. Tagore is a cheat, he stole it from me and arranged it. If you like it, I'll give it to you, because you really are a lonely Fool.

. . .

Translated by Donald Watson

18

ROUEN, THE THIRTIETH NIGHT OF MAY '31 (2001)

VIGNETTE 4: THE TRIAL

Joan:

> Walls walls walls walls
> Walled-in void where thirty years pass each day
> I hear tomorrow coming
> Its fiery wings tripled
> Death comes quickly time is slow
> Nightmare night, I go sleeping
> To the bottom of the world, time is slow, death works fast
> Bedded in matches that forever box me in
> I sleep profoundly, the universe three meters long
> While Joan, upright, keeps watch
> Every country plays in her theater head.
> Do you think I am going mad?
> It is only terror that splits me in two.
> All night long Joan prays aloud to God
> Oh my God Oh Papa help me help me
> Wispy words: the condemned clutches
> The wispy fingers of a word: Oh my God
> Spare me execution. Dying
> The dying woman prays as though crazed: Oh my God
> Oh Papa, keep me from dying. And there is not
> A chance. Only pure prayer
> Without hope. She prays to keep company with her voice.

I rise from behind sleep
Most determined
A red eagle's feather floats
On my hat.
Let Cauchon enter, I still have two questions to ask.
—Bishop, state your name and give
Your reasons, tell us why this temper
And why this talk
In the name of God
Come out of your lair
And tell the truth.

Cauchon:

For two years there has been more talk of your pants
And tight collars than of all the thrones of Europe
An ugly vile girl with teats of tin
And calloused hands eats away at our peace
Worse than a foreign Queen
You—insomnia, witches' round
Sex unknown on earth
I speak to you without guile
For my appraisal holds sway on high
Until after tomorrow when anger takes over
Children to one side, women to the other
One day my current opinion
Will suffer what opinions suffer
In the blink of a morning.

Does she even have regulation blood in her veins?
How does she sow the winds of tempests?
Does she even have soles on her feet?
On her lips she has only saints and blood and "forward!"
How does she raise armies with her tongue?
The arrows that enter the flesh of her neck
Exit through her ear without having found her
Anyone else would have let out a howl
Is Eve's issue inside
Or a child of Adam Kadmon?
Yet she lives!

Where were you all night long
Agnus diaboli? You see her trick?
She leaves behind the rope-encircled body
And hand-forged chains
The sentinel's eye to see only closed face
Sealed lips witch's brow
Magie noire, obviously
Eyelids painted in *trompe l'oeil*
Which do not keep her from roaming the country at midnight
In the form of a cat who fears not the rain
You cannot fool me.

Joan:

Confess, Cauchon.

Cauchon:

Let us confess. We swear that we, Cauchon, Pierre count of
    Beauvais Peer of France
Councilor of the King our lord not the other one
Received from the Government Tax Collector of Normandy
The sum due us for seven, twenty, and thirteen days
Of attending, we swear, to the service of our King
Or some forty-five days including Sundays and holidays
To make sure that Joan the Maid be judged, weighed
And burned without hesitation
For God's sake let it be remembered by one and all
That Cauchon was an honest man.
I say all this in French, but I think it in English
Because French is a hindrance to thought.
Pensons:
Therefore, she is a virgin in the flesh.
But her psyche is totally polluted:
Visions hallucinations *cum angelo fornicationes*
Devil-man has already deflowered her soul
And if her reputation is saved
It will not be because of me.
I leave. He leaves. He comes back. I come back:

First, you should know that I have nothing against you

No prejudice
Your important conceit
I will not deny it is God and after him the Angels
And then men and women all jumbled up,
You see I too have lived in the USA:
No prejudice and I will prove it:
I have three daughters myself. Thus.
No prejudice. The fundamental problem
Connected to the paperwork is a matter of form.
Angels, I mean, your angels, how do you spell them?
I pick up your document and what do I see? She gets advice
   from her *A S S E S*.
There's the rub.
She writes asses for angels.
It's missing a *g* the *n* is an *s*.
Madame, I have said so over and over
Whoever wrote this report is the devil's henchman
It is obvious
You do not distinguish angels from asses?
And people follow you braying in the streets.
Identify, Madame, Identification. I den ti fi ca tion 1 2 3 4 5 6 7.
Calling an ass an angel and vice viceversa
Is nasty.

Joan:

   I never said that.
   My brothers in Paradise are perfect
   Their teeth are lambs climbing Carmel
   They have not one letter missing.

Cauchon:

   Buffoonery. There are letters missing, I am telling you.

Joan:

   They were there Sir. I said everything and sent everything.

Cauchon:

   Well then they were drowned
   In the flood of follies you has sent to us last year

Inundating my office and my entire staircase.

Joan:

Had sent.

Cauchon:

Had sent?

Joan:

Had sent. But last year Sir
We sent you neither letter nor mail
Nothing more than the obligatory humble request
For authorization to continue living and working.
The form filled out as required
Neither too little nor too much. I checked everything.
And I have a copy in front of me.

Cauchon:

You mean you can write?
And she writes no less!

Joan:

I learned. No one told me it was a crime.

Cauchon:

Let's get on with the show. What I want is the plan
Of your organization
Who is responsible? Identification. For each mission
A clearly identified head
What I want and what I do not have
Are names names names
The person, the rank, not a facsimile
Lay out who is who and who does what
We know who you are
But the other one: Margaret Saint Michael
No idea.

Joan:

You do not know Margaret,
Michael, Gabriel? That floors me

No later than Thursday Madame Margaret told me she knew
  Monsieur Cauchon very well indeed!

Cauchon:

  I know the saint. But of what certain saints are capable I am in
    the dark.
  I want identification, name, rank
  Research, nothing is clear
  I myself have three daughters
  There are things that do not jive
  Does Saint Margaret speak to you in English?
  Or in French? Which is the correct answer?
  Does Saint Michael wear shoes?
  Does he have mouth, nose?
  Does he have something like arm, leg, organs?
  Is his hair short, long, fringed?
  Each job should have a neat profile
  Organizational requirements.

Joan:

  Why would they have cut it?

Cauchon:

  What?

Joan:

  His hair.

Cauchon:

  Continue sending me two or three more letters like this one
  And I will take myself off the case. If you want a head-on colli-
    sion, let's go for it.
  And soon enough there will be plaster scaffolding with a full
    load of firewood.
  I know one who will bray.
  I have no aptitude for being patient for nothing.
  The sound and the fury of which certain people are guilty!
  Answer me in clear and understandable responses
  Or I will persist in advancing a very hard evaluation
  You are forever a question and never an answer

And the third problem is numbers.
I confirm what we have noted:
Twenty-three horsemen, of which seventeen with the same
    squadron leader
That is completely abnormal
And not one single Englishman
Nobody can win with such a small number
It cannot all depend on you alone
This is a hyperfragile situation
What I would call a witch's spell.

Joan:

And yet it is turning
That great Wheel of Fortune.
Today you will have killed me
But tomorrow the entire world will be a field of Roses
Some of them called "Joan from Before" others "Joan from After-
    ward."

Cauchon:

Answer or I leave.

Joan:

I see that you threaten me
I am sad I am anguished I am pessimistic
All the answers in the world will not calm your appetite.

Cauchon:

Well I am an optimist
My mental life knows no doubt
All my future decisions
Were taken at the Sorbonne
Before your conception.
So read about it in the *Éclair de Rouen*
Special edition
You will find your latest news
Since your angels give you none.

Translated by Judith G. Miller, with Eric Prenowitz

19

THE BLINDFOLDED FIANCÉE
OR AMELAIT (2004)
SCENES 5 AND 6

(*The Letter comes to look for Reguine.*)

Shakespeare:

Let's take The Library scene.
Call The Stacks.

Assistant:

The Stacks!
(*The Letter enters.*)

Shakespeare:

Action! (*He leads The Letter to The Stacks.*) You will find Reguine either in the shelved books or in the rare manuscripts collection, or perhaps . . .

The Letter:

Please don't trouble yourself. Mr. . . . Mr.?

Shakespeare:

Shakespeare, William

The Letter:

I hurried so quickly that here I am at my destination.

What silence there is! And I'm about to interrupt it.

Reguine!

Reguine:

Is that you Mr. William?

Shakespeare:

I bring you someone who claims to be expressly for your hands only. It appears it's a Letter.

Reguine:

A letter?

The Letter:

THE Letter.

(*The Letter sits down in front of Reguine.*)

My Reguine! Phew! We're very high here.

Es endet Schmerz

So wie die Nacht

You were waiting for me two weeks ago I didn't come night fell.

Today you were no longer waiting for The Letter yet here I am and it's day.

Reguine:

What are you talking about? Who are you?

The Letter:

Who? I'm The Letter to Reguine.

I took the plane and found you as quickly as possible in the rare books collection of the palace.

So this is the question: To say everything or not to say everything?

No, no. I've chosen to say everything.

Here's the text of my monologue (*The Letter holds out a letter*)—typed . . .

On delicate blue paper, single-spaced.
I read to you. Are you listening to me? "Bad news,
My Reguine. I've just learned I am condemned to die."

Reguine:

Give me that paper. (*The Letter gives her the sheets.*)
Typed.

The Letter:

"I beg your pardon. It's because my hands are trembling. I'm not
hiding anything from you.
Here is the name of the illness, the doctors, all of that.
It's a tumor. Tumor, you understand. Tomb errr . . .
I'm talking about death throes, you see, I'll have had a short life,
cut down in the flowering,
Dawn drowned in a hemorrhage.
It's my lungs."
He purposely wrote "lungs." He's playing with words, of course;
he's an artist.
Lung—in French *poumon*—sounds like *langue*, does it not?
And in German *lunge* makes us think of *Niebelungen*.
Yes!

Reguine:

He's playing?

The Letter:

But with lightness, gravitas. Look. Everything is in the word, you
see: destiny, death, duel, youth, tragic surprise. There is a host
of other things I could tell you.

Reguine:

No, no.

The Letter:

From he who is writing me at this very instant. He is so tired,
you know.
Do you see this little drawing?

Reguine:

I'd rather not.

The Letter:

What are you saying? It's he, a tired and naked young man, stretched out on a chaise longue.

Reguine:

But why? Why this drawing with all the rest? I already read: "I'm naked in my deckchair."

Once is enough, isn't it? Besides two times naked are two too many for me.

The Letter:

Does it disturb you? Try to imagine the chaise longue placed before a window through which the sun enters in yellow rays and on which he is stretched out naked, stretched on the chaise longue bathed in yellow, dressed only in yellow sun. Do you see? Next to him on the ground a scarab on its back, desperate. The young man, too, on his back, desperate.

Try to understand him. He's in a position to die. Don't we want to help him? Hold on!

Read further. This will end well—you'll see.

Reguine:

It's endless. (She leafs through five or six sheets.)

The Letter:

Ow!

Ow! Softly!

Just a minute. Look! you see that little upside down sign.

He depicts himself as a scarab. Or a turtle on its back.

He needs help. A simple gesture would be enough.

The truth is that at this moment he can't do any more with his strength than grab hold of the paper.

He can't get up.

He says that he is expiring there where the hasty departure of she to whom he sends me—that is, you—dumped him on his back.

But it's not of that that I ought to speak, but rather . . .

No, don't reject me! Don't reject him!

He is innocent. I understand; the expression angered you!

Reguine:

Not at all.

It's everything else as well. All those fantasies, those little draw-
ings with the little feet trembling, shaking.

It feels like we're in a forest, grotesquely leafy with evil
rustlings.

Enough read.

The Letter:

You're sending me back! It's what I feared. Read page 8 first, at
least—I beg you.

The one that starts by:"You are going to want to throw away this
letter don't do it,

I beg of you."

He knows everything; he reads your heart."Think of the state in
which I come to you,"

he says,"I find you . . . I jump . . . And in the same instance it is
too late!"

"Too late" underlined. Just those last lines: "Life arrives"—life,
that's you—"and the same day my dreams set sail in an
ambulance."

Reguine:

It's horrible! Stop.

The Letter:

It's true about the ambulance. He was at St. John's Hospital when
I left. I told you.

Are you crying? Well look at these last lines: I read: "At this
moment, you're crying, I know it." He foresees everything.
Doesn't he?

Reguine:

You don't understand. Go away.

The Letter:

I won't shout. He humbly asks you to come back.

Reguine:

Come back! Don't count on it!

The Letter:

Will you come back? You will come back.

Reguine:

Are you trying to hypnotize me? I'm not afraid of you. You're a
ruse, that's all you are. Now, go away!

The Letter:

I'll obey you later.
(*The Letter withdraws into a corner.*)

Reguine:

A Letter is nothing. Besides it wasn't a letter, it was a tunnel.
Traveling through, the only portholes open onto obscenity. "I am
naked!" That disgusts me. To write that to a woman. As though
he didn't have a sex organ. What to make of the chaise longue?
And that sentence about the ambulance. It's not my concern.
Only a Letter. I don't understand. Here I am trembling. Why?
(*The sky grumbles.*)
Because of the drawing? Because of me? And a growl from on
high? There's going to be a Judgment. A Judgment? Who up
there is handing down a Judgment on me? What am I saying?
Mr. Shakespeare! Mr. William!

Shakespeare:

I'm here. I'm here.

Reguine:

I'm without friends, Mr. William. I'm without light. I haven't
sniffled so much since grammar school.

Shakespeare:

Stop rereading that letter.

Reguine:
    He's going to die.

Shakespeare:
    Naturally. Everyone is going to die.

Reguine:
    Right away. Right away. He's sick.

Shakespeare:
    Maybe. He's very young.

Reguine:
    So young!

Shakespeare:
    One could be mistaken. Or deceived.

Reguine:
    Perhaps.

The Letter:
    What have you decided to do?

Reguine:
    Go to him.
    I can't, I can't go to him.

Shakespeare:
    Don't go if he's sick . . .

Reguine:
    His lungs . . .

Shakespeare:
    He needs a doctor.

Reguine:
    It would be better to wait a bit.

The Letter:

What are you afraid of? Two days, three days. He won't lure you to the monstrous crest of the cliff overlooking the sea.

Reguine:

Not to go to him would be normal, would be wise, would be fair.

It would be like my mother. It would be to be sure of not making a mistake.

Shakespeare:

You won't go.

Reguine:

I won't go. I won't go.

The Letter:

Isn't he naked? Transparent? Unarmed? He's not going to all of a sudden hide his normal face under a frightening mask that will topple your good sense and plunge it from the summit of the stairs into the breech of insanity.

Reguine:

I recognize that old fear, but it's not mine. I could go—for only a few days.

Shakespeare:

It will serve no purpose—to try to stop you.

Reguine:

Two or three days, I have no choice. Choice has fled. (*Noise from the back of the room.*)

The Letter:

Do not enter. Didn't you see the sign?
(*A fight between The Mother and The Letter.*)

Voice of The Mother:

You let me go! I'm The Mother!

The Letter:
Who told you?

The Mother:
Told? I'm The Mother, I tell you.

Shakespeare:
The Mother is always there.

Reguine:
Mama, were you listening?

The Mother:
What do you think? I listen, I see, I read, and still I can't stop myself from worrying. And so I see you're going to knock your feet right out from under yourself!

Reguine:
It's because he's going to die, Mama.

The Mother:
I'd send him packing! Die? Station stop, everybody underground. It's because of that Letter, isn't it?

Reguine:
You read it too!

The Mother:
Impossible. It's too weird for me. All those sentences. And all those animals: vultures, squirrels, cockroaches. No thought. Only escape. It's not a letter, it's a tunnel. It's not a tunnel, it's a zoo. It's an elevator shaft. Some guy says, "Come." You jump. You don't love, you tumble. It won't last, in any case.

Reguine:
Love can be that much greater because brief.

The Mother:
So in addition to everything else, you love him.

Reguine:

I didn't say that. I said nothing.

The Mother:

My daughter, you will not go.

Reguine:

I am going. I'll be back in ten days.

The Mother:

Ten? You said two.

Reguine:

Mama, be quiet! I must.

The Mother:

Go! Go ahead! I'm coming with you. We'll write to you, Mr. Silverman!

Reguine:

Mr. Shakespeare.

The Mother:

You don't take after me. The first weird letter I split.
(*They exit.*)

The Letter:

She's going to him. I was sure of it. You see? You probably find me convoluted, insidiously authoritarian, and tortuous—yes, yes—and even obscene. You wouldn't have said it like that.

Shakespeare:

You've nothing to brag about. If there hadn't been that idea of the promise of Death, she would never have gone. You're at your desk. You're reading. Suddenly the idea of Death cries out, from one minute to the next everything veers, books fall, falcons scream the news to heaven, time changes its look.

Assistant:

I don't know if it's William or The Letter who says that.

Shakespeare:

It was me, of course—William.

You love madly the person you didn't love. You love more than
love. And that's what's happened. It's easy.

The Letter:

But if you love the one you don't love, you love all the same, isn't
that so?

Shakespeare:

I don't *love* you and I don't love *you*, old poison. Enough stink!
Go away! Disappear!

The Letter:

Don't touch me! Jealous old man!

Shakespeare:

Get out of here! You ill-tempered heron!

SCENE 6

(*In Gerutha's rooms.*)

Shakespeare:

New take: Gerutha's Rooms. The Levee of the Queen.

Assistant:

I'm sending in the breakfast. Emma and Frigga enter.
Bedchamber of the Queen Mother Gerutha and her servant.
(*The two servants enter.*)

Emma:

We're serving tea? At this hour?

Frigga:

> And cheese. Since the prince has come home, there are no more hours. It was already so late, I had to wake him up. His beastie had been whining for hours. I had to scold him again.

Emma:

> Poor beast to be subject to such a master.

Frigga:

> Poor master.

Emma:

> Poor mother. There she is. Let's leave. We'll stay behind the drapes.
> (*Gerutha enters.*)

Gerutha:

> Yet another beautiful sunrise wasted. When he asked me if he could come for a few days between Brittany and Germany, Paris and Wittenberg, I could only say yes. But . . .
> (*Someone knocks violently on her door.*)
> Is that you, Amelait?
> (*He enters with his mole cage.*)

Amelait:

> "Is that you, Amelait?" Why ask me that? You're asking me if I'm Amelait? Or if Amelait is me? Or if I'm an other who'd do Amelait? Or maybe you'd rather an other come take tea with you. Your little Fredegond.

Gerutha:

> Don't start. Sit down. Will you have some tea?

Amelait:

> Milk! Milk first. And first of all a kiss. What? I can't tenderly hold you? You stretch out two stiff arms and keep me at a distance? What does she have against human kindness—such a hussy . . .

Gerutha:

Stop, my son, stop. You're very late. Did you see the sun? Losing time again! The whole world is working. Duty first. Come, drink your milk.

Amelait:

Late—you're the one who's late. When will you be my mother, Mama?

Gerutha:

Stop Amelait stop.
(*Amelait repeats her lines.*)

Amelait:

Stop Mama stop. All my life these words as soon as I open my mouth.
Stopstop. I embrace her, stop. I enfold her; she pushes away. Do you take me for my father?

Gerutha:

What are you saying? Absolutely not, not that. Here, taste this gingerbread. It's from Germany.

Amelait:

It's delicious. Delicious. I love these small moments of sharing bread. How beautiful life is out the window.

Gerutha:

Don't eat too fast.

The Mole:

Tell her tell her tell her.

Amelait:

Another slice. Here, old friend.
What's wrong? You don't like my mole?

Gerutha:

Did I say something? You're looking for a reason to be angry.

Amelait:

With your eyes, your nose, with your pinched lips you said: dirty animal.

Gerutha:

Of course not. I just don't like beasts who smell like beasts.

Amelait:

But you smell like the beast with two backs. Mama and Fengwhatchamacallit.

Gerutha:

Enough! Enough! You're looking for a reason to make me angry.

Amelait:

I'm lookinglookinglooking for my mother's secret ticks. Do you hear me, little mole? My mother is clucking. It sounds like Donald Duck.

The Mole:

Tell her tell her tell her tell her.

Gerutha:

Poor boy you'd have preferred that I'd left and your father stayed. You wish I were dead, don't you?

Amelait:

Would I like you to die? (*To The Mole*) Let's see, what do you say, little sister?

And for what reason, which folly? She has certainly humiliated and offended me.

What is she doing here with Papa underground, sleeping in this bed—accompanied on Mondays and Thursdays? She survives, she smiles.

I don't really have anything against a nice warm bed. Nor against a very cold one.

Don't look at me with those drowned madwoman eyes, which you didn't have when myfather yourhusband died.

Gerutha:

I'm not looking at you. Stop Amelait stop. Even if I were to die, that wouldn't raise your father out of the ground.

Amelait:

Doesn't the elevator ever return to the top? It's not Papa's death that will stop me. I have no guilt, none, none, none.

Gerutha:

Let's not speak any more about this, my son, please . . .

The Mole:

Tell, tell, tell, tell

Amelait:

I would and I would not like. I'm unstrung, twisted. I want and do not want what I want. I am jealous 1) of your nephew 2) of your little fat friend with the double chin, Fengwhat-chamacallit 3) 4) 5) I am jealous of myself. Of my genius, my craziness, of the sun and the night. I'm jealous of my adored father whom I would so much like to resemble. I croak like a rat and you are not helping me. Is that what a mother is? Or is that exactly what a mother is? Yesterday, seated next to you, I take your hand, I hold it, I breathe, you pull it away, you ask: "Don't you have anything to say to me?"

Gerutha:

It's the truth, you don't say anything. You arrive at the palace, you've traveled, you've crossed seas, spent months in England, you've studied, fought; what do I know? And not a word.

Amelait:

Words, words, words! When I come to Elsenore it's for this: for holding your hand, being quiet, and feeling good.

Gerutha:

And yet it's certainly you who places words of death on my bed while I'm sleeping. This note, found this morning near my pillow, it's in your hand, isn't it? (*She gives him the note.*) "I wish you were dead." That's you, isn't it?

Amelait:

Does it hurt you?

Gerutha:

It has been written, we desire in vain. This play was finished before it began and we can't do anything about it.

Amelait:

If your death could give Papa back to me, would you give me your death—his life? You aren't answering?

Gerutha:

That's a stupid question. Stop playing the fool. Or are you truly mad?

Amelait:

Do I hurt you? Answer me. Yes or no?

Gerutha:

Yes, you hurt me.

The Mole:

Tell tell tell tell tell

Amelait:

I hurt you? So let me give you some pleasure. Today I have something to say, Mama. Sit down!

Gerutha:

What's this about?

Amelait:

Mama, I'm engaged.

Gerutha:

With whom? Not with a foreigner, I hope?

Amelait:

Mama, Mama, Mama!

Gerutha:

What?!

Amelait:

That's all you have to say?

Gerutha:

Engaged, engaged, I still want to know who it is.

Amelait:

Will you come to our wedding?

Gerutha:

Where? When? It's gone this far and you haven't said a thing to me?

Amelait:

All right, then. We won't talk about it any more. I said nothing.

Gerutha:

Is this another joke?

Amelait:

And your wedding: Where? When? We could have a double wedding, a canopy for four. That's an idea, it would save some money. What do you think?

Gerutha:

These jokes in bad taste—ever since puberty . . .

Amelait:

Everything is tangled up, what's good tastes bad, tragedy is hilarious, death is holding its sides. Give me some more of that pâté. You didn't poison it, I hope? Because I want to give her some.

Gerutha:

No! It's for you. You're not going to give my delicious pâté to your ferret.

Amelait:

My mole is not a ferret.

Gerutha:

It's a female?

Amelait:

It depends.

Gerutha:

Depends? (*She laughs. He laughs.*)

Amelait:

Depending on the hour and the mood, it's a boy or a girl mole, or a cat, a mouse, a woman, a best friend, a cherished sister. She is everything for me, except my mother. Forgive me Mama. You know how I am, my heart is tender and divided.

Gerutha:

I also have a heart, so I know.

Amelait:

I know I know.

Gerutha:

Does your knee hurt?

Amelait:

Right now I hurt everywhere. My neck aches. I'm as stiff as a corpse.

Gerutha:

Do you want me to massage you?
(*The Mole is agitated. The Ghost enters.*)

The Mole:

There, there, there

Amelait:

What are you saying, Chana? Her name is Chana.

The Mole:

There there there. Your father. Get up!

Amelait:

Where? There there? Armed?

The Mole:

There there there. Dressed in a black coat, down to his feet.

Amelait:

Oh yes, there!

Gerutha:

What it is?

Amelait:

His face a little tanned by death.

Gerutha:

What are you doing to my drapes?

Amelait:

Upright, burning without noise like a black flame, the bearing of a rabbi.

Gerutha:

A rabbi?

Amelait:

Why are you mad at me, adored father: Am I too heavy? Too slow? Too lazy? You were quicker, sharper, more elegant? I do what I can.

Ghost:

You don't have any money at least?

It's money that rots kings.

In my days there ruled an absolute distinction between those who ran after money and those who were pure, like me.

Amelait:

You can relax about what I think about filthy lucre. Why do you think I chose to cut off my income? I do everything not to earn money. It was painful not to be able to buy a necklace for my fiancée.

The Ghost:

You're engaged?

Amelait:

I had to borrow from Horatio for the ring.

What have I ever done for myself since you left, except go to the movies?

The Ghost:

It seems you write books.

Amelait:

They don't sell. I feel very loyal toward you. I could be famous. I hold back.

I won't surpass your glory by as much as a hair.

The Mole:

It's the truth.

The Ghost:

And the Swedes?

Amelait:

A success. Swedes and Courlanders: men, women, cattle, children, pigs, sheep quartered, roasted, sautéed. Only the seagulls escaped.

Aren't you happy?

Not a day when I don't get up as braced as the string of your
bow, ready to shoot the arrow of your look into your enemy's
eye. And you're not pleased with my corpsecalendar?
Do you smile at me, dearest father?

The Ghost:

A little. Next you'll subjugate the Icelanders. And your mother?
She never understood me. She loves life too much. I feel slightly
betrayed. Where are we with yourmother?

Amelait:

I'm doing everything I can to crush her.

The Mole:

It's the truth.

Amelait:

But it's not easy. She lives, she lives.

The Ghost:

You said it. She prefers life to the dead.
Don't forget my heroic stature. Don't forget. Don't for . . .
don't . . .

Amelait:

What are you saying?? Finish (*The Ghost disappears*) your
sentences!!!

The Mole:

He said not to forget to pierce her heart.

Amelait:

He said that?

The Mole:

Oh! If I'm lying, finish the sentence yourself.

Translated by Judith G. Miller

NOTES

HÉLÈNE CIXOUS: BLOOD AND LANGUAGE

1. Derrida, *Geneses, Genealogies, Genres, and Genius.*

2. Conley, "Preface," *Hélène Cixous.*

3. "The Laugh of the Medusa," published for the first time in French in 1975 as an article in a journal number devoted to Simone de Beauvoir, can be considered very close to "Savoir," a longer version included in Hélène Cixous and Catherine Clément's *The Newly Born Woman,* which appeared the same year. However, the English version of "The Laugh of the Medusa," translated by Keith Cohen and Paula Cohen and published in 1976, was already revised by the author and does not correspond to the French original. The coexistence of multiple versions of the *same* text—Cixous makes it a practice to take up short texts in book-length ones, but they are often altered, cut, or significantly revised—can be considered typical of the author's polymorphic writing and results in a very original case of intertextuality or even intratextuality as it occurs within her oeuvre.

4. Cixous and Jeannet, *Rencontre terrestre.*

5. Cixous's titles are given in English only when they correspond to texts that have already been translated into English; the dates always refer to the original edition.

6. In Cixous and Calle-Gruber, *Rootprints.*

7. Hélène Cixous, "Entretien avec Françoise van Rossum-Guyon," *Revue des Sciences humaines* 168 (October-December): 479–93.

WRITING AND DREAMING THE FEMININE

1. Emphasis in the original.

2. "Le Rire de la Méduse," *L'Arc*, no. 61 ("Simone de Beauvoir et la lutte des femmes") (1975): 39–54.

3. A phrase that inspired the American artist Nancy Spero for her installation "Let the Priests Tremble . . . " (1998).

4. Judith Butler, *Precarious Life: The Power of Mourning and Violence* (London: Verso, 2004).

5. Jacques Derrida, *Monolingualism of the Other; or, The Prosthesis of Origin*, trans. Patrick Mensah (Stanford, Stanford University Press, 1998); published in French in 1996.

6. Gilles Deleuze and Félix Guattari, *Anti-Oedipus. Capitalism and Schizophrenia*, trans. Robert Hurley, Mark Seem, and Helen R. Lane (New York: Viking, 1977); published in French in 1972.

7. Roland Barthes, *Mythologies*, trans. Annette Lavers (London: Jonathan Cape, 1972); published in French in 1957. In this collection of short essays, previously published in the magazine *Les Lettres Nouvelles*, Barthes analyzes what he considers "modern myths," covering a wide range of practices and objects, from tourist guides to wrestling. An enlarged volume in English was published later: *The Eiffel Tower and Other Mythologies*, trans. Richard Howard (New York: Hill and Wang, 1979).

8. "The Emperor's New Clothes," adapted by Hans Christian Andersen from a popular tale, tells the story of a king who is cheated by two tailors: they make a new suit for him, with a special cloth that can be seen only by intelligent people. The emperor himself and his ministers cannot see anything at all, but they do not acknowledge it for fear of looking stupid. When the emperor shows his new clothes in a procession, everybody claims to see it, until a small child reveals that the emperor is, in fact, naked.

9. Cixous refers here explicitly to "Circumfession," a text by Derrida published in 1991 (after this conference was given), in Geoffrey Bennington and Jacques Derrida, *Jacques Derrida* (Chicago: University of Chicago Press, 1993). Cixous devoted an entire book, *Portrait of Jacques Derrida as a Young Jewish Saint*, to an analysis of this text; see part 4.

10. Jacques Derrida, *Mémoires d'aveugle: L'autoportrait et autres ruines* (Paris: Réunion des Musées Nationaux, 1990).

1. THE LAUGH OF THE MEDUSA

1. Men still have everything to say about their sexuality, and everything to write. For what they have said so far, for the most part, stems from the opposition activity/passivity, from the power relation between a fantasized obligatory virility meant to invade, to colonize, and the consequential phantasm of woman as a "dark continent" to penetrate and to "pacify." (We know what "pacify" means in terms of scotomizing the other and misrecognizing the self.) Conquering her, they've made haste to depart from her borders, to get out of sight, out of body. The way man has of getting out of himself and into her whom he takes not for the other but for his own, deprives him, he knows, of his own bodily territory. One can understand how man, confusing himself with his penis and rushing in for the attack, might feel resentment and fear of being "taken" by the woman, of being lost in her, absorbed, or alone.

2. I am speaking here only of the place "reserved" for women by the Western world.

3. Which works, then, might be called feminine? I'll just point out some examples: one would have to give them full readings to bring out what is pervasively feminine in their significance. Which I shall do elsewhere. In France (have you noted our infinite poverty in this field?—the Anglo-Saxon countries have shown resources of distinctly greater consequence), leafing through what's come out of the twentieth century—and it's not much—the only inscriptions of femininity that I have seen were by Colette, Marguerite Duras, . . . and Jean Genet.

4. *Dé-pense*, a neologism formed from the verb *penser*: hence "unthinks," but also "spends" (from *dépenser*). —Trans.

5. Standard English term for the Hegelian *Aufhebung*, the French *la relève*.

6. Jean Genet, *Pompes funèbres* (Paris, 1948), p. 185.

2. COMING TO WRITING

1. "*Terreur: l'arrêt de vie, l'arrêt de mort.*" The word *arrêt* (stop) is a homonym in French, and can be translated both as "arrest" and "sentence;" here, "life arrest, death sentence." All notes are by the editor of *Coming to Writing and Other Essays*—Ed.

2. *"Mon refus de la maladie comme arme. Il y a une même qui me fait hor-reur. N'est-elle pas déjà morte? Sa maladie: c'est le cancer. Une main malade. Elle est elle-même la maladie."* In this passage Cixous employs a characteristic form of wordplay: usage of the pronoun *elle* to refer interchangeably to more than one noun, including both fictional female subjects and things that are feminine nouns in French. Here the feminine nouns for "sickness" and "hand" overlap with the identification of a feminine self—*une même*—and this plurality of references leaves the reader uncertain as to whether *elle* indicates that the sickness or the woman is already dead (*déjà morte*), whether the hand or the woman is the source of the sickness (*elle-même la maladie*), and so on.

3. *"Tu as deux mains. Tu as demain."* In this passage on the rejection of sickness as a weapon, the echo of the homophones *deux mains* ("two hands") and *demain* ("tomorrow") creates the suggestion that even if one hand does not work, the other remains a resource, like the future.

4. *"On tue une fille."* The title of this passage echoes the title of Freud's essay "A Child is Being Beaten."

5. "Peut pas s'empêcher de voler!" / "En ce cas, nous avons des cages extra." The verb voler means both "to fly" and "to steal." In this scene, a young girl irrepressibly steals—apparently language, in this case—and simultaneously flies (from the scene of the crime, in a flight of words). She is punished with "special cages," meaning not only prison for the thief, but foot-binding to restrain the mobility of the girl who "flies." See Nancy Kline's introduction to *The Tongue Snatchers,* by Claudine Hermann, for a gloss on Cixous's development of this term.

6. "Le souffle 'veut' une forme." The word souffle means both "breath" and spirit, as in *le souffle créateur,* "the breath of God." It is also used to indicate inspiration, as in *avoir du souffle,* "to be inspired." Throughout this passage (and elsewhere in Cixous's work, such as the 1975 fiction *Souffles*), the vocabulary of breathing, or respiration, is aligned with a parallel vocabulary of inspiration.

3. TALES OF SEXUAL DIFFERENCE

This lecture was delivered during a joint session with Jacques Derrida at a conference entitled "Lectures de la différence sexuelle" (Readings of Sexual Difference) organized at the Collège International de Philosophie, Paris, in October 1990 by the Centre d'Etudes Féminines of the Université de Paris 8. The lecture was improvised from notes, and the text retains many characteristics of this unscripted oral presentation. Derrida's talk, which immediately followed Cixous's, was entitled "Fourmis," the English translation by Eric Prenowitz: "Ants," *Oxford Literary Review* 24 (2002): 17–42. All notes are by the translator.

1. "The fairy that makes," *la fée qui fait*, is echoed in *la fée différence*, "the difference fairy."

2. This "D. S.," the initials of "sexual difference" in French (*différence sexuelle*, a feminine noun), is a homophone of *déesse*, the "goddess" of the next sentence.

3. "Pleasure," "orgasm," etc.

4. Cixous is making use of the difference in French between the familiar singular second-person objective personal pronoun (*toi*, referring to Derrida) and the plural (or formal singular) second-person personal pronoun (*vous*, appropriate for the audience). The expression "'*you*' is all of you" translates "'toi' *c'est vous*," in other words, she is now in a position where she says "you" to him but in the direction of, and thus apparently to, the audience.

5. Neologism *prévoie* (though this word does exist as a subjunctive form of *prévoir*, "to foresee," which would be ungrammatical here), homophone of *prévois* ("foresee" in first- or second-person singular indicative), but composed with *voie*, meaning "path."

6. This last word, *péril*, is repeated here partially italicized (*pér*il): *pér* sounds like *père*, "father" ("Playing with the father . . . "), and *il* is the pronoun "he."

7. *Homme mère*, "man mother," is homophonous with *Homère*, the blind Homer.

8. Play on the question of who precedes or follows whom. She only "follows" him because in describing him as "the circumcised one," she is only reading his own text about himself, but circumcision happens to the infant "before" the so-called constitution of the subject ("before you who are here," i.e., Derrida the adult sitting next to her).

9. The word *circoncis* (past participle functioning as a noun: "circumcised one") starts and ends with the sound *C* (roughly the English pronunciation of the letter), which can admit these three spellings in French.

10. *Circonfession* appeared later in Jacques Derrida and Geoffrey Bennington, *Jacques Derrida* (Paris: Seuil, 1991), translated by Bennington as *Circumfession* in *Jacques Derrida* (Chicago: Chicago University Press, 1993).

11. Translates *décapement*, neologism based on *décaper* (to strip, scour, sandblast, etc.), but very close to *décapiter*, to behead.

12. The expression here, "'*à la saignature*,'" is based on a neologism combining *signature* and *saigner* (to bleed).

13. *Plus-de-prépuce*: the *plus* meaning both "more" and "no more."

14. The feminine noun *merci*, in the expression *à la merci* (at the mercy of), is homophonic with *mère/scie* (mother/saw). We might also translate this sentence: "Do (all) men come from/belong to the mother-who-cuts?

15. *Déprépucelage*, neologism combining *dépucelage* (losing of virginity) and *prépuce*.

16. "Choice" here translates *gré* ("liking," "thankfulness," in various expressions), which has just figured in *malgré*, translated as "in spite of."

17. This sentence, "*Une femme se sent* comme différente," differs from the "masculine" version (a man "*se sent différent*") essentially in the additional *comme*, which can indicate a function ("it is as "different" that a woman feels" or "feels herself") or suggest an approximation ("a woman feels sort of different, somewhat different").

18. In *Circumfession* Derrida recounts how he discovered "very late" that he had been given a secret name, Elie (Elijah in English), which was never officially registered or inscribed on his identity papers.

19. A series of homophones of *Elie*: "and link, and read/bed, l, i, she there . . . "

20. *Elle* = she; *aile* = wing.

21. *Cassandre* (= Cassandra) here says "case/Cinder."

22. Apparently a play on *pas*, meaning both "not" and "step": "Si simple pas. Pas si simple."

23. This "stars" (*étoile*) seems to be a verb: the (Christian) cross becomes a (Jewish) star. But this "star(s)" calls up "you": the next sentence begins "Et toi, là [. . .]" ("And you, there [. . .]"), a near homophone of *étoile*.

24. "People begrudge you" translates *on t'en veut*, an idiomatic expression that Cixous reconfigures, taking it literally, as *on en veut, de toi*: they want some of you.

25. This "of a she" translates *d'un elle, d'une elle*, the pronoun (*elle*) preceded first by the masculine article (*un*) and second by the feminine article (*une*).

26. Personal pronoun used in particular with reflexive verbs: *se toucher* = to touch oneself/one another.

27. *Doux* (= soft, sweet) and *d'où* (= from where) are homophones.

28. *Deux mains* (= two hands) and *demain* (= tomorrow) are homophones.

29. "We write ourselves" translates *nous nous écrivons,* a reflexive construction that can mean either "we write ourselves" (each one him/herself) or "we write each other." The corresponding ambivalence applies to what is translated as "we invent ourselves."

30. This *qui-nous sont-je* is homophonous with *qui nous songe:* who dreams us.

31. Idiomatic expressions that would translate literally as: "a word that promises, that returns from afar, and that announces a sacred voyage."

THE ORIGINS: ALGERIA AND GERMANY

1. As described by Christa Stevens in "Hélène Cixous, auteur en 'algériance'" (*Expressions maghrébines* 1, no. 1, pp. 77–91), in 1997 Cixous published four texts related to her Algerian origins: the book *OR: Les lettres de mon père*; and the short stories "Pieds nus" in Leïla Sebbar, ed., *Une enfance algérienne* (Paris: Gallimard, 1997), pp. 53–63, "Stigmata, or Job the Dog," and "My Algeriance" (the last two translated by Eric Prenowitz and included in *Stigmata: Escaping Texts*, 1998).

2. Italics in the original in all quotations from *Osnabrück.*

3. In particular, in Jacques Derrida, *The Animal That Therefore I Am*, ed. Marie-Louise Mallet, trans. David Wills (New York: Fordham University Press, 2008).

4. "Letter to Zohra Drif," trans. Eric Prenowitz, *Parallax* 4, no. 2 (April–June, 1998): 189–96.

LOVE (AND) THE OTHER

1. See Naomi Schor, "Cet essentialisme qui n'(en) est pas un: Irigaray à bras le corps," *Futur antérieur:* "Supplément: Féminismes au présent" (Paris: L'Harmattan, 1993), pp. 85–109, for an account on Beauvoir's, Irigaray's, and Cixous's theories on women and alterity.

2. Cixous, *Angst.*

3. Peggy Kamuf, "To Give Place: Semi-Approaches to Hélène Cixous," *Book of Adresses* (Stanford: Stanford University Press, 2005), pp. 114–31, quotation on p. 127.

4. Gayatri Chakravorty Spivak, "Cixous sans frontières," in Mireille Calle-Gruber, ed., *Du féminin* (Grenoble: Publications de l'Université de Grenoble, 1992), pp. 65–81.

5. Cixous, *La*.

6. A development of this analysis of "Love of the Wolf" can be found in Marta Segarra, "Friendship, Betrayal, and Translation: Cixous and Derrida," *Mosaic* 40, no. 2 (June 2007): pp. 91–101.

7. Jacques Derrida, *The Politics of Friendship*, trans. George Collins (London: Verso, 2005), p. 186.

8. This quotation comes from the French enlarged revised edition of this text, in the book *L'Amour du loup—et autres remords*.

9. Ibid.

10. Ibid.

8. LOVE OF THE WOLF

1. Clarice Lispector, "A favor do medo," in *A Descoberta do mundo* (Rio de Janeiro: Noveira Fronteira, 1987), p. 42.

2. Marina Tsvetaeva, *Mon Pouchkine,* followed by *Pouchkine et Pougatchov,* trans. André Markowicz (Paris: Clémence Hiver, 1987), p. 26.

3. Ibid., p. 27.

4. Ibid.

5. Marina Tsvetaeva, *Le Gars* (Paris: Des femmes—Antoinette Fouque, 1992), p. 129.

6. Ibid, p. 26.

7. Ibid., p. 33.

8. Written in 1922 after having read the folktale "The Vampire" in Afanassiev's collection.

9. Tsvetaeva, *Le Gars*, pp. 16–17.

10. Aeschylus, *Agamemnon,* from the translation by Ariane Mnouchkine (New York: Viking, 1975), p. 135.

11. Tsvetaeva, *Mon Pouchkine,* pp. 32–33.

12. Tsvetaeva, *Pouchkine et Pougatchov,* pp. 78–79.

13. Tsvetaeva, *Le Gars*, p. 28.

14. The French word *gars*, or "kid," is pronounced without sounding either the *s* or the *r,* hence *ga.* Consequently, the signifier *gars*, when pronounced sounding all its phonemes, means "beware," a warning which, when the word is pronounced ordinarily, is suppressed. —Trans.

THE ANIMAL

1. Jacques Derrida develops this idea in *The Animal That Therefore I Am*, ed. Marie-Louise Mallet, trans. David Wills (New York: Fordham University Press, 2008).

2. Cixous, "Prologue," unpublished MS. My translation.

3. This can be translated as "thinking concerning the animal" (as David Wills does in his translation mentioned earlier), but also as "animal's thinking."

4. *The Animal That Therefore I Am*, p. 11.

5. Hélène Cixous's seminar, March 5, 2005.

6. A study on Cixous and animality can be found in Marta Segarra, "Hélène Cixous's Other Animal: The Half-Sunken Dog," *New Literary History* 37, no. 1 (Winter 2006): 119–34.

7. Hélène Cixous, "Stigmata: Job the Dog," trans. Eric Prenowitz, *Philosophy Today* 41, no. 1 (Spring 1997): 12–17; reprinted in Cixous, *Stigmata*.

8. Cixous, "Prologue."

10. DEDICATION TO THE OSTRICH

"And as birds, risen from the shore, as if rejoicing together at their pasture, make of themselves now a round flock, now some other shape, so within the lights holy creatures were singing as they flew, and in their figures made of themselves now *D*, now *I*, now *L*." *The Divine Comedy*, trans. Charles S. Singleton (Princeton: Princeton University Press, 1975). [All notes are by the translator.]

1. A black-earth steppe region in south-central European Russia; also, its capital. When Mandelstam was arrested on May 13, 1934, he tried to commit suicide in a mental hospital in Cherdyn. Thanks to the intervention of Nadezhda and others, Stalin himself agreed to allow Mandelstam to choose another place of exile. He chose Voronezh, because of its associations with Russian poetry, and because it lay in the European part of Russia. The Mandelstams were in exile in Voronezh for three years, until 1937. The poems Mandelstam wrote there, referred to as the "Voronezh cycle" or the "Voronezh notebooks," are considered among his finest. . . .

2. The word *vers* in French commonly means both verse, or line of poetry, and worms. The text plays on these two meanings. . . .

3. Reference to the biblical story of Samson and Delilah (Judges 16:21). Samson was blinded by the Philistines in Gaza for having lain with Delilah. Later, Samson killed himself and the Philistines when he caused their house to fall down around them (Judges 16:30).

4. The Xhosa are a pastoral people living in Cape Province, South Africa. Their language is widely spoken and is characterized by the use of clicks. Winnie Mandela is a Xhosa from the Pondoland. Nelson Mandela learned the Xhosa language in the mission school in Qunu, where he was educated.

5. Maat is the ancient Egyptian personification of the world order, incorporating the concepts of justice, truth, and legality. She is the daughter of Ra, creator of the world. *Pharaoh* means "beloved of Maat, he who lives in her through his laws." A favored venue for judicial hearings was before her shrines, and judges were regarded as her priests. In Egyptian art, Maat is depicted with an ostrich feather in her hair.

6. Winnie's nickname, from her Pondo name Nomzamo. Her full name is Nomzamo Winnie Madikizela Mandela.

7. Zami's native village, Bizana, is in Pondoland, near the Cape-Natal border, close to the Umtamvuna River. Meaning "a small plot," Bizana was an independent territory until 1894, and has historically been the scene of many tribal battles. Zami has described her homeland thus: "The part of Pondoland where I come from is still totally tribal; tribesmen still congregate on the hills, wearing their traditional blankets." (See *Part of My Soul Went with Him* [New York and London: Norton, 1984], p. 46.)

8. "And as their wings bear the starlings along in the cold season, in wide, dense flocks, so does that blast the sinful spirits; hither, thither, downward, upward, it drives them. No hope of less pain, not to say of rest, ever comforts them." Dante's *Inferno*, canto 5. The "sinful spirits" referred to here are Paolo and Francesca, illicit lovers killed by Francesca's jealous husband.

1 1. MESSIAH

1. This is an allusion to Jacques Derrida's "Che cos'è la poesia?" in *Points de suspension: Entretiens* (Paris: Galilée, 1992). —Ed.

DERRIDA

1. In Derrida, *H.C. for Life, That Is to Say* . . .

2. Jacques Derrida, *The Animal That Therefore I Am*, ed. Marie-Louise Mallet, trans. David Wills (New York: Fordham University Press, 2008).

3. Mara Negrón, ed., *Lectures de la différence sexuelle* (Paris: Des femmes–Antoinette Fouque, 1994). This collection of papers presented at a conference held in 1990 includes a text by Cixous, "Contes de la différence sexuelle"—from which we have selected a fragment for part 3, "Dreaming and Writing the Feminine"—and one by Derrida, "Fourmis" ("Ants"), in response.

4. Jacques Derrida: "Circumfession: Fifty-Nine Periods and Periphrases," in Geoffrey Bennington and Jacques Derrida, *Jacques Derrida* (Chicago: University of Chicago Press, 1993).

5. Paper given by Cixous at the conference on Derrida "Le passage des frontières," held at Cerisy-la-Salle in July 1992 and published in *Le Passage des frontières*, ed. Marie-Louise Mallet (Paris: Galilée, 1994), pp. 83–98.

6. Derrida, *Geneses, Genealogies, Genres, and Genius*. This was a lecture given at the conference on Cixous held at the Bibliothèque nationale de France in Paris, in 2003.

7. A *tallith* is a shawl worn over the shoulders or sometimes the head by Jewish men during prayer.

8. Jacques Derrida, *Monolingualism of the Other, or, The Prosthesis of Origin*, trans. Patrick Mensah (Stanford: Stanford University Press, 1998).

9. Jacques Derrida, *Spurs: Nietzsche's Styles/Éperons: Les styles de Nietzsche*, trans. Barbara Harlow (Chicago: Chicago University Press, 1979).

14. ON STYLE

1. Jacques Derrida, *Spurs: Nietzsche's Styles*, trans. Barbara Harlow (Chicago: University of Chicago Press, 1979); the edition is bilingual.—Ed.

15. "TODAY"

1. Jacques Derrida, "Psychoanalysis Searches the States of Its Soul," trans. Peggy Kamuf, in Jacques Derrida, *Without Alibi*, ed. Peggy Kamuf

(Stanford: Stanford University Press, 2002), pp. 242–43. All notes are by the translator.

2. Ibid., p. 257.

3. Ibid., pp. 279–80.

4. *Tu*, the second-person familiar subject pronoun, has the same form as the past participle of *taire*, to silence, as in "Il s'est tu," he fell silent.

5. Jacques Derrida, *Geneses, Genealogies, Genres, and Genius: The Secrets of the Archive*, trans. Beverly Bie Brahic (New York: Columbia University Press, 2006), pp. 30–31.

6. *H.C. for Life, That Is to Say . . .* , trans. Laurent Milesi and Stefan Herbrechter (Stanford: Stanford University Press, 2006), p. 7.

THE THEATER OF HÉLÈNE CIXOUS

1. In a candid essay on her theater practice, "Enter the Theatre" (trans. Brian J. Mallet, in Prenowitz, *Selected Plays of Hélène Cixous*, pp. 25–34), Cixous speaks movingly of her duty to remember: "The mission entrusted to me by my father [was that] I must do everything to ensure that I and the people around me are not swept away by oblivion, indifference. I must keep alive the *qui vive* and preserve the dead, the murdered, the captive, the excluded, from the jaws of death" (p. 26).

2. Cixous recounts in a resonant interview with Eric Prenowitz, "Modernepic Theatre" (in Prenowitz, *Selected Plays of Hélène Cixous*, pp. 1–24), that her earliest theater work, *La Pupille* (1971), and *Portrait of Dora* (1976), was somewhat of an accident. She was first truly "visited by theatrical gods" when writing *The Conquest of the School at Madhubaï* (1984), at which point the central character, Sakundeva, took possession of her before "escaping" into the text.

3. In an October 12, 2006, lecture at La Maison Française of New York University, Cixous reckoned that all actors are dual sexed and degendered at the same time.

4. Cixous discusses how writing for the Théâtre du Soleil, with its many participants, specific actors, and goals of translating world geopolitics, puts certain acceptable and even fertile constraints on her imagination. She is more able to play with the "effects of writing" in dramatic texts not specifically written with and for the Soleil; cf. "Hors Cadre Interview," ed. and trans. Verena Andermatt Conley, in Tim Murray, ed., *Mimesis, Masochism, Mime: The Politics of Theatricality*

in Contemporary French Thought (Ann Arbor: University of Michigan Press, 1997), pp. 29–39.

5. The following, in order of publication, is a list of Hélène Cixous's plays written for and published by the Théâtre du Soleil. The English translation is in brackets. In this essay we will cite in English the titles we discuss: *L'Histoire terrible mais inachevée de Norodom Sihanouk, roi du Cambodge*, 1987 [*The Terrible But Unfinished Story of Norodom Sihanouk, King of Cambodia*]; "L'Indiade ou l'Inde de leurs rêves," 1987 [*The Indiad or India of Their Dreams*, trans. Donald Watson, unpublished]; *La Ville Parjure ou le réveil des Érinyes*, 1994 [*The Perjured City or The Awakening of the Furies*, trans. Bernadette Fort, in Prenowitz, *Selected Plays of Hélène Cixous*]; *Tambours sur la digue, sous forme de pièce ancienne pour marionnettes jouée par des acteurs*, 1999 [*Drums on the Dam: In the Form of an Ancient Puppet Play Performed by Actors*, trans. Brian J. Mallet and Judith G. Miller, in Prenowitz, *Selected Plays of Hélène Cixous*].

6. Cixous spoke of her chamber plays at La Maison Française of NYU, October 12, 2006.

7. Her eight chamber plays include, in order of publication— English titles in brackets: *La Pupille*, 1971; *Portrait de Dora*, 1976 [*Portrait of Dora*]; *Le Nom d'Œdipe: Chant du corps interdit* [*The Name of Oedipus: Song of the Forbidden Body*]; *La Prise d l'Ecole de Madhubaï*, 1984 [*The Conquest of the School at Madhubaï*]; *On ne part pas, on ne revient pas*, 1991; *L'Histoire (qu'on ne connaîtra jamais)*, 1994; *Voile Noire Voile Blanche*, 1994 [*Black Sail White Sail*]; *Rouen, la trentième nuit de mai '31*, 2001; "La Fiancée aux yeux bandés ou Amelait," 2004, unpublished.

8. Charlotte Canning assesses this spatialization in her very astute essay, "The Critic as Playwright: Performing Hélène Cixous's *Le Nom d'Oedipe*," in Lee Jacobus and Regina Barreca, eds., *Hélène Cixous: Critical Impressions* (Amsterdam: Gordon Breach, 1999), pp. 305–26.

9. This latter encourages us to place Cixous's chamber theater within what J. P. Ryngaert has advanced as a new impetus toward language-centered theater, one in which words hold sway over all other elements of the stage ("Speech in Tatters: The Interplay of Voices in Recent Dramatic Writing," *Yale French Studies* 112 [Fall 2007]: 14–28).

10. Our definition of myth is broad and includes historical figures who have achieved mythic status (timelessness and thus the ability to be widely adapted). While Roland Barthes engages with myth in a different way than Cixous in *Mythologies* (Paris: Seuil, 1957), his concern, like hers, is myth's ability to freeze human potential, including thought.

Cixous has tackled classical Greek myths, as well as the master discourses of psychoanalysis based on these myths: hence her participation in the Soleil's House of Atreus project, 1992, for which she translated Aeschylus's *The Eumenides,* and her drafting of *The Perjured City,*
1994. In the latter, the death of children because of HIV-contaminated
blood transfusions brings the avenging furies back to earth.

11. From Cixous's lecture at La Maison Française, New York University, October 12, 2006.

12. *The Indiad,* contrary to the other works (or chamber pieces)
examined here, is chronologically ordered. Scenes are complete in
themselves and do not blend into other scenes (as do the movements
in *Oedipus*). There is a greater sense that characters are incarnated
rather than existing as theatrical signs or "souls," that is, given shape
especially through voicing. Cixous's chamber pieces are also notably
different from *The Indiad* and other pieces written for the Soleil in
the amount of foregrounded intertextuality: *Rouen,* for example, cites
Eliot, Shakespeare, Milton, and Villon.

13. *Oedipus* calls for two actors for Jocasta, Oedipus, and Tiresias.
Doubling the principles also doubles the possibilities of experimenting
with subject positions. In each case, there is a spoken role and a singing role. In the excerpts included here, the speaking Jocasta (in italics)
seems to know much more about her fate than the singing Jocasta.

14. The character Polonius, for example, eliminated from *The Blindfolded Fiancée,* turns up in *Voile Noire Voile Blanche (Black Sail White Sail)*
as the character Pauline. The rotten smell of Denmark invades *The
Perjured City,* as does a parody of Fortinbras in the character of Forzza.
We should note that Cixous also frequently evokes the Holocaust—
the sacrifice of the hemophiliac children in *The Perjured City* being
only one instance that recalls the Jewish children killed by the Vichy
regime.

15. Cixous, La Maison Française, October 12, 2006.

SELECT BIBLIOGRAPHY

ENGLISH EDITIONS OF CIXOUS'S BOOKS

The Exile of James Joyce. Trans. Sally A. J. Purcell. New York: David Lewis/London: John Calder, 1976.

Portrait of Dora. Trans. Anita Barrows. *Gambit International Theatre Review* 8, no. 30 (1977): 27–67. Repr. *Benmussa Directs*, pp. 27–73. Playscript 91. London: John Calder/Dallas: Riverrun, 1979.

Vivre l'orange/To Live the Orange [bilingual French/English]. Trans. Ann Liddle and Sarah Cornell. Paris: Des femmes–Antoinette Fouque, 1979.

Angst. Trans. Jo Levy. London: John Calder/New York: Riverrun, 1985.

Inside. Trans. Carol Barko. New York: Schocken, 1986.

The Conquest of the School at Madhubaï. Trans. Deborah W. Carpenter. *Women and Performance* 3 (1986): 59–95.

—— and Catherine Clément. *The Newly Born Woman*. Trans. Betsy Wing. Minneapolis: University of Minnesota Press/Manchester: Manchester University Press, 1986.

Writing Differences. Readings from the Seminar of Hélène Cixous. Ed. Susan Sellers. New York: St. Martin's, 1988.

Reading with Clarice Lispector. Trans. Verena Andermatt Conley. Minneapolis: University of Minnesota Press/London: Harvester Wheatsheaf, 1990.

The Name of Oedipus. In *Plays by French and Francophone Women: A Critical Anthology*. Ed. and trans. Christiane Makward and Judith G. Miller. Ann Arbor: University of Michigan Press, 1991.

The Book of Promethea. Trans. Betsy Wing. Lincoln: University of Nebraska Press, 1991.

"Coming to Writing" and Other Essays. Ed. Deborah Jenson, trans. Sarah Cornell, Deborah Jenson, Ann Liddle, and Susan Sellers. Cambridge: Harvard University Press, 1991.

Readings: The Poetics of Blanchot, Joyce, Kafka, Lispector, Tsvetayeva. Ed. and trans. Verena A. Conley. Minneapolis: University of Minnesota Press/London: Harvester Wheatsheaf, 1992.

Three Steps on the Ladder of Writing. Trans. Sarah Cornell and Susan Sellers. New York: Columbia University Press, 1993.

The Terrible But Unfinished Story of Norodom Sihanouk, King of Cambodia. Trans. Juliet Flower MacCannell, Judith Pike, and Lollie Groth. Lincoln: University of Nebraska Press, 1994.

Voile Noire Voile Blanche/Black Sail White Sail. Bilingual. Trans. Catherine A. F. MacGillivray. *New Literary History* 25, no. 2 (Spring 1994): 219-354.

Manna for the Mandelstams for the Mandelas. Trans. Catherine A. F. MacGillivray. Minneapolis: University of Minnesota Press, 1994.

The Hélène Cixous Reader. Ed. and trans. Susan Sellers. New York: Routledge, 1994.

Bloom. Dublin: Kingstown, 1996.

—— and Mireille Calle-Gruber. *Rootprints: Memory and Life Writing*. Trans. Eric Prenowitz. New York: Routledge, 1997.

First Days of the Year. Trans. Catherine A. F. MacGillivray. Minneapolis: University of Minnesota Press, 1998.

Stigmata: Escaping Texts. New York: Routledge, 1998.

The Third Body. Trans. Keith Cohen. Evanston: Hydra/Northwestern University Press, 1999.

—— and Jacques Derrida. *Veils*. Trans. Geoffrey Bennington. Stanford: Stanford University Press, 2001.

Selected Plays. Ed. Eric Prenowitz. London: Routledge, 2003.

Portrait of Jacques Derrida as a Young Jewish Saint. Trans. Beverley Bie Brahic. New York: Columbia University Press, 2003.

The Writing Notebooks. Ed. and trans. Susan Sellers. New York: Continuum, 2004.

—— and Tony Godfrey. *Vera's Room: The Art of Maria Chevska*. London: Black Dog, 2005.

Ex-cities. Ed. Aaron Levy and Jean-Michel Rabaté. Philadelphia: Slought, 2006.

Dream I Tell You. Trans. Beverley Bie Brahic. New York: Columbia University Press, 2006.

The Day I Wasn't There. Trans. Beverly Bie Brahic. Evanston: Northwestern University Press, 2006.

Reveries of the Wild Woman: Primal Scenes. Trans. Beverley Bie Brahic. Evanston: Northwestern University Press, 2006.

Insister of Jacques Derrida. Trans. Peggy Kamuf. Edinburgh: Edinburgh University Press, 2007.

Manhattan: Letters from Prehistory. Trans. Beverly Bie Brahic. New York: Fordham University Press, 2007.

Love Itself in the Letter Box. Trans. Peggy Kamuf. Cambridge: Polity, 2008.

White Ink: Interviews on Sex, Text, and Politics. Ed. Susan Sellers. New York: Columbia University Press, 2008.

Hyperdream. Trans. Beverley Bie Brahic. Cambridge: Polity, 2009.

So Close. Trans. Peggy Kamuf. Cambridge: Polity, 2009.

Zero's Neighbour. Sam Beckett. Trans. Laurent Milesi. Cambridge: Polity, 2010.

FRENCH EDITIONS OF CIXOUS'S BOOKS

Le Prénom de Dieu. Paris: Grasset, 1967; repr. 1985.

L'Exil de James Joyce ou l'art du remplacement. Paris: Grasset, 1968.

Dedans. Paris: Grasset, 1969; repr. Des femmes–Antoinette Fouque, 1986.

Le Troisième Corps. Paris: Grasset, 1970; repr. Des femmes–Antoinette Fouque, 1999.

Les Commencements. Paris: Grasset, 1970; repr. Des femmes–Antoinette Fouque, 1999.

Un vrai jardin. Paris: L'Herne, 1971; repr. Des femmes–Antoinette Fouque, 1998.

Neutre. Paris: Grasset, 1972; repr. Des femmes–Antoinette Fouque, 1998.

La Pupille. Paris: *Cahiers Renaud-Barrault* 78, 1972.

Tombe. Paris: Seuil, 1973; repr. 2008.

Portrait du soleil. Paris: Denoël, 1973; repr. Des femmes–Antoinette Fouque, 1999.

Prénoms de personne. Paris: Seuil, 1974.

—— and Catherine Clément. *La Jeune Née.* Paris: Christian Bourgois, 1975.

Révolutions pour plus d'un Faust. Paris: Seuil, 1975.

Un K. incompréhensible: Pierre Goldman. Paris: Christian Bourgois, 1975.

Soufffles. Paris: Des femmes–Antoinette Fouque, 1975; repr. 1998.

La. Paris: Gallimard, 1976; repr. Des femmes–Antoinette Fouque, 1979.

Partie. Paris: Des femmes–Antoinette Fouque, 1976; repr. 1998.

Portrait de Dora. Paris: Des femmes–Antoinette Fouque, 1976; repr. *Théâtre.* Paris: Des femmes–Antoinette Fouque, 1986.

——, Madeleine Gagnon, and Annie Leclerc. *La Venue à l'écriture.* Paris: U.G.E., 1976.

Angst. Paris: Des femmes–Antoinette Fouque, 1977; repr. 1998.

Préparatifs de noces au-delà de l'abîme. Paris: Des femmes–Antoinette Fouque, 1978.

Le Nom d'Œdipe: Chant du corps interdit. Paris: Des femmes–Antoinette Fouque, 1978.

Ananké. Paris: Des femmes–Antoinette Fouque, 1979.

Vivre l'orange. Paris: Des femmes–Antoinette Fouque, 1979.

Illa. Paris: Des femmes–Antoinette Fouque, 1980.

With ou l'Art de l'innocence. Paris: Des femmes–Antoinette Fouque, 1981.

Limonade tout était si infini. Paris: Des femmes–Antoinette Fouque, 1982.

Le Livre de Prométhéa. Paris: Gallimard, 1983.

La Prise de l'école de Madhubaï. Paris: *Avant-Scène–Théâtre* 475, 1984; repr. *Théâtre*. Paris: Des femmes–Antoinette Fouque, 1986.

L'Histoire terrible mais inachevée de Norodom Sihanouk roi du Cambodge. Paris: Théâtre du Soleil, 1985.

Entre l'écriture. Paris: Des femmes–Antoinette Fouque, 1986.

La Bataille d'Arcachon. Québec: Trois, 1986.

L'Indiade ou l'Inde de leurs rêves, et quelques écrits sur le théâtre. Paris: Théâtre du Soleil, 1987.

Manne aux Mandelstams aux Mandelas. Paris: Des femmes–Antoinette Fouque, 1988.

L'Heure de Clarice Lispector. Paris: Des femmes–Antoinette Fouque, 1989.

Jours de l'an. Paris: Des femmes–Antoinette Fouque, 1990.

——, Daniel Dobbels, and Bérénice Reynaud. *Karine Saporta*. Paris: Armand Colin, 1990.

L'Ange au secret. Paris: Des femmes–Antoinette Fouque, 1991.

On ne part pas: On ne revient pas. Paris: Des femmes–Antoinette Fouque, 1991.

Déluge. Paris: Des femmes–Antoinette Fouque, 1992.

Beethoven à jamais ou l'existence de Dieu. Paris: Des femmes–Antoinette Fouque, 1993.

L'Histoire (qu'on ne connaîtra jamais). Paris: Des femmes–Antoinette Fouque, 1994.

—— and Mireille Calle-Gruber. *Photos de racines*. Paris: Des femmes–Antoinette Fouque, 1994.

La Fiancée juive—de la tentation. Paris: Des femmes–Antoinette Fouque, 1995.

La Ville parjure ou le réveil des Érinyes. Paris: Théâtre du Soleil, 1995.

Messie. Paris: Des femmes–Antoinette Fouque, 1996.

OR: Les lettres de mon père. Paris: Des femmes–Antoinette Fouque, 1997.

—— and Jacques Derrida. *Voiles*. Paris: Galilée, 1998.

Osnabrück. Paris: Des femmes–Antoinette Fouque, 1999.

Tambours sur la digue: Sous forme de pièce ancienne pour marionnettes jouée par des acteurs. Paris: Théâtre du Soleil, 1999.

Les Rêveries de la femme sauvage: Scènes primitives. Paris: Galilée, 2000.

Le Jour où je n'étais pas là. Paris: Galilée, 2000.

Portrait de Jacques Derrida en jeune saint juif. Paris: Galilée, 2001.

Rouen, la trentième nuit de mai 31'. Paris: Galilée, 2001.

Benjamin à Montaigne: Il ne faut pas le dire. Paris: Galilée, 2001.

Manhattan: Lettres de la préhistoire. Paris: Galilée, 2002.
Rêve je te dis. Paris: Galilée, 2003.
L'Amour du loup—et autres remords. Paris: Galilée, 2003.
Tours promises. Paris: Galilée, 2004.
—— and Jacques Derrida. *Lengua por venir/Langue à venir. Seminario de Barcelona* [bilingual Spanish-French]. Ed. Marta Segarra. Barcelona: Icaria, 2004.
L'Amour même—dans la boîte aux lettres. Paris: Galilée, 2005.
Le Tablier de Simon Hantaï: Anagrammes suivi de H.C. S.H. Lettres. Paris: Galilée, 2005.
—— and Frédéric-Yves Jeannet. *Rencontre terrestre.* Paris: Galilée, 2005.
Hyperrêve. Paris: Galilée, 2006.
Insister: À Jacques Derrida. Paris: Galilée, 2006.
Si près. Paris: Galilée, 2007.
Le Voisin de zéro: Sam Beckett. Paris: Galilée, 2007.
Ciguë: Vieilles femmes en fleurs. Paris: Galilée, 2008.
Philippines: Prédelles. Paris: Galilée, 2009.
Ève s'évade: La ruine et la vie. Paris: Galilée, 2009.

BOOKS AND SPECIAL ISSUES ON CIXOUS

Blyth, Ian and Susan Sellers. *Hélène Cixous: Live Theory.* New York: Continuum, 2004.
Bono, Paola, ed. *Scritture del corpo: Hélène Cixous, variazioni su un tema.* Rome: Luca Sossella, 2000.
Bray, Abigail. *Hélène Cixous: Writing and Sexual Difference.* New York: Palgrave Macmillan, 2004.
Calle-Gruber, Mireille. *Du café à l'éternité: Hélène Cixous à l'œuvre.* Paris: Galilée, 2002.
—— *Hélène Cixous Portfolio.* Paris: ADPF, 2005.
Calle-Gruber, Mireille, ed. *Hélène Cixous, croisées d'une œuvre.* Paris: Galilée, 2000.
Calle-Gruber, Mireille and Marie-Odile Germain, eds. *Genèses Généalogies Genres.* Paris: Galilée, 2007.
Conley, Verena Andermatt. *Hélène Cixous: Writing the Feminine.* Lincoln: University of Nebraska Press, 1991 [1984].
Derrida, Jacques. *H.C. for Life, That Is to Say . . .* Trans. Laurent Milesi and Stefan Herbrechter. Stanford: Stanford University Press, 2006. French original *H.C. pour la vie, c'est-à-dire . . .* Paris: Galilée, 2002.
—— *Geneses, Genealogies, Genres, and Genius: The Secrets of the Archive.* Trans. Beverly Bie Brahic. New York: Columbia University Press, 2006. French original *Genèses, généalogies, genres et le génie: Les secrets de l'archive.* Paris: Galilée, 2003.

Diocaretz, Myriam and Marta Segarra, eds. *Joyful Babel: Translating Hélène Cixous*. Amsterdam–New York: Rodopi, 2004.

Fiorini, Monica. *H.C. libera viaggiatrice dei margini*. Florence: Alinea, 2003.

Guégan Fisher, Claudine. *La Cosmogonie d'Hélène Cixous*. Amsterdam: Rodopi, 1988.

Ives, Kelly. *Hélène Cixous I Love You: The Jouissance of Writing*. Maidstone (UK): Crescent Moon, 2000.

Jacobus, Lee A. and Regina Barreca, eds. *Hélène Cixous: Critical Impressions*. Amsterdam: Gordon and Breach, 1999.

McQuillan, Martin, ed. *Reading Cixous Writing: The Oxford Literary Review* 24 (2002).

Michaud, Ginette. *"Comme en rêve" (Derrida, Cixous): Suivi de Songes de juillet*. Montreal: Le Temps volé, 2009.

Motard-Noar, Martine. *Les Fictions d'Hélène Cixous: Une autre langue de femme*. Lexington, KY: French Forum, 1987; repr. Paris: Klincksieck, 2001.

Penrod, Lynn Kettler. *Hélène Cixous*, New York: Twayne, 1996.

Prenowitz, Eric. *Hélène Cixous: When the Word Is a Stage. New Literary History* 37, no. 1 (2006).

Renshaw, Sal. *The Subject of Love: Hélène Cixous and the Feminine Divine*. Manchester: Manchester University Press, 2009.

Schiach, Morag. *Hélène Cixous: A Politics of Writing*. New York: Routledge, 1991.

Segarra, Marta, ed. *Hélène Cixous, Expressions maghrébines* 2, no. 2 (2003).

—— *Ver con Hélène Cixous,* Barcelona: Icaria, 2004.

—— *L'Événement comme écriture: Cixous et Derrida se lisant*. Paris: Campagne Première, 2007.

Sellers, Susan. *Hélène Cixous: Authorship, Autobiography and Love*. Cambridge: Polity, 1996.

Sellers, Susan, ed. and trans. *The Hélène Cixous Reader*. New York: Routledge, 1994.

Spanfelner, Deborah. *Hélène Cixous: A Space for the Other*. Saarbrücken: VDM Verlag Dr. Müller, 2008.

Stevens, Christa. *L'Écriture solaire d'Hélène Cixous: Travail du texte et histoires du sujet dans Portrait du soleil*. Amsterdam: Rodopi, 1999.

Van Rossum Guyon, Françoise and Myriam Diocaretz, eds. *Hélène Cixous, chemins d'une écriture*. Amsterdam: Rodopi, 1990.

Wilcox, Helen, Keith Mcwatters, Ann Thompson, and Linda R. Williams, eds. *The Body and the Text: Hélène Cixous, Reading and Teaching*. Hemel Hempstead: Harvester Wheatsheaf, 1990.

Zupančič, Metka. *Hélène Cixous: Texture mythique et alchimique*. Birmingham, AL: Summa, 2007.